SPORTS AND GAMES
OF MEDIEVAL CULTURES

Sally Wilkins

Sports and Games Through History
Andrew Leibs, Series Adviser

Greenwood Press
Westport, Connecticut • London

Library of Congress Cataloging-in-Publication Data

Wilkins, Sally E. D.
    Sports and games of medieval cultures / Sally Wilkins.
      p. cm.—(Sports and games through history)
    Includes bibliographical references (p.) and index.
    ISBN 0–313–31711–9 (alk. paper)
    1. Games—History—To 1500.   2. Sports—History—To 1500. I. Title. II. Series.
GV1200.W55   2002
790'.09—dc21   2001040553

British Library Cataloguing in Publication Data is available.

Library of Congress Catalog Card Number: 2001040553
ISBN: 0–313–31711–9

First published in 2002

Greenwood Press, 88 Post Road West, Westport, CT 06881
An imprint of Greenwood Publishing Group, Inc.
www.greenwood.com

Printed in the United States of America

The paper used in this book complies with the
Permanent Paper Standard issued by the National
Information Standards Organization (Z39.48–1984).

10 9 8 7 6 5 4 3 2 1

⊞ CONTENTS

▦ SERIES FOREWORD

I am pleased to introduce Greenwood Publishing's Sports and Games Through History. I feel this new series offers readers the greatest geographical breadth and historical depth of any study on the games we play, how we play them, and what they tell us about the variations and the resounding similarities of the world's cultures.

The first four volumes in this series explore the sports, games, and physical activities during important periods in world history: from the first ancient Olympiad to the Fall of Rome (776 B.C. to 476 A.D.); from the start of the Dark Ages to the invention of printing (476 A.D. to 1450); from the beginning to the end of The Renaissance (1450 to 1649); and from Colonial America to the first modern Olympiad (1700 to 1896). The world's seven major regions (Africa, Asia, Europe, Latin America, the Middle East, North America, and Oceania) are all represented, though one of the series' great discoveries is how often sports and games cross geographic boundaries and historical time lines.

In the series' opening volume, Steve Craig notes that some sports, such as archery and wrestling, are indigenous to every culture in the Ancient world. From the Pyramids of Egypt to the ruins of Rome, antiquity is strewn with references to, and artifacts from, what look like many sports and games we still play today. Although the lack of detailed accounts and written rules often prevents absolute knowledge of sport history, the knowledge compiled by scholars such as Craig provides valuable insight into the nature of games played in the ancient world.

Each entry in the series provides a detailed description of sport, game, or activity, traces its development, explains how essential equipment can be made or adapted, and provides the rules of play. One goal of the series is to include enough information so students can recreate an activity as well as read about it.

Along with the simultaneous development of sports around the world, the shaping powers of military and cultural imperialism are the driving force behind the series' final volume, on the eighteenth and nineteenth centuries. Bob Crego's book demonstrates the inexorable influence of Great Britain, both for the games they carried across their empire (the World Cup is awarded in soccer, not baseball), as well as the native games and traditions they banned while building colonies.

Above all, sports and games from all cultures offer insights that help us understand our own culture. One sees casinos on reservations differently after reading Sally Wilkins' book on the Middle Ages, where we learn about the vital role that games of chance played in the spiritual and emotional lives of most Native American tribes.

Entries on major modern sports such as baseball and basketball are included, but the series ends with the first Modern Olympiad in 1896. Thus, the series sets the stage for the twentieth century, during which sports were transformed by economic, cultural, and political realities into industries and their own myths, each needing its own encyclopedia.

One of the best things to take into the reading of this series is your own knowledge and love of the sports and games you play, watch, and follow. The ensuing pages offer many adventures in learning where these came from and thus provide ideas on how to have the most fun as you explore the universe of play.

Andrew Leibs
Award-winning sportswriter and author of
A Field Guide for the Sight-Impaired Reader

▦ INTRODUCTION

GAMES AND HUMAN HISTORY

The history of humankind and the history of play are inextricably linked. Children play without needing to be taught. Some kinds of play and toys, such as dolls, cook sets, miniature weapons, and toy phones, are imitative behavior. Children pretend to do the things they see adults around them doing. There is no doubt that this is training for later life, but it is also fun, and if you ask the children, "Are you studying to become adults?," they would look at you in bemusement and say, "No, we're playing." Other games are less obviously linked to useful skills in later life but can still be seen as training. Tossing and catching and running and jumping develop muscular strength and coordination. Counting, guessing, and memorizing develop intellectual abilities. Competition develops loyalty within a group and trains minds and bodies for the challenges of adult confrontation.

No doubt the "who can jump higher or further" contests date back to the beginning of history. Chase-and-capture games preserve the fears of our ancestors, preyed upon by lions or wolves. Arch-and-trap games such as "London Bridge" are universal, too. Marbles and tops, hoops, and keep-away and keep-aloft games are found on every continent. English visitors to Africa reported with some surprise that children played at hopping from one stone to another without touching the ground in between, as well as running up termite mounds in a game identical to their familiar "king of the mountain."

As individuals get older, their games become more complex. So too, it seems, as cultures develop. Rules can be as simple as "when I shoot you, you have to fall down" or as complex as the elaborate rituals of mahjong or cricket (both too recently developed to have been included in this volume.) People in simple cultures seem to have played relatively simple games. People in more highly developed cultures played more complex games. However, people in primitive societies spent more time playing. At one time scientists assumed that modern people would have more leisure, and therefore more play, as they spent less time securing food and shelter. The truth seems to be that as people spend less time filling their basic needs, their lives become more complex with less time for strictly leisure activities.

In primitive societies, sports are for everyone: grannies and toddlers played palitún, bowgitee, and campball. As sports grew more complicated they often became a profession for the few, providing entertainment for the many. When training in the ancient skills of warfare and hunting were transformed into sports competitions, the same young men who would have been hunters and soldiers became athletes.

Many games probably began as rituals for divining the future. Anyone who has ever dealt a hand of solitaire and thought, "If I win this game, it means I'm going to get a raise" (or even, "If I win just one game, I can go to bed") has experienced the apparent though unrealistic connection between the random chance of the game and the unknown future.

People almost everywhere have traditionally played games for some kind of stake or prize. In order to provide a prize for the winner, every player put up some kind of a stake. The winner took home all or most of the stakes, and the losers lost what they had contributed. This is the simplest form of gambling. The stakes could be trivial, or they could be items of great value. The addiction to gambling, only recently determined to have a biological component, has always been a part of the human experience. People could and did gamble and lose tremendous amounts on trivial games. Men bet their wives, their children, their freedom, and sold themselves into slavery when they lost. Both Asia and Latin America have legends of rulers who bet—and lost—their kingdoms. It's no wonder many religious traditions have warned against gambling, even condemning it.

Sometimes, as with chess, games were deliberately changed to eliminate the element of chance. Sometimes prizes were eliminated or valueless "counters" were substituted for money. Sometimes a fortune-telling device or gambling tool gradually became a toy or a children's party game. Colored spinners took the place of dice, and pictures of animals or cartoon characters replaced the numbers on playing cards so that the connection between an ancient ritual and a preschooler's educational activity is completely obscured.

THE MIDDLE AGES

The thousand-year period covered in this volume (476–1476), defined roughly "from the fall of Rome to the invention of the printing press," is a time known in Western history as The Middle Ages. Most of us have a mental image of that medieval era that is made up of equal part Chaucer, Tennyson, and Monty Python. Knights in shining armor ride through the land; Robin Hood swashbuckles and redistributes wealth. Vikings sail in to pillage and burn, while Crusaders march off on fruitless quests, and St. Francis preaches to wild animals. It is quaint, colorful, and almost entirely European.

The Middle Ages was a time of tremendous development and change inside Europe, beginning in the so-called Dark Ages—dark because the collapse of the Roman Empire left a power void that led to nearly constant fighting among the clans and tribes of Europe. Gradually the leaders of the various tribes divided Europe under the feudal lords, eventually consolidating power in what would become the nation states.

Outside of Europe, we in the West sometimes forget, it was not the Middle Ages. In some parts of the world conditions were very different than in others. While Europe was reeling from the reverberations of Rome's crashing fall, the eastern part of the Roman Empire continued with some stability for several centuries. It became what we call the Middle East, where the Middle Ages saw the flowering of a new civilization fueled by the rise of Islam. In Asia the great civilizations of India, China, Japan, and Korea were counting their ages in dynasties that often lasted many centuries. The Mongols, nomadic people of the Eurasian plains, were a living bridge between Asia and the Middle East. After the Crusades, international trade would connect Europe to Asia along routes established by the Mongols.

Civilization existed in the Americas, too, though in a very different form from the European model. Unfortunately for historians, the written records of the Amerindian civilizations were minimal. Their oral records, which were detailed and extensive, died out along with the people when the combined ravages of war and disease spread across the continents with the European explorations. What we can know of those people's lives during the era of this book must be reconstructed from the archaeological record and the notes made by those early explorers.

So, too, in Oceania. The written history of the peoples of those islands scattered across the South Pacific dates back only three hundred years, to the voyages of Captain Cook and others like him. That people had been crossing that vast sea, exploring and settling the islands by canoe and raft, is still mind-boggling. Linguistic and anthropological evidence has many scientists convinced, however, that prehistoric explorers from both South America and Southeast Asia traveled through the Pacific to New Zealand and Australia and to the edges of Antarctica. In these regions during the period of this book the most people were living in the Stone Age; that is, they did not do metalwork. They also kept no written records, and few organic artifacts survive in the tropics. Again we rely on the observations of the earliest European explorers, especially when they took the time to record the oral histories they were told. With this information we extrapolate back in time to develop a picture of what the leisure time of these early peoples may have been like.

METHODOLOGY

In Oceania and the Americas, and to some extent in Asia and sub-Saharan Africa, I have relied heavily on notes taken by European explorers and anthropologists. These records reflect the opinions and experiences of the foreign observers, but they are often all we have.

The newcomers described what they saw using terms from their own familiar games. English sailors in Australia called the local board game "draughts," though it bore little resemblance to checkers. Spaniards in Mesoamerica were astounded at bouncing rubber balls but quick to describe the rubber ball games in terms borrowed from European pelota. In Canada the French were just as comfortable calling the indigenous ball-and-stick game "lacrosse," though it had perhaps less resemblance to their own game of "la soule et la crosse" than it did to Byzantine polo.

I've made an assumption that the games being played in a region when Europeans arrived were representative of games that were played by the ancestors of those peoples. In one way this is indefensible, since we know that games do change over time. On the other hand, the activities of childhood tend to be extremely conservative, carrying on traditional activities and rhymes long after their original contexts have been lost. "Traditional games" really do carry on traditions.

SOME NOTES ON THE THEORIES OF GAMES

Does the existence of an identical or similar game in multiple societies thousands of miles apart demonstrate that those peoples had contact with one another? Does it show that those peoples descended from common ancestors in the relatively recent past? Or is it possible for games developed spontaneously among different groups to be virtually identical?

Scholars have different opinions about this question. Stewart Culin

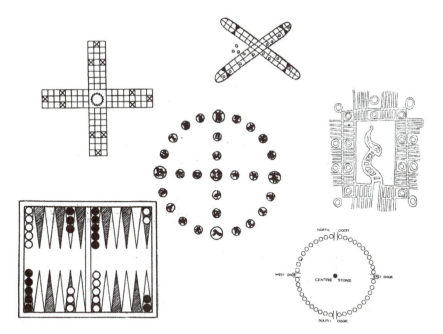

Figure 1.1. Some scholars believe the Indian chaupur (top left), European tables (bottom left), Central American patoli (top right), totoloque (middle right), and North American zsetilth (bottom right) all developed from the Korean nyout (center). *Sources*: Chaupur, tables, and patoli based on Murray (1952); totoloque and zsetilth from Culin (1975); and nyout from Culin (1896), courtesy of the Brooklyn Museum of Art.

was confident that the cross and circle of the Korean nyout board (Figure 1.1) was the origin of India's cross-shaped pachisi board, and that the European chess board was a remnant of its center. He also considered it the source of the circuit board of several American games. The way we understand the evidence revealed by archaeology and anthropology is shaped by our underlying beliefs about how games developed. Believing that related games must all have come from the same source leads to the conclusion that primitive people had contacts of which we may have no other evidence. Elaborate outlines of geographical diffusion have been drawn based on this belief. Believing that individuals widely separated in space and time may spontaneously come up with the same idea leads to a very different conclusion.

My personal bias is in favor of the "separate and spontaneous" theory. If modern scientists can stumble upon the same complex theories independently of one another, why is it impossible that primitive players had the same experience? Ordinary parents can attest that small children play with found objects in predictable ways. They throw stones, make piles of objects and knock them over, compete with one another to run faster, jump higher and yell louder without anyone teaching them how to do so. It seems logical to conclude that human beings have been playing and competing in this way since prehistoric times. Even the more complex notion of a board game—moving markers along lines of points or grids—could certainly have developed from the common behaviors of dividing territory and mapping journeys. That the four points of the compass could become the four sides of a board both in India and in North America's desert southwest does not seem terribly far-fetched.

At the same time it is clear that some games did develop in one area and then spread into other regions, frequently changing dramatically as they were adapted into different cultures. Chess, playing cards, and mancala are all examples of such games. In the histories included in this book I have reported the common theories of diffusion when they are generally agreed upon. The reader should be aware that nationalist loyalties frequently lead to disputes over the origins of games.

The regional introductions will explore these cultures in more detail.

DEFINITIONS

Within each geographic region, the entries are divided into a section on games, a section on play, and a section on sports. For purposes of this series I have defined games as sedentary pastimes with recognized rules of play. These include board or table games, card games, dice games, and string games. They also include riddles and word games, but these are beyond the scope of the book. I have defined sports as organized, competitive physical activity. Individual and team sports are both included. Dance is an activity that is often very physical and sometimes can be competitive, but for the most part it has not been included here. Play covers a broad category in between games and sports: active games and outdoor play. Some of these games have their origins in prehistoric rituals that were intended to invoke a good harvest, insure fertility in marriage, or protect against predators and enemies. Others are adaptations of adult activities for childish amusement. It's worth remembering that sports are play, and almost every sport can be adapted for play if the element of competition is ignored.

A few entries are not games per se, but are descriptions of game equipment or of groups of games of which several examples are listed alphabetically. Because many games were played in more than one region, the reader will occasionally be referred to another section of the book for more detail to avoid redundancy.

ADAPTATIONS

I've attempted to include suggestions for adapting many of the games in the book for modern use (*in italics*). Sometimes no adaptation is necessary: today's children can play "London Bridge" or "Hawk and Chickens" exactly as their ancestors did nine hundred years ago. Sometimes no practical adaptation seems advisable. The reader is encouraged to use caution and common sense in attempting these activities.

Sometimes the ancient sources give only brief, tantalizing descriptions of games, particularly the games of children. In these cases I've counted on the universality of certain games to fill in the blanks. If ancient manuscripts say children played a game with marbles in which they tried to get the marbles into a hole, but nothing else, I have selected one of the many marbles games that involve shooting into a hole for instructions. I've tried to use different games in different regions, even though it's likely that many variations were played in every region. As most of us can report from our own experiences, new games develop from old as players attempt to make a game more challenging or more variable.

For most games, you can decide whether to be more or less authentic. Rubber balls existed only in Mesoamerica during this time frame. Many European games changed dramatically when the explorers began to bring rubber balls back from the New World, but during the time covered in this book those games were all played with "dead balls." An inflated leather ball or bladder had some loft but still no real "bounce." Stitching and stuffing balls with leather, cloth, reeds, feathers, and horsehair are easily done, and will make for a much more authentic adaptation of the game. But playing the same game with a "dead" tennis or soccer ball may well be perfectly acceptable for your purposes.

Simple suggestions are included in the descriptions of games. More complicated instructions have been gathered into an Appendix, where you will also find some recipes and hints on finding materials for creating a collection of medieval games.

⊞ AFRICA

Africa is an enormous continent with a very diverse population. Although Westerners tend to see the people of Africa as uniformly "African," scholars divide the people according to more than one hundred language groups. Several distinct racial types are also evident among the indigenous people. Most regions of Africa were home to some hunter/gatherers, some agriculturalist/farmers, and some pastoralist/herders. These groups lived in a relationship that was both antagonistic and symbiotic. Even when they relied on one another they often regarded each other with disdain (not unlike modern society, where professionals and the wealthy may look down upon blue collar and service workers, without whom the economy would fail).

The Sahara desert divides the northern part of the continent from the rest of Africa, and during the period covered by this book the Berbers of the north had much more in common with the people of the Middle East than with those of sub-Saharan Africa. Nevertheless, there was trade up and down the Nile River even in ancient times. Commerce and empire building bridged the miles between the far-flung nations of Africa throughout the Middle Ages and laid the way for the explorers who sailed from Europe during the Renaissance.

The Middle Ages was marked in Africa by an enormous population shift. About one hundred years B.C.E. Bantu-speaking people from Nok began moving south and east across north-central Africa. Their migrations continued for more than one thousand years. The Nok were an iron-working people of the Sahel, a region of fertile grasslands in West Africa south of the Sahara. As they settled across the continent they tended to conquer, absorb, or push out the indigenous people. Slave selling was a common and profitable motive for warfare. Many of the power struggles on the continent today can be seen as continuations of that migration, which were temporarily hidden by the artificial divisions of European colonial governments.

In the eighth century Arab Bedouin from the Middle East introduced camels to the Sahara, revolutionizing trade across the desert. The Sahel became the center of three great empires that rose and fell in central Africa during the 1,000 years covered by this book. In the fourth century the kingdom of Ghana grew powerful, trading goods and slaves from sub-Saharan Africa across the desert with the Berbers. When religious dissention split the Ghanan empire at the beginning of the thirteenth century, some converts to Islam rose to power in the kingdom of Mali. The Mali city of Timbuktu became one of the great cultural centers of the medieval world. A century later the Edo empire of Benin was established in what is now Nigeria. The Ashanti, Igbo, and Yoruba peoples of West Africa are among the descendants of the Benin Empire.

While Islam spread through central Africa, some kingdoms in the east remained primarily Christian until the end of the fourteenth century. Trading with Egypt via the Nile and with India and Arabia across the Red Sea and Indian Ocean, the kingdom known as Axum (or Aksum) at its height controlled Arabia, but its influence waned as Islamic states around it became more powerful. The emperors moved from the city of Axum to Roha, and the remnant of the empire, known as Ethiopia, remained virtually isolated in the Horn of Africa until the twentieth century.

Central and eastern Africa came to be dominated by the recurring immigrations of Bantu speakers. The newcomers from the northwest never moved deep into the jungles, which became refuges for the indigenous people. The Bambuti (generally called Pygmies by the Europeans), were skilled hunters native to the deep forests of central Africa. Bambuti clans developed symbiotic relationships with the more recently arrived agrarians, trading meat, nuts and mushrooms for grain, cloth and metal objects. The Aka were associated with the Mangbetu, the Efe with the Mamvu and Lese, the Mbuti with the Bila, and the Sua with the Budu people.

In eastern Africa the Hutu (or Bahutu) arrived in the sixth century, driving the native Twa Bambuti into the rainforest. Toward the end of the Middle Ages another group of Bantu speakers, the Tutsi (or Watusi), arrived and conquered the Hutu. The Tutsi, like the Maasai on the eastern coast and the Nuer of the Nile Valley, were tall, aristocratic cattle herders. Each of these groups looked down on their farming neighbors, the Hutu of the highlands, the Kikuyu in the Rift Valley and the coastal Chagga.

Trade up and down the Nile and contact with the Arab world led to a mixed Moslem-African culture and the development of a common language on the continent, Swahili. The primary export of Africa in those days was slaves, and Swahili was the language of the slave trade. Today many people would like to eradicate Swahili, but its usefulness keeps it alive despite its dark beginnings. The great cities of the Arab-Africa trade route, Mogadishu, now in Somalia, and Mombasa in present-day Kenya, were built around a thousand years after the birth of Christ.

By the twelfth century the Bantu speakers had reached the southernmost parts of the continent. The Bantu-speaking Ngoni drove the Xhosan or (Khoisan) peoples into the Kalahari Desert south of the Savannah. The Xhosan, with their distinctive languages spoken nowhere else on Earth, include the groups called by the Europeans "Bushmen" (the San) and "Hottentots" (the Xho). Some of the Xhosan adapted their hunter-gatherer culture to a nomadic desert life, while others became agriculturalists. The Zulu, Swazi, and Lovedu are among the peoples descended from the Ngoni.

From southeastern Africa the newcomers developed an empire, Mwanamutapa, based on trade both with the cities to the north and across the ocean to India and even China. The great stone city at Zimbabwe, now a ruin, was built around the end of this book's time frame.

Africa presents some interesting challenges for this study. Our knowledge of the games and sports of the time is limited; as in Oceania, by the lack of written records; and as in the Middle East by the prevalent disapproving influence of Islam. Much of our information comes from the reports of European explorers and colonists from the seventeenth through the nineteenth centuries, whose own experiences and biases often shaped their descriptions.

Activities we classify as sports today were very much training for daily life in sub-Saharan Africa. This does not suggest that these activities were not fun or competitive. Knowing human nature, we can be sure that they were both. It is not clear, however, whether organized competition between villages existed before European colonization. Some scholars have suggested that competitive dancing is an ancient tradition; others that it developed as a response to cultural restrictions under colonial rule. There is some evidence that intervillage and even intertribal athletic demonstrations were held in the precolonial period. There was always competition among individuals, and demonstrations of fighting skill and the acrobatics of ritual dance provided opportunities for the selection of spouses. A few of these traditional competitions have been included here.

The games of Africa are intriguing and challenging because many of them require complex mental arithmetic. Many of the indigenous languages of Africa had no written form, and some had a limited vocabulary for numeric concepts, yet mancala and magic squares, to name just two common African pastimes, depend on and develop a great facility for calculation.

Anthropologists have noted that many of the traditional gambling games of Africa probably developed as methods of divination. The throw of the cowries or the pattern of tossed carved chips would be interpreted as answers to questions about the outcome of battles or the coming harvest. It seems that they have long been used for entertainment as well. Both Moslem and Christian missionaries to Africa spoke of the prevalence of gambling and its deleterious effects on the culture. Many of the people sold as slaves in precolonial Africa had staked their freedom on the outcomes of games.

The peoples of medieval Africa lived in a complex society. Trade and economics, military campaigns, immigration, and the missionary efforts of Islam all contributed to blending the culture. It should be no surprise to find the same games being played by different peoples, sometimes with different names but only slightly varying rules.

GAMES

⊞ Abbia

This ancient Yauonde gambling game from east-central Africa has virtually died out, but the carved wooden playing pieces are still reproduced today and have become symbolic of the country of Cameroon. The pieces were carved from hard nuts or bark of the calabash tree. The nuts were split in half and the designs, which ranged from figures of people and animals to symbols representing activities and ideas, were carved on the curved outside of the chip (Figure 2.1).

Abbia could be played by any number of people who would sit in a circle in the market. Each would put up a stake, and then by laying out their own chips, players would predict how the chips would fall when tossed. Finally the player whose turn it was would toss the chips. If one of the other players had accurately predicted the results, that player won the toss, collecting all the stakes and the turn to play next. If no prediction matched the outcome, the tosser collected the stakes. Variations on the game rewarded intermediate winning combinations, very much in the way a lottery does.

To play abbia you need to make a set of chips for each player and choose something to use for stakes. Split almonds are the shape of traditional chips. Color the curved side of the chip with indelible markers, based on the designs in the picture or other simple figures of your own imagining. Be sure each player's set has the same basic designs. Traditionally abbia was played with about a dozen chips, but the odds of winning are higher with a smaller number

Figure 2.1. Abbia chips were carved to represent animals, people, and abstract symbols. *Source*: Adapted from Siegel (1940).

of chips, so you may decide to play with just four or five chips instead. For stakes you may use nuts you haven't colored, or small candies.

You may play all-or-nothing: if anyone's pattern matches the fallen chips exactly, that player takes all the stakes. If no one's does, the person who tossed the chips takes all. Or you may reward partial matches: two stakes to any player who matches all but one of the chips, one to a player who matches all but two, and the remainder to the player whose toss it was. (If you plan to play this way you will need to put up higher stakes to begin, so that there is enough in the pot to pay out the rewards.)

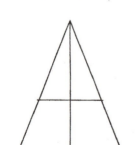
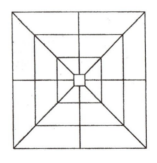
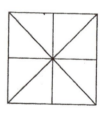

Figure 2.2. *Left to right*: Boards for tsoro yematatu and Zimbabwean merrels (discussed later in chapter), and achi could be traced in the dirt or carved on wood or stone.

Achi

Variations of this simple tic-tac-toe game were played throughout the Old World from ancient times. It was known in ancient Egypt and probably came into the heart of Africa along the Nile with traders. The board was a square twice divided into quarters (lines from corner to corner and bisecting the board vertically and horizontally). This board could easily be traced in the dirt or carved on wood or stone (Figure 2.2). Each player had three or sometimes four pieces; most commonly in Africa peeled sticks for one player and unpeeled for the other.

In phase one of achi the players took turns placing their pieces on the board, one at a time. In phase two, once all the pieces were on the board, players taking turns moving their pieces. Pieces could only move along the lines, one point at a time, and only on to a vacant point. There was no jumping and no capture. The game was won by placing three pieces in a row.

No modern adaptation is necessary for this game: peel some sticks; scratch a board on a stone, and you're ready to play.

Bao

Bao is a Mancala game played even today in sub-Saharan Africa.

The board, which may be ornately carved or simply scooped out in the dirt, is four rows of eight cups each. Each player has an outer row (closest to the player) and an inner row (in the middle). The two outside cups of the inner row are called *kimbi*. The end kimbi are called *kichwa*. The fourth cup from the player's right in each inner row is larger than the rest and is called *kuu*. Some boards have an extra cup for the store. The playing pieces may be shells, stones, bits of clay, or even coins. At least fifteen should fit into a cup, and sixty-four are needed for the game.

The object of the game is to leave your opponent's inner row empty. Each player sows only in his own rows, but captures from the opponent's rows. A play which results in capture is called *mtaji*. A noncapture play is called *takana*.

Two versions of this game are described here.

Version 1. Set up the board by putting two pieces into each cup. Toss a cowrie to decide who will go first. On your turn, pick up the pieces in one of the cups of your outer row and sow or drop them, beginning in the cup next to the one you've emptied, one in each cup, around the cups of your own two rows. On each turn you may choose whether to sow either clockwise or counterclockwise, but you may not change directions except after certain captures (explained below).

If your last seed falls into an occupied inner-row cup, you capture the seeds from the adjacent cup in your opponent's inner row and sow those captured seeds in your inner row. If the captured seeds came from one of the four cups in the center of your opponent's inner row, continue sowing in the same direction; beginning at the left kichwa if the turn was moving clockwise and from the right kichwa if the play was counterclockwise. If the captured seeds came from one of the kimbi, begin sowing from the nearest kichwa. This may reverse the direction of the turn. If the last captured seed falls into an occupied cup, capture the seeds from the adjacent cup and keep going.

On any turn, if there are no seeds in the cup adjacent to where the last seed falls (or if it falls into an occupied cup in the outer row), collect all the seeds from that cup (including the one just dropped) and continue in the same direction (this is called a relay). When the last seed falls in an empty cup, the turn ends.

Mtaji may begin from either an inner or outer row. A player may not play takana if a mtaji is possible. Takana must begin in the inner row unless there is no inner-row play possible. On each turn, players must say whether they are making a takana or mtaji play. If a play begins as takana, no captures can be made even if after a relay the play ends in an occupied cup with pieces adjacent. Instead another relay is made.

If there are more than fifteen seeds in a cup they may only be sown in takana or relay. A single seed cannot be lifted and sown. A player with only singletons left has lost because he cannot play.

Version 2. Once the players are comfortable with the game, try this more advanced, two-stage version. Instead of beginning with all the pieces on the board, begin with eight pieces in each kuu and two pieces in each of the cups between the kuu and the kichwa. In the first part of the game, each turn begins by placing a seed from the store (a nemo) *into one of the occupied cups (not the kuu), lifting the seeds from that cup, and sowing them.*

The kuu have special rules during this part of the game: No takana begin from the kuu, and a takana that ends in the kuu ends the turn. If a mtaji ends in the kuu, the player may choose to end the turn (sleep) or to relay.

You may not capture the seeds in your opponent's kuu unless the cup opposite your own kuu is empty. If the kuu is the only occupied cup in your inner row and there are no seeds to be captured in your opponent's inner row, you may place a nemo in your kuu and then take out just two seeds, sowing one on either side of the kuu. This is called taxing the kuu. (If there are exactly eight seeds in the kuu when this happens, the kuu is not taxed, instead all nine seeds are lifted and sown.)

The second stage of the game begins when the nemo are gone and is played according to the basic rules. Once the kuu are emptied they are treated like any other cup for the rest of the game.

▦ Building a House

This is a fairly simple string figure still practiced in Central Africa that looks more complicated than it is. *Make a loop from a string about five feet long. To begin, hang the string on your left little finger, and pick it up with your left thumb. Hold your left hand up so the string runs across your palm and hangs straight down. Put your right hand through the loop, turn your left hand so the palm faces you and your right hand is behind your left. Pinch the thumb string with your right thumb and index finger, bring it under the left hand through the hand loop and loop it over the left index finger (do not get a twist in this loop). Now with your right thumb and index finger, pinch the string across the palm just before it goes between the ring finger and little finger, and loop it over the left thumb. Reach over your left hand with your right and pull the string that runs across the back of the left hand up and over the fingers. Keep pulling it up, turning your left hand palm up, and you see the four posts of your house rise to the roof.*

▦ Choko

This two-person game is still played in West Africa. The "board" is a five-by-five-square grid that may be simply scooped out in the dirt. Each player has twelve pieces—usually sticks. One player uses longer sticks, called *kala*, and the other shorter sticks, called *bono*. Pebbles, dung balls and even small onions also served as game pieces in various parts of the region. In the first part of choko, players take turns placing their pieces on the board, but they can begin moving pieces around before all the pieces have been entered. Pieces can be moved either horizontally or vertically, one step at a time. If the next space is occupied and the space beyond is vacant, the player can jump over the opponent's piece and capture it. An unusual feature of choko is that each capture entitles the player to remove any other one of the opponent's pieces from the board. The winner is the player who has the most pieces left when the game is over.

▦ Dara

This game of the Dakarkari of Western Africa was a sophisticated "three-in-a-row" type game. Five rows of six holes each were scooped out of the dirt to form the board. Each player began with twelve pieces: stones, twigs, or bits of pottery. In the first phase of dara, players took turns placing their pieces in the holes (no more than one to a hole). After all the pieces were on the board, the players took turns moving a single piece one space, horizontally or vertically, trying to make rows of three (diagonal threes did not count, nor did rows of more than three). Each time a player completed a three-in-a-row, she removed any one of her opponent's pieces from the board. When one player could not make any more rows of three, the other was the winner.

▦ Fa Kor

This game from West Africa is the familiar "pick a hand" game, made more interesting by the use of a board for keeping score and multiple simultaneous guessing pairs. The fa kor board was a series of seven concentric circles, with a dot in the center. Sometimes this design was painted on a board, but it could be simply scratched in the sand. Any even number could play, so long as they would fit around the board. Players sat around the board, each across from an opponent. Each player had a distinctive chip or marker to move across the board, and each pair of opponents had a smaller chip for hiding in the hands. All the pairs played simultaneously, so the game could become quite loud.

To play fa kor, draw the board on the ground. Each player can make a distinctive marker by drawing a symbol or picture on a nutshell or wood chip. You also need objects for hiding (nuts, shells, stones, or sticks). Each pair decides which player will go first (using the same "pick a hand" method is simplest). When everyone is ready, all the pairs of opponents begin at once. Within each pair, player A places his hands behind his back and hides the small object in one hand, then holds his hands out in front of himself. Player B guesses which hand she thinks A has the chip in. If she is right, she gets the chip and it is her turn to hide. If she is wrong, then A keeps the chip and wins a point, moving his marker into the outermost circle. Each time the guesser is wrong, the hider moves one space closer to the center. The first player to reach the center dot wins the game. The faster you and your opponent guess, the better the chance that one of you will win, so you are playing both against each other and together against the rest of the players.

▦ Hidden Stone Game

Basuto children in southern Africa played this hidden stone game.

To choose who would be "it," a child took as many pieces of grass as there were players, tied a knot in one piece, and held them all in his hand so the knot was hidden. Each player took one piece, and the player holding the knotted piece of grass was "it."

A group of children sat in a circle with the player who was "it" in the center. The others passed a small stone or bean from one to the next. No matter who had the stone, everyone kept shuffling their hands back and forth, behind their backs, under a blanket or around their knees, so that it appeared that anyone or everyone might have the stone. When the player in the center said, "stop," everyone froze, and the player guessed who had the stone. If she was correct, she joined the circle and the hider became the guesser. If she was mistaken, the stone passing began again.

▦ Igba-ita

This Igbo pitch-and-toss gambling game from what is now Nigeria was a favorite pastime for men on market day. Anywhere from two to a dozen men could play at one time, sitting or squatting in a circle, each with his pile of lucky cowrie shells in front of him.

The player to go first picked up twelve shells, and the others, to play, could stake shells in multiples of six, separating them from their piles. Once everyone betting had set out his stake, the player tossed up the twelve shells. If they should fall with all twelve facing in the same direction, he collected the complete stake from everyone. If they split, six up and six down, he collected a half a stake from each player. If the split was eleven and one, he collects one from each player. For any of these throws, the player could throw again. If the player threw a four to eight split the turn passed to the next player. Any other split didn't count, so the player would toss the shells again.

Play ended when one player had obtained all the shells, or more likely, when the players were called back to work!

The cowrie shells are basically two-sided dice in this game: each falls up or down, mouth or back. You can buy cowrie shells in craft supply stores or play igba-ita with any small objects that have two obvious sides: pennies, bottle caps, or wooden chips.

⊞ Ipenpen

This Yoruba guessing game from the Guinean coast is simple to describe but hard to play. Two players put up stakes, and a large number of seeds (about three hundred) were poured on the ground. Player A divided the seeds into two piles of approximately the same size. Player B tried to guess which pile had the larger number. They counted the seeds, and if B was correct, she won the stake. If she was wrong, A claimed the prize.

Beans or okwe seeds were commonly used for Ipenpen. Navy beans are about the right size for this game.

⊞ Kafir Row Game

This game, played by the Xhosa people of South Africa, developed dexterity and careful attention. It could be played alone or by any number of players taking turns.

This game was played with heads of grain from which the seeds had been stripped. Corn, or maize, was introduced to Africa from South America in the 1500s and this game is played with corncobs today. A type of sorghum called "kafir corn" was the grain native to southern Africa. (*Kafir*, the Swahili term for the Xhosa people, came from the Arabic word for "infidel.")

The grain heads were laid out in two rows, with the heads about two inches apart and a space about six inches wide between the rows. The first player sat beside the rows and closed his eyes. (Another player watched to make sure there was no peeking!) The player had to take the first head from the far row and drag it across the space, between the first and second heads in the closer row without touching them to capture it. He repeated this task with each head in order, drawing each one toward him between the next two heads in the line. To win the player had to "capture" all the heads. If the heads touched, the turn ended and the heads were laid out again for the next player.

You can play this game with sticks or corncobs.

⊞ Labyrinth Drawing

Labyrinths have fascinated people throughout history. There are two types: the maze, which is designed to confound, with dead ends and false paths; and the true labyrinth, which leads by a circuitous path to a

Figure 2.3. Labyrinths were challenging to make and to solve. *Source*: Kidd (1969).

center that is somehow a reward: a sacred space of wisdom, the treasure house, even the hiding place of a bride. In precolonial Africa labyrinth patterns were woven into cloth and etched in pottery and stone. (Figure 2.3). Children and adults enjoyed drawing complex labyrinths of both kinds in the sand. The labyrinth became a game by challenging another to trace the path from the outer edge to the center, without lifting the finger or retracing any lines.

The difficulty in drawing a labyrinth of any size is to be sure that there really is a way to the center. The simplest way to do this, for a beginner, is to trace the correct path first, then fill in the twists and turns, and finally remove the original line. To trace a complex labyrinth in the sand, where you cannot erase your guideline, requires excellent planning and attention to detail!

▣ Li'b el Merafib (Hyena)

Hyena is a race game still played by the Baggara (Arabs who moved into northern Africa in the seventh century). It is derived from an ancient Egyptian game called the "Coiled Snake." To this day the Baggara are nomads who cross the desert with the seasons, grazing their cattle in the grasslands during the rainy season and moving into the Nile River Valley during the dry season. The story of the hyena game is their story, as the players move from camp to camp, driven by the need for water.

The board for hyena is a spiral line with a random number of spaces scattered along it. If the board is traced in the sand, the spaces are scooped out. The starting point, at the outside end of the spiral, is the village. The center point is the oasis, and the spaces along the way are the camps. Three pieces of stick, split lengthwise, serve as dice. These are green on the curved, bark side and white on the flat split side. Each player has a distinctive marker, which represents the player's mother, and there is another, larger piece which is the hyena.

Each move is determined by the throw of the stick dice. Three green sides up are worth six spaces, while three whites up are worth three. In either case the player tosses the dice again. Two white sides up are worth two spaces, and the player's turn ends. One white side up is called a *taba*. A player must throw a taba before his "mother" can leave the village. After she leaves the village, a taba does not advance the mother, but is banked—each player keeping track of how many tabas his mother has. She will need them later. A player continues to throw the dice and move his mother until he throws a two.

Two or more mothers can occupy the same camp—they do not capture. When the mothers reach the center, they must have an exact throw to enter the oasis. A long throw, then, is a lost turn. If they are short, they can spend tabas from their store to reach the oasis—one taba per camp. Once there, the mother must pay two tabas to wash her laundry, and two more for water to take back to the village. If her "son" or "daughter" (the player) does not have enough tabas, the mother must remain at the oasis until they are accumulated. While she is waiting, any 6, 3, or 2 throws she cannot use can be "saved" and once she has paid for her water she can move quickly, using the accumulated scores.

The mothers return to the village by the same path and according to the same values. The first one to reach the village is the winner, but the game is not over. The winner pays two tabas to release the hyena, and now she tosses the dice to move this larger piece. The hyena is fast—every toss of the dice is doubled for the hyena. On its way to the oasis, however, the hyena is not dangerous. When the hyena reaches the oasis, the player pays ten tabas for the hyena to drink. Then the hyena returns to the village, eating any mothers still on the path as it overtakes them. So the first object of the game is to be the first to return to the village and release the hyena. The second object of the game is to get back to the village before the hyena catches you!

To play hyena you'll need to make stick dice by splitting some small branches in half. (You can use craft sticks painted on one side instead.) Stones or buttons can be used for the mothers. Make sure each player's mother is distinctive. Find a larger stone for the hyena. You may find it easier to keep track of your taba with paper and pencil. Finally, draw the spiral on pavement with chalk and divide it into places with cross lines, or trace it in the sand and scoop out places along the line.

▦ Mancala

"Mancala" is an Arabic word that refers to a group of games often called "count and capture" or "pit and pebble" games.

Mancala games date back to ancient times in Africa. There is evidence that the game was played in Egypt more than one thousand years B.C.E. It spread from Egypt through Africa, probably with traders moving up and down the Nile. In the Middle Ages mancala games spread through the Middle East and into India and Southeast Asia along with the Muslim faith. Later African slaves brought it to the Caribbean.

All mancala games involved scooping up playing pieces and dropping them around a board. Seeds were often used as playing pieces and the move was called "sowing." It looked a bit like planting a garden.

Many variations of the game are known today. They are grouped according to the number of ranks, or rows of cups (or pits) on the board. Two-rank versions are the most common; three-rank are the rarest. North of the Sahara and in Asia the *wari*, a two-rank board is most common. In southern Africa boards often have four ranks.

Mancala boards have been found carved in stone in Egypt. Most are made from polished wood. Years ago many were carved from ivory. In coastal areas boards are carved to resemble fish. Some stand on four legs and have covered sections for storing playing pieces. But it is also common to see people playing mancala on the ground, with pebbles or coins for pieces and cups scooped in the dirt.

The number of cups on the board varies greatly. There may be as few as four on a side or as many as ten. Larger "storehouses" are often built into the board. In some variations they are included in playing the game.

More than 250 names are known for mancala games. Mancala itself comes from the Arabic word for "move" and refers to the moving of the pieces. Many African variations of the game are called *wari*, from the word "houses," referring to the cups on the board. Sometimes the game is named for the type of wood used for the board, or for the word "board," as in the game of bao. In other countries the name of the game comes from the playing pieces, which may be pebbles, seeds, or other common objects. The name *congkak*, from the Malay word for "counting silently," best describes the skill necessary to succeed at mancala games.

Mancala games are games of skill, particularly math and logic skills. The basic game is simple enough for a child to learn, but adults find a challenge in planning strategies and comparing possible outcomes. One variation, *omweso*, allows players to move either backward or forward around the board, which adds the concept of negative numbers to the skills involved. There is no element of chance in mancala.

Rules for mancala games vary from place to place and no doubt also vary from one time to another. Thousands of local variations exist and historians can sometimes track ancient migrations of people by noting which games are played in different regions. It is not possible to know exactly how the game was played in a particular city at a particular date, but it is reasonable to assume that the rules in use today are similar to those used in that part of the world in medieval times (see Bao in Africa, Congkak in Asia, and Wari in the Middle East).

▦ Nigbé

This variation on the universal game of "heads and tails" came from West Africa in the region now called the Ivory Coast. It was most often played with cowrie shells, though chips or nuts with one side marked could be used instead. The game was simple: each player took a turn tossing the four shells into the air, and points were awarded depending on how they fell. If two fell open side down and two open side up, the tosser received two points. Four openings up earned five points and four down were worth ten. The three-and-one combination earned no points. Players kept track of their points in the dirt, and when one player reached the number agreed to in the beginning (usually one hundred) that player erased all the others' points.

You can buy cowrie shells in craft stores.

▦ Panda

Panda was an example of the math games so popular in Africa. The Mbuti people of central Africa used to challenge travelers and traders to play panda. The challenger tossed an agreed-upon number of beans on the ground, and then scooped up a handful. The other player, looking at the beans left on the ground (but not with time to count them) had to ask for one, two or three beans to be returned to the ground. The object was to make an even multiple of four. After the requested beans were added to those on the ground, the total was counted. If the estimator wound up with an exact multiple of four, he won. If not, the tossing player won. (It is intriguing to compare panda to witcli, a game from North America involving estimating multiples of four.)

This game is easier if you use a mixture of differently colored beans. The more spread out the beans are on the ground, the easier the estimation is, too. Start with a small number (twenty or forty) and work up as your skills improve.

▦ Place-keeping Game

This game from what is now Nigeria and still played today is a challenging bit of mental math, requiring observation and concentration. It resembles some modern card tricks.

Any number can play. Sixteen small stones are arranged in two lines of eight. One player moves out of earshot of the rest while they choose one stone to be the goal. When the player returns, she must figure out which stone they have chosen. She does this by asking which row the chosen stone is in, then rearranging the stones and asking again. She can ask and rearrange only four times, so careful planning and attention to detail is essential in order to narrow down the possibilities.

Players may compete for a prize, but more often the reward is simply the respect of her peers.

This game is simpler to play if the stones are somewhat distinguishable from one another. By far the easiest method is to mark them with numbers or letters, but designs of animals, birds, and fish are more authentic-looking.

⊞ Qakela

This was a child's guessing game among the Xhosa of southern Africa. All the players sat in a circle. The first contestant was sent far enough away to be unable to spy on the group. Each player selected a small object (a bean, a kernel of grain, a stone) and hid it in one hand. The guesser was called back and stood in the circle while the others held out their clenched fists. The guesser chose one hand and was required to guess what was inside. If she guessed correctly, she joined the circle and the person whose hand was chosen guessed next. If the guesser was wrong, she had another turn. A second wrong guess and the guesser was out.

To play qakela it is not necessary for each player to be hiding a different object, and in fact the game can be made simpler if there are only four or five possible objects for the guesser to choose among.

⊞ Tarumbeta

Tarumbeta is a challenging mental math puzzle still played in East Africa. A number of beans are laid out in a triangle: a single bean, then a row of two, then three, and so on. (Forty-five beans are used for the full game, but beginners start with ten.) One player, the "chief," sits at the point of the triangle, two pickers sit one on either side, and the challenger sits at the base of the triangle facing away from the beans. The pickers take away beans, one at a time, beginning at the base of the triangle. After each bean is taken away the chief asks "which one" and the challenger has to tell which bean has been removed (by number). To add to the challenge, when the lowest-numbered bean of any line is taken away the challenger must remain silent. (The beans are always picked up in the same order: the picker on the left takes away the first bean on the bottom row, the picker on the right takes away the last bean on the bottom row, then the left picker takes away the next one on the left, etc.) The challenger must hold the diagram of the triangle in his mind, keep track of which beans have been taken, and remember which numbers begin each row. If a player calls the wrong number his turn ends, and players rotate positions for the next turn.

▦ Tsoro Yematatu

This tic-tac-toe game from Zimbabwe in southern Africa was played on a board drawn in the dirt: a triangle with one line from the point to the base and another perpendicular across the center, forming seven points (Figure 2.2). Each player had three stones, which they took turns placing on the points. In the second part of the game, players moved their stones to try and get three in a row. There was no capturing.

▦ Wadi

This odds and evens game was played by the Bacongo people of central Africa. Players brought their own *mpanza*, or game disks, which they had made from pieces of calabash rind or bark. One side of each disk was light colored and the other side, dark. For a game each player used eight disks. Any number of people could play. Each player put in a stake, and everyone shook their disks and rolled them at once. Even numbers of white sides turned up were losing rolls. Odd numbers were winning rolls, and the stakes would be divided among the winners. (If several players rolled odd numbers, either the highest number would win or the pool would be divided among them, with the higher numbers winning a larger proportion of the stakes.)

If you have access to a pile of firewood you can make mpanza from sheets of bark. Dried squash rind is also authentic, but painted wooden disks from a craft store will work, too.

▦ Xhosa Stone Game

Every culture seems to have a "jackstones" game. This version came from the Xhosa people of southern Africa. Children sat in a circle and dug a small hole in the center. Fifteen small stones were placed in the hole. The first player took one stone and tossed it up in the air—before it fell, he scooped all the other stones out of the hole, then caught the one. Now he tossed it up again, and before it fell, he had to return all but one of the stones to the hole, and then catch the falling stone. If he succeeded, the stone he kept out was his, and he had another turn. If the player failed to catch the tossed stone or to scoop out or return the other stones, he lost his turn and the next child played. When only two stones were left in the hole, the play changed—the player had to toss up the stone, take the two out and place them one on either side of the hole before catching the tossed stone. If he was successful, he got to keep both stones, and the game was over. The player who had captured the most stones was the winner.

To play this game you need fifteen stones and a sandy spot to dig the hole. The stones do not need to be identical, but they must be small enough for the player to hold them all in one hand, and large enough to be easy to pick up.

▦ Zimbabwean Merrels

This two-person board game was one of the more complex version of merrels. The board was four concentric squares, with lines from the four corners and four midpoints of the central square out to the corners and midpoints of the outer square, forming twenty-four points or intersections (Figure 2.2). Each player had twelve stones. In the first phase of the game the players took turns placing their stones on vacant points on the board. Completing a line of three entitles the player to remove one of the opponent's stones. In the second phase players moved their stones, one point at a time, along the lines, to try to form mills and capture opposing pieces. In the third stage, when a player had only three stones left, he could move one stone to any free spot on the board (no longer restricted to moving along the lines one point at a time.) When a player was reduced to two stones, he had lost.

You can draw the board on paper or scratch it in the dirt. Each player's stones must be distinctive: use colored stones or checkers, or mark stones with crosses and circles.

PLAY

▦ Ampe

This game was most often played by girls of the Ewe people in western Africa. The players stood in a semicircle. The girl chosen as the first leader stood facing the semicircle. She turned to face the first player. As all the players sang, the leader and the first player clapped their hands and jumped up and down three times. The fourth jump was higher and when they landed, each player put one foot forward. If the player extended the same foot as the leader, the leader moved on to play with the next person in line. If they didn't put out the same foot, the leader repeated the routine with the same player. If they repeated three times without matching feet, the leader went to the end of the line and the next player in line became the leader.

▣ Antoakyire

This Akan version of the "drop the object" game was traditionally played only by boys in what is now Ghana. Players stood in a circle, each holding a piece of cloth with a knot tied in one end. A tree or other object some distance from the circle was designated as the sanctuary. The first player to be "it" walked around the outside of the circle, singing: "anto, akyire, anto aiyire" ("it's not behind you") All those in the circle sang the response: "yie, yie, yie" after each line. Suddenly "it" dropped his cloth behind one player, continuing to circle as before. If he reached that spot again without that player realizing it, all the others chased the designated player, beating him with their clothes, until he reached the sanctuary. Once he touched the tree, the beating stopped and the circle re-formed, with the beaten player as "it." If the selected player noticed that the cloth had been dropped, he grabbed it and chased the first player, beating him with the cloth until he reached the sanctuary. Then that player would be "it" again. (In some versions the singer sang a different line when he dropped the cloth, and then ran around the circle while the other player chased him.)

▣ Ata So

This game rewarded close observation and good guessing. Players drew straws to see who would be chief, and the chief went off and sat alone. The other players sat in a row with their feet out in front of them. The chief called to a few players to be his messengers, and they joined him. He whispered to each the name of a bird, animal, or fish, which they tried to imitate. The messenger children returned to the group, imitating their assigned animal as they approached. Each messenger selected a player and touching her outstretched toes, said, "What do you eat?" The player had to guess what animal the messenger was imitating. If she guessed correctly, she earned a point and the messenger returned to the chief for a new assignment. If the guesser was incorrect, the messenger moved on to the next player to try again. If no one guessed, the messenger revealed the animal by saying "I'll take my ____ back to the chief." Guessers kept track of their points and the first one to reach ten points was the winner and became the chief for the next game.

Because we are not as observant of the natural world as the people of medieval Africa, players may find it difficult to distinguish different types of birds or fish.

A modern version of this game could require messengers to imitate eating different foods instead.

▦ Ball Dance

This was a game played almost exclusively by women in the southern part of Africa. The ball was made of root, and described as being about the size of an orange. From ten to twenty women could play, forming two lines facing one another across a space of thirty to forty feet. The game consisted of tossing the ball under ones right leg, across the space to the player opposite, who would toss it back to the next player in line and so on down both lines. After passing the ball the players would change sides, so that they "followed" the ball back and forth. The object of the game was to keep the ball in play as long as possible.

A tennis ball will do for this game, although the original wooden ball would not bounce and a croquet ball would be more authentic. You can buy and paint wooden balls of many sizes from craft supply stores. Begin with the rows closer together and gradually increase the distance as your skills improve.

▦ Caba

Caba was the Xhosa word for tag. This version of the universal chase game was played in southern Africa. One player began the game by touching another player on the shoulder and running away. The one touched had to chase the others until she managed to touch one; then that player became the chaser. Some versions of the game included a "home" where players cannot be tagged.

▦ Che

This game from southern Africa was played only by men. The ball, which bounced almost like a rubber ball, was made from the thickest part of a hippopotamus' hide, the back of its neck.

The players formed a circle around a large flat stone. The leader threw the ball hard against the stone, aiming it so it would bounce toward the next player in the circle. That player caught it and threw it again, so that it bounced to the next player, and so on around the circle—but at any point a player might instead throw the ball against the stone so that it bounced high up into the air. At this signal the players began to leap and shout, each trying to distract the others while keeping his own eye on the ball. The player who caught the ball when it fell became the leader for the next round.

In a variation of this game two players stood inside the circle, bouncing and catching the ball off the rock. If one missed, the player in the outer circle who caught the ball took the place of the player who missed. *You can play che with a tennis ball.*

▦ Ekak

This West Africa variation of the nearly universal hidden object game was played with a ring made of a piece of vine. The ring could be as much as two inches in diameter—the smaller the ring, the more challenging the game. Several children gathered around a pile of sand, and the first hider buried the ring. Each child had a stick or a long thorn. They all plunged these into the sand to try to hook the ring. The one who captured the ring became the hider for the next game. If no one succeeded in pulling the ring from the sand, the hider tried. If the hider was successful, the others placed their hands on the sand and the hider pounded her fist against their hands. If even the hider could not find the ring, everyone helped unbury it, and the next player became the hider.

▦ Fion

This multistaged "leap frog" game for four was typically played by young boys in Cape Verde, off the west coast of Africa. It was more challenging and more competitive than the usual leap-over-everyone version.

The frog bent down with his hands braced on his knees, while the others jumped over him (from the side). The leapers could place their hands on the frog's back as they jumped but could not touch the frog with any other part of the body. If a leaper bumped the frog, he became the frog. The frog could bend as low or stand as high as he desired, as long as he kept his hands on his knees and could stay balanced. If the leaper did not leap before the frog could count to thirty, the leaper became the frog. The first leap was called the *fion*, the second was called *tape*. The third leap was called the *marton*, and on this jump the leapers were permitted to kick the frog's behind while they jumped. If they chose not to, they were required to say "purdab" or become the frog.

Finally the leapers hopped in a circle around the frog, and each kicked the frog's buttocks as he passed by. If any player touched the frog anywhere else, they changed places.

▦ Hoop-rolling

In the central African jungle, Bambuti children made hoops from vines and rolled them with sticks. This could be a solitary amusement or a contest in which boys would race to see who could roll their hoop the furthest or reach a designated point first without letting the hoop fall.

▦ Ido

Ido was the Yoruba version of a boys' game from West Africa. It was generally played by from two to six players. It could be played anywhere the ground was slightly inclined, or soft enough to be built up into a hill. (If this was not possible, a board might be set on a slight incline instead.) At the bottom of the incline a hole was dug in the ground, about the size of a fist. Each player began the game with a handful of "horses": ido seeds—from four to ten each, about the size of a marble. In the first round, players took turns placing two seeds at the top of the incline and rolling them into the hole, trying to get one to land on top of the other or on top of the growing pile of seeds in the hole. The order of play for the second round was determined by the order in which the players accomplished this object. In each turn of the second round the players rolled a seed down the incline, again with the object of landing it on the top of the pile. In this case, landing a seed on the top of the pile won the entire pile of seeds for the player.

Further west, in the Yauri version of this game, each child dug a hole and piled the dirt beside it to create the incline. The first player put two seeds into his hole, and for that round each player rolled two seeds into the first player's hole. The first to land a seed on top of the pile was the winner for that round, and the play passed to the next player's hole.

Ido is readily adapted for play today. Ido seeds, called "nickernuts" or "sea-beans," drift on the current from West Africa across the Atlantic. Today they grow along the shores of Florida, South America, and in the South Seas. People often bring them home from vacations to tropical beaches where they wash up on shore. They can be polished and saved from year to year, although in Africa the game was usually played just in the fall when the seeds were plentiful and just right for rolling. If you can't locate anyone with a cache of nickernuts, make one-half-inch-diameter balls from paper maché. Small wooden balls from the craft store will do as well (marbles are heavy and don't pile up).

▦ Ige

Tossing and catching stones, bones, or other small objects is a nearly universal game. It develops dexterity and hand-eye coordination as well as counting skills. This West African version was played with pebbles. Tossing a pebble into the air, the player scooped up a pebble and then caught the falling pebble. On the next turn the player had to scoop up two pebbles before catching the tossed pebble, then three and so on. The Yoruba version of ige was played with seven pebbles, but among the Dogon, who live in what is now Mali and Burkina Faso, as many as twenty pebbles were scooped up.

Another version of this game was played with a larger stone. The player tossed the pebble into the air, picked up the large stone, and had to catch the falling pebble on the stone (or, for a harder challenge, on the back of the hand holding the stone).

In some regions, seeds or smalls bones were used for the same game.

⊞ King of the Mountain

Racing to the tops of rocks, piles of snow, or other heights must be a universal impulse. Throughout much of Africa termite mounds provided towering challenges to young competitors (Figure 2.4). The termites build their nests above ground in these towers, which act like chimneys, drawing air through them and cooling the nests. The hard, rugged mounds can reach heights of ten feet or more, and children loved to race each other to see who would be first to clamber up to the top. Jumping down again was part of the fun.

⊞ Lions and Leopards

Still played today, this game is very similar to the English "London Bridge." Two players link hands and raise their hands to form a "trap." The others line up and march under the trap while the group sings, "Lions and Leopards, lions, and leopards, hunting at night. Lions and Leopards, lions, and leopards, catch them tight!" At the end the trap comes down, capturing the "game." Captured players form new traps, so that the line passes through more and more traps as the game goes on.

⊞ Melon-tossing Game

This was a game !Kung women of the southwest Kalahari region played when members of different clans gathered. The women formed a circle and turned counterclockwise throughout the game. Each in turn took the melon, ran into the center of the circle, and danced while tossing the melon into the air. The more complex the dance, the better. Then the dancer tossed the melon to the next woman in the moving circle, and they traded places. Obviously since a ripe melon breaks easily if dropped, the object of the game was to keep the melon in the air.

Figure 2.4. Children raced up towering termite mounds. *Source*: Kidd (1969).

⊞ Mpeewa

Clapping or rhythm games are still very popular in Africa, as they are in parts of the United States. Players often chant to help establish and maintain the rhythm. In medieval times clapping games were primarily played by girls, perhaps because the object is cooperative rather than competitive. The game is successful only when everyone manages to match the complex motions in time with the other players.

The basic form of mpeewa is a series of claps: both hands together, both hands against your partner's hands with the palms facing away from you, and both hands against your partner's hands with one facing up and the other facing down. In addition players may cross-clap, clapping their right hand against the partner's left. These games can be played in circles as well as pairs, increasing the complexity.

⊞ Ndoma

This was a herder's stick-and-ball game from the Kalahari of southwest Africa. Boys divided into two teams and used their goatherd's sticks to manuever a wooden block back and forth around a field. The object of the game was simply to keep possession of the block.

You can play ndoma with any stick. African herding sticks do not generally have a "hook" on the end. The "block" would actually have been a small piece of a branch or root, so it was a cylinder rather than a cube.

⊞ Nut Toss

Some variation of this game appeared in virtually every culture in Africa. This version came from the Ivory Coast. A small hole was dug in the ground. In the first round players stood in a circle a few feet or more from the hole (the distance agreed upon before the game) and simultaneously each tossed a palm nut into the hole. The one whose nut fell closest to the hole gained a point and became the first guard. In the next round, the other players took turns throwing their nuts into the hole, while the guard tried to hit the incoming nut with his own to keep the opponent from scoring. Each time a player managed to get a nut into the hole, he scored a point and became the guard. The game ended when every player had scored, and the one with the largest number of points was the winner. Or players could agree that when one player reached a previously agreed-to number of points, she won the game.

Use acorns or hazelnuts to play this game.

⊞ Ognazhiii

This Benue game from West Africa rewarded speed and encouraged deep breathing! At least four players were needed but any number could play—the more players, the harder the game became. Players formed two lines and chose which side would go first. The first team selected a runner, who broke suddenly and raced around the opposite team, while her teammates repeatedly called out the word "ognazhiii," or rainbow. The goal was for the runner to return to her place before her teammates ran out of air!

⊞ 'Tiang Kai Sai

Any number of children could play this game from the Kpelle people of West Africa, which combined breath-holding with counting and a tongue twister. Ten to twenty-five stones were laid in a row. The player took a deep breath and touched each stone in turn, repeating "'tiang kai sai taang (one), 'tiang kai sai fele (two)," and so forth. If he inhaled, missed a number, or mispronounced the phrase, the turn passed to the next player. In a Ghanan variation of this game a player who got to the end of the row without taking another breath captured the last stone, and the player who had the most stones at the end of the game was the winner.

It's not necessary to be able to count in Kpelle to play 'tiang kai sai, but if you want to try, here are the numbers from one to ten: taang, fele, saba, naang, lolu, lol maida, lol mai fele, lol mai saba, lol mai naang, and pu. Otherwise, choose any tricky phrase and repeat it before each number in English: Big Toy Boat One, Big Toy Boat Two, and so on.

⊞ Tossing Cowries

Tossing cowries was one common way to determine which player or team would go first in a game. Cowrie shells have one "open" side. In Africa even today they are tossed the way we toss a coin: one player tosses the shell into the air and the other calls "up" or "down." If the shell falls as called, that player goes first. If it falls the other way, the player who tossed the shell goes first.

SPORTS

⊞ Cross-country Running

Today East Africans are recognized throughout the world as champion runners. It is often observed that for the people of Kenya and Tanzania running is the primary means of transportation, and that is true. But it is also an activity the people have always enjoyed for its own sake as well. Children, adults, and even elderly people in East Africa have competed in footraces from ancient times.

The track of a footrace was typically from one village to the next. Runners ran up and down steep paths, jumping over roots, rocks and streams as they ran. A distance of eight to ten miles was not uncommon. Spectators sometimes joined the runners, accompanying them for several miles before turning back. Prizes were sometimes awarded to the fastest runner, but the most important prize to be won was the honor of the community.

For an authentic race you can select a path with a significant amount of hilly terrain, and run in bare feet!

⊞ Empatia

The Maasai were cattle herders from eastern Africa. Young boys tended the cattle that were the people's wealth. In their late teens Maasai men were initiated into a time of warriorhood by circumcision. The new warriors formed an age group: working, hunting, and fighting together until they were deemed ready to become adults. Warriors left the responsibilities of herding and took up spears. Their task was to defend the community. One goal for the warrior was to kill a lion, and if he accomplished this task he could wear a headdress made from its mane. If he killed a buffalo, he could carry a shield made from its hide. Another ritual, the *eunoto*, marked the end of a Maasi age group's warrior years and entry into the responsibilities of adulthood in their late twenties.

One of the distinctive activities of the Maasi warriors was the *empatia*, a sort of competitive dance in which the young men leapt straight up into the air. Although it was not a formal competition with "winners" or prizes, the community recognized and honored those who leapt the highest and the most gracefully.

Leaping straight into the air is difficult! Stand in a circle, bend the knees just a bit, and on signal everyone jump as high as possible. If spectators are sitting on the ground they'll be better able to judge who leaps the highest.

⊞ High Jump

Watusi youths competed in high jumping at festivals. Two reeds stuck into the ground with a third reed balanced between them formed the hurdle, some three or four feet off the ground. This jump was positioned next to a small, hardened anthill that served as the jumping platform. The jumpers ran from a distance of about twenty feet, leaping from the anthill over the reed. Any jumper who struck or knocked the reed down was eliminated. When all had jumped at the first level, the reed was raised and the jumpers began again. It was not unusual for the jumpers to leap over rods eight or more feet from the ground.

All you need to try the high jump are two sticks for uprights with notches cut at different levels to hold the cross-piece, and a cross-piece light enough to remain on the notches but fall harmlessly if struck. You can set up a small inclined board for a jump, being careful that it is solid.

⊞ Inzema

Inzema was a game of the Xhosan and Ngoni peoples that taught skills needed for hunting on the African savannahs.

This game was played by teams of equal numbers of children. Sharpened sticks were used as spears, with a round gourd as a target. When the game began the teams lined up on each side of a long field. One player rolled the gourd along the field, using his spear to bowl the gourd along. Both teams chased the gourd and threw their spears, trying to spear the gourd. The player who brought down the gourd became the bowler for the next round.

To play Inzema you will need a long open field, a target that can be rolled along the ground, and a set of spears or sticks. A ball will work as a target but cannot be speared. A small pumpkin is more authentic. On the other hand, if your sticks are sharp there is some risk to the bowler (which is also authentic but not, perhaps, desirable). For a safer game, use a playground ball as a target, and make blunt spears by gluing soft foam balls securely to the ends of broomsticks or dowels. For a more authentic game, use a small pumpkin for a target and pointed sticks or arrows for spears, and put padded shin guards on the bowler.

⊞ Katag

Wrestling in Africa was both a sport and a rite of passage. Wrestling matches (katag) among friends could be just for fun and practice. Villages held wrestling festivals where the young men demonstrated their skills and young women chose their future spouses. (In some cultures only unmarried men were allowed to wrestle. In others women wrestled, too.) Wrestling matches were sometimes arranged to settle conflicts between villages and clans. Skills developed in wrestling could prove lifesaving for a hunter or warrior in the field.

An intervillage match was an event for the whole community. Each village would put together a team of their best wrestlers. The team was accompanied by singers, drummers, and sometimes a village shaman. The host village was responsible for providing a feast for all the wrestlers and spectators, though the visitors would bring contributions to share. The wrestlers dressed in bright colors and wore decorations representing their village, clan, and totems.

On the appointed day a drummer would begin to play in the wrestling ring, often in the center of the village, summoning all to the match. Gradually more musicians would join the drummer, and then the wrestlers and some spectators would begin to dance. The dancing became more complex and enthusiastic as the number of dancers and drummers increased. Dancing served as the warm-up for the match, as well as getting everyone into the competitive spirit.

While they danced the wrestlers were both demonstrating their strength and agility and sizing up their opponents. After about an hour the wrestlers paired off, selecting a member of the opposing team who seemed about their equal in size and strength. A wrestler raised both hands as a challenge to an opponent. The selected opponent could accept the challenge by raising his hands in response, or shake off the challenge and select someone else.

African wrestling was a test of strength and agility. Tripping, pulling, and biting were generally prohibited. Different clans had different styles of wrestling, and trainers would teach their protégés their trademark holds. One description can only approximate the complexity of the sport. Generally the two wrestlers faced off, each placing one arm under and one over the arms of the opponent (never both under). In a match between unequal opponents the stronger wrestler sometimes agreed to use only one arm or to wrestle from a kneeling position in order to make the match more balanced. Depending on the ground rules accepted by both sides at the beginning, to win a wrestler had to touch both his opponent's shoulders or the nape of his neck to the ground.

Several bouts between pairs of wrestlers could take place at the same time, with the youngest and least experienced pairs opening the match. Referees watched each pair for illegal moves and to declare a winner. In some places the wrestler needed to win two out of three rounds to claim the bout. Once a bout ended, both victor and loser rejoined the milling crowd of spectators, and either might issue a challenge to another opponent and wrestle again later. The final bout, however, would be between the champions representing each village, and every eye would focus on that one pair of wrestlers.

When the champions had completed their bout the victor's teammates would carry him in triumph around the ring as wrestlers and spectators danced again. Finally everyone adjourned for a feast to celebrate and cement the good relations between the villages.

To stage an African-style wrestling tournament you will need several pairs of wrestlers, dancers, singers, and referees. Pair wrestlers by size and weight. Wrestle on grassy ground or on wrestling mats.

▦ Mpondo

Striking and parrying with sticks was a common play in most African communities, and important training for the use of weapons in battle. In some cultures two sticks were used, and the fighter could thrust or parry with either hand, while in other groups fighters carried shields of wood or metal in one hand to turn away blows. Mothers trained toddlers in parrying (defending against a blow by turning the stick away with your own stick). Children played at parrying each other, and by the time they reached their teens young boys would organize "tournaments" where the winner of one bout would take on the next challenger until a champion was determined. Spectators circled around the fighters, shouting their encouragements and sizing up potential opponents.

Each year the courtship season of the Surma people of what is now Ethiopia and Sudan culminated in the *Donga*, a stick-fighting tournament which was a ritual opportunity for the young people to demonstrate their prowess and desirability. Each village sent its eligible young men to the tournament, where fifty or more men might participate. The men were armed with long wooden poles, and wrapped their heads, necks, and ribs with cloth before dueling. Opponents squared off in pairs, swinging their poles with both hands in an effort to knock each other over. Although some injuries occurred, the object of the duel was not to hurt the opponent—killing another fighter resulted in banishment. As some fighters were eliminated, those remaining turned their attention to one another until a final victor was declared for that round. After several rounds the champion would be carried on the shoulders of the others to be presented to the young women, one of whom would choose him as her husband before the other young people selected their chosen spouses.

You can stage a stick fight in an open area. Use foam sticks or poles padded with layers of cloth taped around them. Cloth head and arm wrappings are simple and authentic, although a bike helmet and several layers of thick clothing might be simpler. Remember that the object is not to hit the opponent but to knock him over by getting him off-balance as you swing and parry.

⊞ Ox Racing

Many sub-Saharan African people were cattle raisers, so it is not surprising that young people who spent their days herding cattle might also entertain themselves by riding and racing on them. Among the Sotho, oxen racing was an organized sport, with designated courses covering many miles of rough terrain. Among other peoples, riders rode on the backs of camels, ostriches, and horses.

A cross-country bicycle race can take the place of an ox race, particularly if you ride dirt bikes across bumpy, rocky ground.

⊞ Oyo

Oyo, also called Ekoi, is a team game often played to this day by children and young men. At first glance it seems a lot like badminton, but once the teams start taking prisoners it becomes something quite different! The *ikpo-oyo* is a racket made by fastening a loop of string made from piassava fibers back to itself, creating a handle about eighteen inches long with a small "noose" on the end. The oyo is made of palm fronds tied with the same string. The stem ends are heavier and the leafy ends act like a tail, so the oyo flies when thrown rather like a shuttlecock.

The court is an open area, at least thirty-six feet long, with a line drawn across the midpoint. Players are divided into equal teams, and line up parallel to and about halfway across the court from the centerline, so that they face each other across the empty center of the court.

Team captains toss cowrie shells to determine which team will begin the game. A player on the starting team throws the oyo so that it will fall toward the opponents and land with its stem end down. The receiving players try to catch the oyo in their nooses. If one succeeds, they score a point, and the player who caught the oyo makes the next throw. If the oyo hits the ground, there is no point, and the oyo is returned to the starting team for another throw. Players develop a variety of throws in order to make it difficult to catch the oyo, but in order to be a valid throw it must come across the midcourt line higher than the players' heads.

When a team scores a point, the player from the other team who threw the oyo is captured, and crosses over into the opposing side of the court. He does not become a member of that team, however. He competes with the others in trying to catch the oyo. If the captive catches the oyo, he tries to run back with it to his own side. The others try to stop him and retrieve the oyo before he can cross the line. If he makes it back to his own team, he throws the oyo to the opponents. If the captors stop him, he remains a captive and they win the point.

If two or more players catch the oyo at the same time there is no captive, but the point counts. Some players smash the noose with the oyo against the ground as a symbol of their superiority (rather like the slam-dunk in modern basketball) but if the noose breaks or the oyo slips out, they forfeit the point and the captive goes free.

Teams may negotiate an exchange of captives. One team may require several captives in exchange for the return of a valuable player.

The game is over when one team has so few players left that it must surrender, or when one side or the other reaches an agreed-upon number of points.

To play oyo you will need to make an ipko-oyo for each player. Make a loop from grapevine or braided rough twine and fasten it to a dowel or stick handle. (The small "fiddlesticks" sold for children to practice lacrosse will also work and will make for easier catching.) The solid end of the oyo should be small enough to fit into the noose, while the "feather" end must be large enough to catch in it. You can make an oyo from cornhusks (especially if you leave them attached to the stalk end) or any stiff leaves, or use commercial shuttlecocks. Play on a lawn or sandy area to avoid smashing the ipko-oyo.

▦ Simbo-Sangnoulou

This Yakoba dance from what is now the Ivory Coast was a prime example of dance as athleticism, involving intricate acrobatics as well as strength and agility. Two *simbo* were muscular young men in their twenties; four *sangnoulou* were young children, most often girls younger than ten. All the dancers wore elaborate costumes and masks. The sangnoulou stood on the shoulders of the simbo while they danced, leapt and twisted in imitation of a serpent. The simbo tossed the sangnoulou into the air, swung them around by their hands or ankles (the way figure skaters do), and spun them in the air. All these movements were synchronized between the two simbo. In the closing movement of the dance the simbo tossed the sangnoulou back and forth between them, catching the children in their crooked arms while holding daggers in their hands. In one variation the two simbo tossed a child and a dagger back and forth, so that the dagger passed between the child's legs. (It is perhaps unnecessary to point out that they practiced with sticks before graduating to daggers.)

This dance is similar to some of the acrobatic acts performed by cheering squads today. You can stage a competition if you choreograph a dance for dancers carrying other dancers on their shoulders. Make a list of specific steps or moves each pair must do. Some possible steps for the dancers on the ground include spinning around, raising one foot and then the other, and dancing in figure eights, stars, or circles. "Riders'" movements can include leaning to one side and the other, reaching for the outstretched hands of other dancers, and waving streamers or fans. More ambitious moves might include hanging upside down while the dancer holds their knees, or swinging dancers by their arms and legs. Allow the pairs to create their own "dances" incorporating those steps. Have some drummers to accompany the dancers when they compete. Judge the competition on creativity as well as whether the dance includes all the required steps.

▦ Target-shooting Competitions

The Bambuti people of the Central African jungle were renowned for their archery skills. Their bows were small, about twenty inches long, and as the people themselves were very small they did not have tremendous force behind their arrows, yet with them they hunted and brought down all the large game of the jungle, including elephants. This required tremendous accuracy: a single shot through the eye, for example. African rulers sometimes staged competitions, to which people from all the surrounding lands might come. In target shooting the Bambuti frequently outdid their taller agrarian conquerors, who used long self-bows. At the same competitions other warriors would demonstrate their skill and accuracy with spears.

For an African target-shooting competition provide a variety of weapons, including small bows, self-bows, long darts, and light and heavy spears (see Appendix). Hang targets painted on paper or cloth on hay bales. All players, regardless of their weapons, begin from the same distance and take turns trying to strike the target. The winners of the first round then shoot again from further back, until a champion is determined for each weapon.

⊞ ASIA

Asia is the largest continent and even in the Middle Ages had the largest population of any continent. Asia is home to the world's oldest civilizations. India and China both had complex cultures and significant technological achievements thousands of years B.C.E.

During the time frame covered by this book, much of Asia was in political turmoil. The end of the Han dynasty in the 200s opened centuries of struggle in China. The land was repeatedly divided and reunited by a series of dynasties. Feudal lords levied heavy taxes and conscripted thousands of men into their armies. Toward the turn of the millennium trade flourished as China exported silk over land and sea, but increasing wealth brought invaders from the north and west—the Mongols, under Chingas (or Genghis) Khan.

In Japan the Yamato family had consolidated power by the end of the fourth century and began to struggle with Korea for control of that peninsula. These conflicts would continue throughout the Middle Ages. The Japanese maintained trade and diplomatic contacts with China, absorbing many Chinese cultural and religious traditions.

Religion defined and divided Asia. India's ancient religion was Hinduism, with its many gods and rigid class structure. But the Buddha was an Indian prince, and the faith he founded 2500 years B.C.E. was adopted by many of India's rulers. Medieval India also had a small Christian population (legend says that the apostle Thomas preached and was martyred in India). Increasing trade throughout Asia helped spread Buddhism during the early part of the Middle Ages. Japan's emperors became Buddhists at the end of the sixth century, although the majority of people continued to practice Shinto. China, which had been governed by the tenets of Confucian philosophy since the second century, adopted Buddhism in the 600s.

At about the same time Mohammed was preaching in Mecca. Islam spread into northwestern India, dramatically reshaping the culture of that people, and from India into Southeast Asia. In Southeast Asia geography and climate preserved some pockets of ancient traditions, while migration from the central part of the continent shaped the dominant cultures of those lands.

Like religions, games and sports spread with traders and invaders. Chess probably began in India and spread into both China and the Middle East. Playing cards almost certainly began in China, which was using paper long before anyone in the West. Nyout or yut from Korea may well have been the forerunner of India's chaupur/pachisi. Polo was certainly spread by the Mongols, in some cases directly as they introduced it into countries they occupied, in other cases indirectly as their enemies adopted the game to train soldiers to better fight back the horse-borne invaders.

In each country the history and traits of the people shaped the games they played. Japan's intensely formal, communal society encouraged cooperative games with elaborate, complex rules. Patterns of feudal conflict became ritualized in colorful local competitions in China. Korea, repeatedly conquered by Mongols, Chinese, and Japanese armies who banned the use of weapons, developed the "empty-hand" fighting style we know today as Tae Kwan Do.

Perhaps the best-known sports of Asia are those we call the martial arts. Unlike the military training of the West, Asian martial arts emphasized mental and spiritual training as well as physical skills. This emphasis grew from the ancient religious beliefs of the Asian people. The ancients believed that the universe was driven by two opposing principles: labeled *yin* and *yang*. Everything was made up of a combination of opposites: male and female, light and dark, good and evil. In China during the fifth century B.C.E., two related movements built on this underlying belief. Taoism directed people to live in simple imitation of nature, meditating on the lessons of the natural world. Confucianism taught that ethical living, according to the principles of *li* (etiquette) and *jen* (love) would bring yin and yang into balance and harmony.

Over the centuries covered in this book each of the Asian cultures developed distinctive methods of combat, always incorporating these ideas of balance, harmony, and the imitation of nature. While advanced training in the martial arts was the work of a lifetime for professional fighters, even ordinary people could and did benefit from the basic training of the body and mind.

Asian board games developed mental acuity and rewarded patience and foresight. Westerners attempting to learn Go or Shogi (Japanese chess) find the number of possible variations overwhelming at first.

Papermaking technology, unique to Asia through most of the Middle Ages, had a significant influence on the games and toys of the Asian people. Kites were popular with adults and children. They would have been impossible without a ready supply of lightweight material. I've observed that playing cards originated in China. Game boards in Asia were frequently painted or printed on paper, too, making them completely portable and easily replaced: players kept score in the margins. Paper games were also, of course, more subject to destruction than boards etched in stone or painted on wood.

A thousand years is not so long ago in China as it is in North America. Many of the games played then are still popular today. This makes research into their medieval forerunners both complex and fascinating. My sources of information about recreation in medieval Asia are varied. A variety of paintings and books have been preserved, some giving detailed descriptions of activities while others contain only tantalizing references. Many of the ancient documents have not been translated, so I have been forced to rely on secondhand descriptions for information. Other sources come from the reports of travelers, traders, and explorers. Marco Polo, the most famous of the European travelers to Asia, made his journey in the thirteenth century, but he was not the first traveler to make that trek. Many missionaries, traders, and adventurers crossed the Middle East and traveled the "Silk Road" into India, China, and Southeast Asia. Asian explorers traveled west over land and sea as well. The Chinese admiral Zheng He led numerous voyages into the West, bringing back not only spices and jewels but wild animals and, no doubt, games. Arab traders and Mongol raiders brought the cultures of Asia and those of Europe into far more contact than we generally realize.

An important note about Asian terminology: Chinese, Japanese, and Korean are all written in characters developed over centuries from ancient pictographs. These characters represent ideas, not sounds, so the same written characters can be read and understood by people who speak different languages. Western languages are written phonetically: the letters represent sounds. In order to write Asian languages in western (Roman) script, several systems of "Romanization" have been developed. The first such system, developed in the 1850s, is called the Wade-Giles method, for the man who developed it and the one who made its use widespread. A different method, the Gwoyeu-Romantzyh, was developed by scholars in the National Republic of China (Taiwan). The version in common use today is called *Pinyin*. It was developed by scholars in the Soviet Union and was adopted in a literacy campaign within the People's Republic of China. For political reasons, therefore, Pinyin is rejected by the people of Taiwan. Transliterations in this book may represent different systems used by various scholars, as well as the varying pronunciations found in a group of languages spoken by more people than all the other languages on the planet.

GAMES

▦ Ashtapada

Ashtapada, or ashta-kashte, is a race game from ancient India that was probably the ancestor of chaupur and, eventually, pachisi. The ashtapada board was later adapted for chaturanga. The older game continued to be popular in India during the Middle Ages, and over the years variations of the game spread into other parts of Asia along the trade routes.

An ashtapada board was an eight-by-eight-square grid (Figure 3.1). The board was not checkered, but on each side of the board the center two squares were marked: these were "castles." Each player entered and exited the board through his "castle," and pieces in castles could not be captured. On some boards the four corner squares and the four center squares were also castles. In India these boards were carved from wood, often with intricate and beautiful designs, but they could also be scratched in the dirt, and you can still see the game played this way in Southeast Asia today.

Two, three, or four players could play. Each had an even number of playing pieces (two or four). Four cowrie shells were tossed to determine the moves. A piece moved the number of "mouths" facing up, except that if no mouths faced up, the throw was worth eight spaces. Players entered their pieces on their first throw. In some versions a player had to get a specific throw to enter, generally the four or the eight (all up or all down). The pieces moved clockwise around the outside of the board, then turned and moved counterclockwise in a spiral until reaching the center, where they were removed. An exact throw was needed to remove a piece from the center square. If a player's piece landed on a space occupied by an opposing piece, that piece was knocked out and had to be re-entered (unless the occupied space was in a castle, where pieces were safe from capture).

These are other ashtapada variations:

- Dasapada had a ten-by-ten board.
- Saturankam had a nine-by-nine-square board with only five castles (the four sides and the center) and was played with two four-sided dice (four-sided dice are rectangular and marked only on the four sides, not the ends.) The four sides were marked 1, 3, 4, and 6, and players were required to roll a double one to enter a piece.

Figure 3.1. Boards for chaupur (top left) were often embroidered on cloth. Surakarta (top right) and len choa (bottom left) boards were painted on wood. Ashtapada boards (bottom center) were often carved on wood. A kono board (bottom right) is quickly drawn on paper.

- Sadurangam was played on a five-by-five-square board with five castles, but used four cowries to determine play.
- Thaayam was also played on a five-by-five-square board, using cube-shaped tamarind seeds for dice. In thaayam a piece could only enter the board on a throw of one. Thaayam also had the concept of "twinning" later seen in chaupur: if a player arranged to land two pieces on the castle square opposite her own she could declare them a "twin" and move them together around the board. A twin could only be knocked off the board by another twin.

To play ashtapada you can draw a board on paper. Each player needs two distinct playing pieces, and you need four cowrie shells or any other two-sided "dice" (coins, counters with dark and light sides, or bottle caps).

▦ Chak T'in Kau (Throwing Heavens and Nines)

This Chinese game was played with dice and later adopted for dominos. Eleven combinations were called the *civil* suit. In descending order they were: double sixes, called *heaven*, and double ones, called *earth*. Double fours were *man* and a three/one was *harmony*. Double fives were *plum flowers*. Double threes were *long threes*. Double twos were called *bench.* A six/five was a *tiger's head*, a six/four was a *red-headed hen*, a six/one was a *long-legged seven*, and a five/one was a *red-mallet six*. The other ten possible rolls were the military suit and were ranked strictly by numeric value: nines (five/four and six/three), eights (five/three and six/two), sevens (four/three and five/two), six (four/two), fives (three/two and four/one), and three (two/one).

Players rolled the dice and the one with the highest number became the first banker. All players put up stakes (which did not have to be equal), and then the banker rolled to determine which "suit" they would be playing. If the banker rolled heaven or "nine," she collected from every player. If she rolled the red-mallet six or the three, she paid every player an amount equal to what they had risked. If the banker rolled anything else, she gave the dice to the next player. That player had to roll in the same suit as the banker, any rolls in the other suit being disregarded. The player rolled again until he got a score in the suit being played. If his roll was lower than the banker's roll, he paid the banker and the next player had a turn. If any player's roll beat the banker's roll, the banker paid that player, who became the new banker. If a player matched the banker's roll there was no stake paid, and the dice passed to the next player.

⚏ Chaturanga

Chaturanga was a battle game played by four people; two loosely aligned against the other two. It was always played for stakes, which were agreed upon at the beginning of the game, paid as the game progressed, and eventually divided by the winners. When gambling was condemned by the Hindu (and later Muslim) cultures, the stakes and the dice were removed and the game began its transformation into Shatranj and a number of other chess variants. (See Shatranj in the Middle East and Chess in Europe as well as Shogi and Xiangi in this chapter.)

The chaturanga board was adapted from the board for ashtapada. It was an eight-by-eight-square grid, divided into quadrants by marking the four corner squares of each quadrant (so the board had four corner squares, four central squares and two squares on the middle of each side marked). Each player—black, yellow, red, and green—controlled an "army" consisting of a rajah or king, one elephant, one warhorse, one ship, and four infantrymen or pawns (Figure 3.2). The game began with the ships in the four corners of the board (one ancient document shows black on the north quadrant, red on the south, green in the east, and yellow in the west); then the horses, then the elephants, and finally the rajahs, on the inner square of the player's quadrant, known as the throne. The infantrymen were lined up in the next row.

Figure 3.2. Ornately carved chaturanga pieces represented the divisions of the military. *Source*: Falkener (1961).

On each turn, the throw of a long die (a wooden or ivory rectangle marked with two, three, four, or five pips on its four faces) determined which piece a player would move. Infantrymen moved on a throw of five, one square at a time forward across the board, except to capture, when they moved one square diagonally. Rajahs could also be moved on a five, one square in any direction. The elephant moved on a throw of four, horizontally or vertically in any direction, any number of vacant spaces, but could not jump. The horse moved on a throw of three, one square forward, backward or sideways, and one square diagonally, and could jump over any piece. The ship moved on a throw of two, two squares diagonally in any direction and could jump over an intervening piece. All pieces captured enemy pieces by landing on a square occupied by an opponent's piece, but ships and infantrymen could capture only each other, not any superior piece.

After throwing the die to determine which player moved first, the play passed to the left. Each player had to move according to the die, even if that would be to his disadvantage. If the play indicated was impossible, the player would lose that turn. (Because the elephant could not jump, an opening throw of four meant losing the first turn.)

Moving the rajah onto the throne of an opponent's rajah won a stake from that opponent. If the same move captured either opposing rajah the stake was doubled. Capturing the second opponent's rajah with your rajah won a double stake—quadruple if the capture was made on the rajah's own throne. Capturing the second rajah with an elephant or horse won a single stake. Mounting the throne of your ally's rajah gave you control of your ally's pieces and his turns. Then you could choose whether to move your own or your ally's pieces on either turn. Capturing both the opposing rajahs and taking control of your ally's forces was called "building an empire" and won a quadruple stake from your opponents.

A captured rajah could be regained by the ally: if your rajah had been captured and your ally captured the rajah of one of your opponents, the two players still holding rajahs could agree to exchange the captured rajahs, which would then reenter the board at their own thrones or the nearest vacant square. The opponent could, however, refuse the exchange. If one player captured all three other rajahs, that player could reenter her ally's rajah without any exchange. The ally would then regain control of his pieces, since he would have his rajah back.

Ships did not capture each other directly, because although they moved through the same spaces they never landed on the same squares. They could be captured by establishing a concourse of shipping: if three ships were aligned in adjacent squares and the fourth ship moved in to complete the square, the fourth ship captured the two opposing ships and took control of the allied ship. There were just five places where this could occur, the center four squares and the four squares in the center of each quadrant.

An infantryman reaching an unmarked square on the opposite home row could be promoted to the piece which originally occupied that square—either a horse or an elephant, but only if the player had already lost at least one infantryman. Since pawns could not move backward or sideways, if an infantryman could not be promoted it remained in place until it was captured or, if another infantryman was captured first, it received a delayed promotion. The one exception to the promotions rule occurred if a player had only a ship and a single infantryman left. In that case the infantryman was considered "privileged." If a privileged infantryman was in or reached the home row it could be promoted to any piece at the discretion of the player.

If a player lost all his pieces except his rajah the game was drawn. If a player lost all his pieces he was out of the game. In either case the ally might choose to continue, although at a distinct disadvantage since she would have only one turn to her opponents' two.

You can play chaturanga on a modern chessboard by marking the quadrant corners. Use the king, bishop, knight, rook, and infantryman pieces from differently colored chess sets, or make your own pieces from wood or clay.

⠿ Chaupur

Chaupur, the ancestor of the game we now call Parcheesi, was immensely popular in India during the sixteenth-century Mogul dynasty. Huge boards were laid out in courtyards and nobles played with servants as playing pieces. Even before that time, however, the game was well known in the subcontinent.

Chaupur boards were made from cloth and lavishly embroidered. They consisted of a cross, with four equal arms that were three-by-eight-square grids joined at the center by an open square. On each arm there were three spaces known as "castles" or "forts" where the pieces could not be captured: these were generally marked with crosses. These safe spaces were twenty-five spaces apart, and the game was sometimes called "Twenty-five."

The game was for four players, and each sat by one arm of the board. North and South were partners and played against East and West. Each player had four pieces of the same color (typically red and black play against yellow and green). Chaupur pieces were traditionally beehive-shaped.

All pieces began from the central square. Each player's pieces moved down the center of that player's arm of the board, turned and moved up the right side of that arm, and then continued around the whole board, out the left and back the right side of each arm until returning to his own arm, which he came out the left side of and then turned down the middle to return to the square. (Pieces returning up the middle track were laid on their sides to distinguish them from pieces coming down the track.) The object was to get all four of ones pieces safely home, but partners won or lost together, so sometimes one partner would hang back to enable the other to get around the board. A player could pass on a turn or waste a roll without penalty.

Cowrie shell dice determined the movement of the pieces. A player shook six cowrie shells in one hand and rolled them out on the table. If all six fell with the open sides down, the player moved twenty-five spaces and received a "grace," an additional one. (More on these later.) If the shells fell five down and one up, the roll was worth ten plus a grace. Otherwise the rolls were worth however many shells were turned up: 2, 3, 4, 5, or 6. Any roll of 6, 10, or 25 entitled the player to roll again. A single roll could not be split, but if a player won a roll again the second roll could be used by a different piece.

A player's first piece could enter the board on any roll, but each subsequent piece could only enter on a "grace." Capture was by moving into a space (other than a castle) occupied by an opposing piece or pieces. A single piece landing on a space occupied by multiple opposing pieces drove them all off, unless they were twinned. Captured pieces were returned to the square and had to reenter and begin the race again. The player who captured another piece earned a roll again. Any number of aligned pieces (those of partners) could occupy a castle but an opposing piece could not enter the castle while it was occupied, so occupying a castle could block an opposing piece's movement. Pieces could only be borne off the board by an exact roll.

As in Thaayam, if a player had two pieces in the same square she could choose to twin those pieces, moving them together around the board. A pair of twinned pieces could only be driven off the board by an opposing twin, and a single piece could not move on to a square occupied by a twinned pair, so the twin could create a blockade preventing an opponent from moving through a section of the board.

▦ Chu Zi Jin

During the Tang dynasty (620–907) people in China began keeping crickets in cages in their homes. They enjoyed the music the crickets made and considered them amusing pets. Later, in the Song dynasty, the practice of fighting crickets became a national obsession. Male crickets are naturally aggressive. In the wild they "fence" with their antennae, lock their jaws, tug at each other, and wrestle with their forelegs. In medieval China people chose and even bred crickets for strength. Fighting crickets were kept in pots, and fed seeds and insects to build up their strength. Then in the days leading up to a fight they would be kept hungry to increase their aggressiveness. Some cricket fights were continued until one cricket killed the other, but in the natural world crickets wrestle until one "gives up" by retreating, and then the other proclaims its triumph with a victory song. Chinese cricket owners discovered that vanquished crickets could be encouraged to fight again by shaking them and tossing them up into the air, rather like dice. They may have begun treating the crickets like dice because they were usually gambling on the outcomes of the fights, but modern science has learned that making a losing cricket fly a short distance causes a release of hormones that restore its confidence!

▦ Congkak

Mancala games originated in Africa but spread quickly throughout Southeast Asia along with Islam. (You can read a general description of Mancala in the chapter on African games.)

Congkak, or chunca, is a mancala game still played in Southeast Asia. It is a fast-moving game that begins with two players sowing simultaneously. In the second stage, the players must remember which cups are "burnt" or out of play.

The congkak board has two rows of cups or depressions, called houses. Generally there are seven houses on each side, and a storehouse on each end. Players own a storehouse to their left. The boards are sometimes elaborately carved of mahogany or teak, but plain wooden boards or a series of cups scooped out of the dirt can also provide for a game.

Ninety-eight playing pieces are used. In Southeast Asia cowrie shells or tamarind seeds are most common. At least fifteen pieces should fit into one cup. Wider cups are easier since it's important to play quickly. The board is set up by placing seven seeds in each cup, leaving the storehouses empty. The object of the game is to capture the most pieces.

In the first stage of the game, both players move at the same time. They begin by scooping up all the seeds from one cup on one side and sowing them (dropping one into each cup) clockwise around the board. They drop a seed into their own storehouse but skip the opponent's.

Where the last seed drops determines the next move. If the seed falls into a player's storehouse, he begins again from any one of his cups. If it falls into an occupied cup (the player's or his opponent's), he scoops up the seeds from that cup and continues around the board. If it falls into one of his empty cups, he captures the seeds from the opponent's adjacent cup, adds them to the one in his cup and places them in his storehouse. The continues by sowing the seeds from another of his cups. The first stage of the game ends when one player's side is empty.

In the second stage, players take turns. The player with fewer seeds takes the first turn. He sows the seeds from his storehouse, seven in a cup, on his side of the board. If there are not enough seeds to fill all the cups, the empty cups are considered "burnt." Burnt cups are "out" for the rest of the game. If there are more seeds in the storehouse than are needed to fill all seven cups, the excess seeds are returned to the storehouse.

Now the player scoops up and sows seeds as in the first round, except that he must skip burnt cups. If he accidentally drops a seed into a burnt cup, it goes into his opponent's storehouse.

When the player sows his last seed, if his opponent's adjacent cup is empty, he moves the last seed to his storehouse, and his turn ends. If the player's last seed drops into an empty cup on the opponent's side, his turn ends and the last seed remains in his opponent's cup. When the player's turn ends, his opponent distributes the seeds from her storehouse and then plays.

The players continue taking turns, distributing and sowing, until all of one player's cups are burnt.

⊞ Dice

The Chinese began playing games with cubic dice in ancient times. Both Chinese dominos and playing cards began as representations of the possible combinations of dice throws. Chinese dice were marked, as modern Western dice are, with pips so that the total of two opposite faces equaled seven. The single pip on a Chinese die was large, and on the side with four pips, the pips were painted red. Players usually tossed the dice into a small dish (see Chak t'in kau and Szi'ng luk).

⊞ Dominos

Scholars believe the Chinese invented *kwat pai* (dominos) after adopting cubic dice from India. Each domino represents one possible throw of two dice. Chinese dominos are bigger than European dominos, about three inches long. The one and four spots are painted red; all the rest are painted white except on the double six, where one half is red and the other half white. There are no blanks. A complete set of Chinese dominos has one domino of each possible combination plus duplicates of all the doubles: the 1/3, 1/5, and 1/6, and the 4/6 and 5/6 (for a total of 32). Almost all dominos games begin by shuffling the dominos (spread out face down on the table) and then stacking them in a "woodpile," eight across and four high.

Like dice, dominos were used for many gambling games. Some of these have immensely complicated scoring systems based on the odds of particular combinations arising. Two relatively simple games (tjak ma tcho ki and tsung shap) are included in this chapter.

You can make Asian dominos from wood, or play Asian dominos games by combining sets of Western dominos, or make domino cards: paper dominos which have been used in China for more than one thousand years.

⊞ Go

Go is a deceptively simple game that takes a few minutes to learn and a lifetime to master. It began as wei'chi in China, was played in Korea as patok, but it reached its height of popularity in Japan, with millions of casual players, thousands of touring professionals, state-sponsored academies, and an official ranking system much like the one that governs Sumo today.

A go board has 361 points, the intersections of the lines on a nineteen-by-nineteen-square grid. In China the boards were printed on paper. In Japan they were lacquered on thick, solid boards hollowed out on the bottom so the placing of a stone made a resonant "click." In Korea the hollow board was strung with wires so that each play resulted in a musical note! Most boards have some markings on several points, generally the center point and those in the center of the four quadrants. These are mostly to help players follow the location of the pieces, but also mark the places that stones are placed when a strong player gives a weaker opponent a handicap.

Beginners are strongly urged to learn to play on one corner of the board (a nine-by-nine-square grid) before attempting to play on a full-sized board. Even experienced players begin a game by concentrating in the corners of the board, then moving into the sides and finally into the center of the board.

The playing pieces are 180 white disks, traditionally made of shell, and 181 black disks made from slate. Black goes first and has a slight advantage, so the weaker player plays with the black pieces.

The object of the game is to control territory by enclosing it. Opposing pieces trapped within the enclosed space are captured, removed from the board and used at the end of the game to reduce their owner's territory. If there are vacant spaces within the enclosure, the pieces are imprisoned but still "alive" and are not removed (see below).

Players take turns placing their pieces on the points of the board. Once a piece has been placed it does not move. A piece is "live" as long as it has a "liberty," a vacant point to which it could "escape" along a line. A whole chain of pieces can be live by virtue of one liberty, and a vacant space provides a liberty even if it is completely enclosed. This is called an "eye." A cluster of pieces with two vacant eyes, both of which are connected through the chain to all the pieces in the cluster, cannot be captured. So on each turn a player is trying to create fences and clusters that are strong, having spaces built into them, while at the same time trying to close up the spaces in the opponent's fences and clusters. Novices frequently fall into the trap of building "false eyes," which appear to protect their clusters but actually leave some portion of the cluster vulnerable to capture—it is notoriously difficult to keep track of all the interconnections on the board. Territories along the edges of the board are easier to enclose and defend because the edge of the board "counts" as an enclosure.

A player cannot place a piece on a point that is already surrounded (*atari*, or "committing suicide") unless doing so will simultaneously capture an opposing piece (the rule of atari, Figure 3.3). And because interlocking squares of four points could lead to perpetual atari moves, the rule of "ko" dictates that when a player has been captured by atari, he or she must play somewhere else on the board before playing another atari in that ko. If three ko develop on the board the game is a draw.

If one section of the board is so interlocked that neither player can play without endangering his pieces, the players agree to declare that section *seki*, or stalemated, and both leave it untouched until the end of the game. The territory contained within the seki does not count for either player.

On the other hand, if a cluster develops where the capture of a cluster is inevitable, the players can declare those pieces "virtually dead" but leave them in place until the game is over.

A go game ends by mutual agreement, when each player believes there is no further advantage to be gained. Go games average one to three

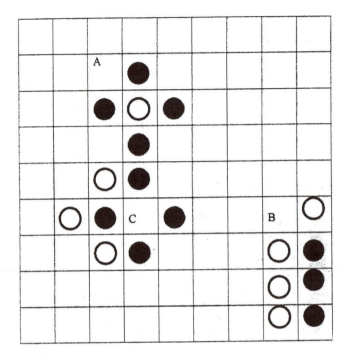

Go positions: A Black captures one white
B White captures three black
C Atari/ko

Figure 3.3. In go, pieces are captured by surrounding them. Rules prohibit *atari* (suicide) unless an opposing piece is captured in the same move, and also prohibit repeating atari in the same spot.

hours long, although tournament games between well-matched players can last for days. When players agree to end the game, they fill in any nonenclosed vacant spaces with leftover pieces to facilitate counting. Next any "virtually dead" pieces are removed from the board. Finally, players use their captives to fill in their opponent's captured territory. The enclosed vacant spaces remaining are counted, and the player with the larger number of enclosed vacant points is the winner.

To make a go board, draw the nineteen-by-nineteen-square grid on paper. Use carbon paper to transfer the grid to a board if you want a permanent board. Black and white stones are traditional go pieces. Look for stones at garden or aquarium supply shops. You can also make pieces from modeling dough and paint them. Buttons are an easy substitute.

⊞ Hasami Shogi

Hasami Shogi is a Japanese alignment and capture game played on one corner of a "go" board (a nine-by-nine-square grid) using the same pieces. No doubt it was developed by parents and children trying to adapt "go" to a child's level, but it is still a challenging game.

Players begin with eighteen pieces each, lined up in the squares of the two rows closest to the player (so there are five empty rows between them). The object of the game is to form a row of five pieces in those center rows. A piece can move any number of vacant squares horizontally or vertically, in any direction. A piece can also jump over a single adjacent piece into a vacant square (this is not a method of capture). A piece cannot move through vacant spaces and jump in the same move.

Trapping an opposing piece (or pieces) between two pieces in a row or column is a capture, and captured pieces are removed from the board. One pair of pieces can capture several opposing pieces between them as long as there are no vacant spaces in the chain. A player can move a piece between two opposing pieces without being captured.

Five in a row, horizontally, vertically or diagonally in the center of the board, wins the game.

⊞ Kono

Kono is a name for several different medieval Korean games of position, some of which are still played today. They seem simple but are more challenging than they appear.

Simple kono is played on a board that is a square, divided on the diagonals, with one of its sides missing. Each player has two pieces, which begin on the four corners of the square. A piece moves from intersection to intersection along a line, one space on a turn. The object of the game is to block the opponent so he cannot move.

Four-field kono is played on the sixteen points of a three-by-three-square grid. Each player begins with eight pieces on his side of the board (there are no vacant points). Capture is by replacement: a piece has to jump over one of its own pieces and knock out the opposing piece on the next point. When not capturing, pieces move one space along any line. A player wins by capturing all the opposing pieces or blocking the opponent so he cannot move.

Despite sharing the same name, five-field kono is a completely different game. The game is played on the twenty-five points of a four-by-four-square grid. Each player has seven pieces and begins with them aligned on the home row and the outside points of the second row. The object of the game is to move all the pieces to the opposite side of the board in the same arrangement. Pieces move diagonally across squares and can move either forward or backward, and there is no capture.

⊞ Len Choa

Leopard games come from Southeast Asia. They are similar to the "fox and geese" games of Europe but most scholars believe they developed separately. This version was played in Siam, the kingdom that is now the country of Thailand. The len choa board was an isosceles triangle, bisected from the top to the base and with two lines across it, so that it was divided into six sections and had ten points or intersections. One player had a single piece, the leopard, while the other controlled six pieces, the sheep (or in some versions one tiger may chase six leopards).

The game began with the leopard piece on the point of the board. In the opening moves the sheep player entered one piece per turn on any empty point. On her turn the leopard player moved her single piece one space at a time along any line. The leopard captured by jumping over a sheep onto a vacant point beyond, and the object for the leopard player was to capture all the sheep. The object for the sheep player was to surround the leopard so it could not move.

A len choa board is easy to draw on paper, paint on wood, or scratch in the dirt. The leopard piece is usually bigger than the six sheep pieces. Toss cowrie shells or throw fingers to determine who will be the leopard for the first game. For repeat games, players alternate playing the leopard or the sheep.

⊞ Luk Fu

Luk fu is a game still played with Chinese money cards. Luk fu is sometimes translated as "six tigers," because the word "fu" can mean either "tigers" or "points," depending on the way it is said, and the object of this game is to collect sets of six cards by winning tricks. The rules given here are somewhat simplified.

Luk fu is a three-sided game. If only three play the *leeten* ("wild card" ace) is discarded. If there are four players the leeten is used, but one player (either the dealer or the player opposite the dealer) receives only one card and doesn't play until the end of the game. The three active players receive twelve cards each. Players look at their cards but do not reveal them.

After the cards are dealt the dealer declares whether or not he thinks he can win (*tsoh*) or not (*um tsoh*). If he declares um tsoh, the player to his right may declare. If that player also states um tsoh, the next active player (not the player with a single card) declares. If all three declare um tsoh, the hand is redealt. If the player who declares tsoh does not win the round, she pays the stake both for herself and for the other losing player.

Play passes counterclockwise, beginning with the dealer (even if he declared um tsoh). A player can lead either a single card or a cluster. The next players must either beat the cards already played or discard an equal number of cards, upside down. Discarding is called *pug pai*.

Single cards are valued according to their rank, so a three outranks a two, and so forth. If a single card is led, the other players must follow suit, so by leading the highest-ranking outstanding card of a suit the player is guaranteed to win the trick.

Multiple-card clusters can be three or four cards of the same rank (*gok*), or any consecutive sequence of three or more cards of the same suit (called *sun*, except in the highest-ranked suit, when they are called *kia*). Clusters of higher-ranking cards (in number or suit) beat clusters of lower-ranking cards. Because the red cards outrank the others, a cluster with a red ace beats any other cluster except a cluster of nines. The cluster of all five aces beats all other gok.

The rule of *lao sui* states that if a player holds the highest outstanding card of the highest remaining suit in his hand he must lead it. This rule does not apply to the player who declared tsoh; that player may lead the lao sui (highest outstanding card) of any suit. Because discarded cards are unrevealed it is possible that the lao sui is unknown, but then it cannot be used to win a round, either. (Note that this rule is preserved as the hukm in Persian ganjifa games.)

The player who wins a round places the winning card or cards in front of her. The losing cards and any discards are piled in the middle of the table. The first player to accumulate six winning cards wins the hand. If there is a fourth player, that player becomes the winner if his single card matches the rank of any of the six winning cards.

⊞ Moksha-patamu

Moksha-patamu was an Indian game designed as a tool to instruct children in the moral virtues. According to the Hindu sages the forces of good and evil within each individual grew stronger or weaker depending on the person's actions. Since the way to nirvana, "heaven," was through gradual perfection, a person could shorten the journey, and reduce the number of reincarnations necessary to achieve perfection, by doing good deeds and avoiding evil ones. On the moksha-patamu board good deeds enabled the soul to climb ladders to higher levels of enlightenment, avoiding many passes across the board. Wicked deeds caused the soul to slide precipitously downward on the backs of serpents, necessitating retracing steps already taken. So too, a soul could escape to heaven by striving for enlightenment, or be condemned to repeated cycles of reincarnation by indulging in evil deeds.

The moksha-patamu board was a ten-by-ten-square grid (100 squares). Pieces moved across the board, beginning at the bottom left corner and moving to the right, then from right to left in the second row and so on, climbing toward the top. The virtue ladders were faith (square 12 to 36), perseverance (51 to 91), giving alms (57 to 75), piety (60 to 97), good conduct (63 to 85), compassion (66 to 88), knowledge (76 to 94), and most virtuous, self-denial (78 to 100). The snakes' heads represented the vices disobedience (41 to 4), vanity (44 to 23), impure thoughts (49 to 10), thievery (52 to 7), deceit (58 to 19), drunkenness (62 to 21), debt (69 to 31), murder (73 to 1), anger (84 to 13), greed (92 to 34), pride (95 to 26), and, worst of all, desire (99 to 29). Vivid paintings often represented both the virtues and vices and the heights or depths to which they might bring the soul.

Passage was determined by the throw of six cowrie shells: players moved the number of mouths facing up, and a roll of six entitled the player to another turn. The first to reach 100 won, but had to finish by an exact throw. If the throw was too large the player had to move up to the 100 spot and then back however many excess spaces were left, a vivid reminder of the danger of attachment!

The game will feel very familiar to anyone who has played the commercial children's game "Chutes and Ladders." ™

⊞ Nyout

Nyout is a Korean race game that goes back at least 3,000 years. It is an example of the "cross and circle" games that some anthropologists believe are the ancestors of almost all board games. Nyout is still popular in Korea today.

A nyout board is a circle of twenty spaces, with the spaces at the cardinal (compass) points larger than the rest. Five spaces are marked across the circle, from North to South and another five from East to West (the center of the circle forming the center of both diameter lines). This board can be easily drawn on paper or scratched in the sand. It has been found carved in wood, charcoaled on bark, and etched in stone.

The playing pieces, called *mal* (horses), are made of wood, plastic, stone, clay or even scraps of paper. If two people play, each has four horses. If three play, each has three horses, and if four play, each has two horses and they play as a team (sitting across from each other). Players sit at the compass points, and each one's horses enter and exit the board from their own side.

Moves are determined by throwing dice. Korean dice, called *pam-nyout*, are small pieces of stick, flat and white on one side, slightly caved and blackened on the other. Different combinations have different values: all black are worth five spaces; all white four spaces; three white and two black, three spaces; two white and three black, two spaces, and one white, one space. All black or all white also win an additional turn.

Players begin off the board, toss the dice, and enter their horses one at a time. A single toss of the dice cannot be divided between horses, but on any turn a player can choose which horse to move. If a horse lands on one of the compass points, it can "take the short cut" across the diameter line back to the exit. If a horse lands on a space occupied by an opponent's horse, that horse is knocked from the board and the owner has to reenter it on another turn. With four players, if a horse lands on a space occupied by the partner's horse, the two continue as a "pair." In addition a player can choose to move a partner's horse instead of his own if it is to the team's advantage.

The premise of the game is simple. Each player enters pieces at one point and tries to be the first to get around the circle and back out again.

You can draw a nyout board on paper and play with any small pieces. Make Korean-style dice from small blocks of wood or plastic, colored dark on one side and light on the other.

▓ Playing Cards

We know playing cards were invented in China before the year 1000, since there is a historical reference to the Emperor Mu-tsung playing cards with his wives on New Year's Eve in the year 969. Chinese playing cards were about an inch wide and about three inches long, much like the dominos from which they were derived. The markings on these cards represented the various combinations of dominos. It is most likely that these cards were used originally to play dominos games, and then other games developed based on the fact that a player could hold paper cards in one hand and hide their values from other players. Paper cards were also used very early in a "forfeits" sort of drinking game in which players had to perform the actions marked on the cards. These may have developed into the poem cards used in shi karuta (discussed later). Yet another form of paper cards represented the playing pieces used in xiangqi (discussed later), retaining the four colors of chaturanga, which are still used for card games today.

"Money cards," the most common form of Chinese cards in use today, were probably a slightly later development, though still medieval. Luk fu, described in this chapter, used money cards. Chinese money cards have four suits based loosely on Chinese currency: *tyen* (coins), *sok* (strings or knots—medieval Chinese coins had holes drilled in them and were strung for safekeeping), *gong* (myriads of strings), and *sup* (tens of myriads.) Different regions of China name the suits differently.

The backs of the cards are usually plain black. In each suit the cards are numbered from one to nine, with aces low. There are also two extra cards in the deck, one of which is not used in any known game, rather like the jokers included in American decks of cards. The other card, the *leeten*, is a "wildcard" ace. The four nines, the aces of the lowest and highest suit, and the eight of the highest suit are all colored red. These red cards outrank other cards, acting almost like trump cards.

Korean playing cards were very long and narrow: seven or eight inches long and as narrow as a quarter- or one-half inch wide. They probably developed not from Chinese cards but independently, perhaps from an ancient arrow game; in fact, the traditional marking on the back of the cards looks like a feather, and may have represented the fletching on an arrow. There were ten cards in each suit, numbered one to nine, with a single court card called the *tjyang*, or "general." A deck might have six or eight suits. The suits were *sa ram* (man), *moul ko ki* (fish), *ka ma koui* (crow), *khoueng* (pheasant), *no ro* (antelope), *pyel* (star), *htok ki* (rabbit), and *mal* (horse). Unfortunately no complete instructions for games with these cards have been found: the game described in this chapter is a simple counting game.

The Japanese did not adopt playing cards from their Chinese or Korean neighbors, perhaps because cards were considered games of the lower classes in those countries. Japan does have a unique tradition of playing cards, but it developed from the cards introduced to Japan by Portuguese sailors in the sixteenth century.

Chinese money cards are readily available in communities with Chinese immigrant populations, or from the Internet. You can make Chinese or Korean playing cards from card stock. Since the characters are complex and will not be easily recognized, it will probably be simplest to mark the cards with Arabic numerals and pictures representing the suits. (You can print copies of Chinese cards from the World Wide Web and paste them on stock. See the bibliography.)

▦ Shi Karuta

Chinese shi karuta cards probably began as a teaching tool. The game resembled modern bingo. There were two hundred cards in a deck, one hundred with the first line of a poem or proverb written on them, and one hundred with the last lines.

Any even number of players could play, although two was the usual number. The last line cards were dealt to the players, who arranged their cards face up in front of them. The dealer read the first line cards, one at a time, and players touched the matching last line card. When a player was first to touch a card dealt in front of another player, he gave that player three of his own cards. The first player to run out of cards was the winner.

You can make shi karuta cards with familiar nursery rhymes, epigraphs, or song lyrics. For more authentic cards use the proverbs of Confucius, which you can find in many books or on the Internet.

▦ Shogi

Shogi is a version of chess that developed in Japan. It probably developed from an intermediate Chinese version of the game, something between chaturanga and xiangqi (discussed later). Legend says that early shogi variations, played on go boards, had more than 300 pieces. The somewhat simpler version of shogi played in Japan today developed between the twelfth and fifteenth centuries.

A shogi board is a nine-by-nine-square grid. The pieces are played on the cells rather than the points. All the cells, and all the pieces, are the same color. (Captured pieces become part of the opposing army.) The cells are rectangular, not square, because the pieces are flat, elongated pentagons with a point at one end (they look like little tents; Figure 3.4). When the pieces are on the board they point at the opponent, so when a captured piece is reentered it's turned in the other direction. Characters on the tops of the pieces show what they are. Since most pieces can be promoted when entering enemy territory, they are marked with their starting rank on one side and their rank after promotion on the other, usually in a different color.

At the start of the game each player has twenty pieces. In place of the two mandarins and the general of the Chinese game, shogi has three generals with varying moves. The *o-sho*, or jeweled general, can move one square in any direction. The o-sho is in effect the king, and the object of the game is to put the o-sho in a position where it cannot escape capture. The *kin-sho*, or gold general, can move one square in any direction except diagonally backward. The *gin-sho*, or silver general, can move one square in any direction except sideways or straight backward.

Next in rank are the *kakko*, or angel, and *hisha*, or chariot. The kakko has the same move as the bishop in European chess: it can move any number of spaces in any direction on the diagonal. The hisha moves like the castle in modern European chess: any number of spaces in any direction on the horizontal or vertical.

The shogi army includes nine foot soldiers, called *fu-hyo*; two spear-carriers, called *yari*; and two *keima*, or mounted soldiers. Fu-hyo move one square forward on each turn. The yari move any number of spaces

Figure 3.4. Shogi and xiangqi pieces are distinguished by painted characters rather than shape. *Source*: Adapted from Falkener (1961).

straight ahead. The keima move two spaces forward and one to the side (the same as the knight in European chess, but only in a forward direction). Keima are the only pieces that can leap over another piece.

All the pieces except the kin-sho and o-sho generals can be promoted when they move into, out of, or within enemy territory (the opponent's three home rows), but a player is not obligated to promote a piece if he believes it to his advantage to retain one of the different moves. To promote a piece the player just turns it over. The kakko and hisha, when promoted, become the most powerful pieces on the board, keeping their own moves and adding the move of the o-sho general. The promoted kakko is called the *ryo-ma*, dragon horse, and the promoted hisha is called *ryo-wo*, dragon king. Fu-hyo, yari, keima, and gin-sho are all promoted to kin-sho (their promoted sides include a symbol indicating what their original rank was). Once promoted a piece cannot be returned to its original rank except by capture.

All pieces in shogi capture by moving into an occupied space in their usual move. When a player captures a piece, she can choose to enter it as her own piece on a later turn. This is called "dropping" the captive piece. Dropped pieces enter the game at their original rank, but can be promoted on a later turn. A player can drop a piece on any space, except that a player cannot have two fu-hyo in the same column. Dropping is a move, and any piece except a fu-hyo may be dropped in a position to cause an immediate checkmate.

Shogi pieces can be cut from cardboard or light wood. Use markers to put symbols representing the various pieces on the pieces: perhaps a three different crowns for the three generals, spears for the yari, a horse for the keima, wings for the kakko, and a wheel for the hisha. A bow could represent the fu-hyo.

⊞ Ssi-teu-ki

Cat's cradle is played throughout northern Europe and North America today. Its name is a modernization of "cratch cradle," derived from the French *"creche"* (manger), but this string game is not of European origin. It was played throughout the Orient and probably came to Europe along with tea and the other exotics that would one day make the China trade so lucrative. String games are played across Asia by children and adults, both men and women. The figures have different names in different countries. In Korea the game is called ssi-teu-ki, "woof-taking" (the "woof" is the cross-thread in weaving; Figure 3.5).

1. Player A begins with a medium-length loop of string by putting both hands into the string so the loop hangs in front of the thumbs and across the backs of the hands.
2. A brings the right hand toward the left and slides all four fingers under the near string; draws back and loops a circle around the hand; then does the same motion with the left hand.
3. A then slides the right middle finger under the string across the left palm string and draws the hand back.
4. A slides the left middle finger under the string across the right palm string between the middle finger strings, and draws back. This figure is called the *sang-tou-tou-ki*, "a cover for a carriage bearing the dead."
5. Bringing one hand on either side of the figure, player B pinches the left crossed strings between the left thumb and index finger, and the right crossed strings with the right thumb and index finger.

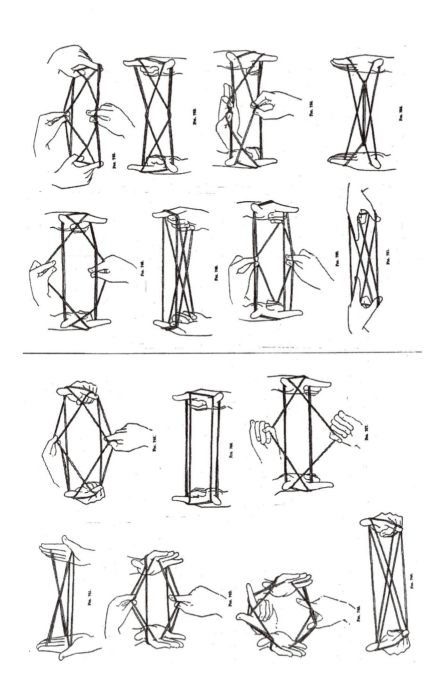

Figure 3.5. Ssi-teu-ki is the Korean original of the game known in North America and Britain as cat's cradle. *Source:* Adapted from Jayne (1906).

6. B draws the strings out to the sides, down and under the figure, brings the hands up through the middle of the hand loop while A removes her hands from the string. As B separates his hands the crosses form loops on the index fingers and thumbs and a pattern of crosses strings appears. This figure is called *patok-hpan*, the chessboard.

7. From the top, A pinches the center of each long X between a thumb and index finger, lifting them up and out, then down and under the side strings and comes up in the center of the figure while B removes his hands from the string. As A separates her hands the strings form four parallel lines, the outer strings doubled and the inner strings single. This figure is known as *tjye-ka-rak*, chopsticks.

8. B reaches across the figure with palms facing upward to hook the left inner string with the right little finger, and the right inner string with the left little finger. Drawing each string across over its opposite outer string, B brings the index fingers and thumbs up under the outer strings, lifting the figure off A's hands and, spreading the thumbs and index fingers, forming the same figure as in step four, only upside down (the hearse cover standing upright).

9. A takes the string off exactly as in step 5, except "upside down"—after pinching the crossed strings between the index fingers and thumbs she pulls them up over the side strings and down through the center of the figure, winding up with the chessboard again (except that her fingers are pointed down, not up).

10. B now takes the strings off just as A did in step 7, pinching the X's between the thumb and index finger and drawing them out, over and around the side strings, and coming up through the center of the figure. Instead of the chopsticks, however, this move results in a figure known as the *soi-noun-kal*, a cow's eyeball: a central diamond shape surrounded by triangles.

11. A pinches the central twist on each of the sides of the figure between her thumbs and index fingers, draws them apart and spreads her thumbs and index fingers apart. The figure that forms is a diamond with a double string across it, held by single loops around the thumbs and index fingers. This is the last figure, called *tjeyl-kou-kong-i*, or "a pestle for grinding rice."

▦ Sugoroku

Nardshir, the forerunner of backgammon, must have traveled into Asia along the Silk Road (the Asia/Persia/Europe/trade route). Games with names that were variations of "double-sixes" are recorded in India and China by the seventh century. Eventually the game was adopted by the Japanese, who called it sugoroku or sonoroku.

The Japanese sugoroku board was flat with twelve lines on each side, bisected the long way by a "river," which seems to have come into the game from xiangqi (discussed later in this chapter). The pieces were upright pins, not flat checkers as in Europe, but the beginning layout appears to have been the same as in Nardshir (see the Middle East chapter). When a player rolled doubles, however, each die had to be used to move a different piece, and there was no extra turn.

Sugoroku was discouraged in the seventh century when it was believed to be interfering with "go." After the game died out the name came to be used for any board game with dice.

To play sugoroku, draw a board divided into two sections by a "river" and divide each section into twelve equal parts. Follow the instructions for Nardshir in the Middle East chapter.

▦ Surakarta

Surakarta is a game for two players still played in Java, part of what is now Indonesia. The board is a five-by-five-square grid, with pieces played on the points, not on the squares (so there are thirty-six places). Outside each corner of the grid two curved "paths" are drawn, one between the second points on each side, and another between the third points on each side (Figure 3.1). A player captures an opponent's piece by moving along one of these eight paths to the spot occupied by that piece.

Each player begins with twelve pieces, generally black lava stones for one player and white coral for the other, lined up on their two first rows. A piece can be moved one space in any direction into a vacant space, unless it is capturing. A capturing piece can cross any number of vacant spots to get to the path.

The player who captures all the opposing pieces wins the game. If neither player can win the game is drawn.

Draw a surakarta board on paper and use stones, coins, or other tokens as playing pieces.

▦ Szi'ng Luk

This popular Chinese dice game is called "string of flowers" in English. In this game with three dice, the only scoring rolls are three-alike (*wai*), 4–5–6 (*szi'ng luk*, or string of flowers), two-alike, and 1–2–3 (*mo lung*, or "dancing dragons"). In the three-alike rolls a higher number outranks the lower ones, and in two-alike, the rank is based on the number of the odd die. To begin, players throw one die, and the first player to roll the red four wins and becomes the first "banker." Players decide what the stake will be, and each puts an equal amount on the table. The banker rolls the dice until a scoring combination appears. If that roll is a three-alike, a two-alike with the third die a six, or the string of flowers, the player collects all the stakes, and is the banker again for the next game. (The other players have to put up more stakes to play.) If the banker rolls the dancing dragons or a two-alike with the third die a one, the banker pays each player a matching amount to the stake they put up and rolls again. If the banker rolls a two-alike with the third die a 2, 3, 4, or 5, the player to the left of the banker takes the dice and rolls until he or she rolls a scoring combination. Then whichever of the two has the higher roll pays the other the stake and becomes the banker for the next game.

⊞ Tjak Ma Tcho Ki

This is a Korean dominos matching game for two, three, or four players. The dominos are shuffled and stacked in a "woodpile" eight across and four high. The first player draws six dominos (one stack plus two from the next) and the others each take five (dividing the half stack, then each taking a full stack, etc.). The first player tries to make a match from the dominos in his hand. If this cannot be done, the player lays one domino face up on the table. The next player may take up that domino or draw one from the pile, and after trying to make pairs in his hand, discards any one domino. Each player repeats this process around the table. The object of the game is to make three pairs. (Since there are only eleven pairs in the set, if four people are playing the 6/6 may be counted as a pair.) Some versions require that the third pair be completed with a new domino (from the woodpile, not from the table).

⊞ Tsung Shap

Two players divide the woodpile between them to begin this ancient Chinese dominos game. The first player takes the top right domino from his pile and lays it face up in the center of the table. The second player does the same, laying her domino next to the first one. They continue to draw and put down the dominos, making a row along the center of the table. With each new addition, the players attempt to "make tens": if the new domino is a match for the domino at either end of the row, the player takes the pair. The spots on the matched dominos are worth ten points each.

If the spots on the new domino plus the spots on the dominos at the ends of the row, or the two dominos at either end of the row, make a multiple of ten, the player takes all three. The spots on these dominos are worth one point each.

If the play clears the table the player stacks that pair distinctively, because the "sweep" earns a bonus of forty. The player then draws another domino from his pile to restart the table.

If a player misses a combination the opposing player may claim it before taking a turn. The game ends when one player is out of dominos, and the winner is the player with the highest score.

⊞ Xiangqi

Most scholars believe chaturanga (discussed earlier) came into China from India in about the middle of the eighth century, although some believe an earlier version of the game had originally come to India from China. Xiangqi, the Chinese version, is an interesting example of the influence of the culture on the game: the cannons only make sense in the context of the Chinese use of gunpowder, but the Indian elephants remain in play although they were unknown in China.

The traditional pieces in xiangqi are disks inscribed with the symbols of the pieces (Figure 3.4). For the Indian rajah the Chinese substituted a general, reportedly at the behest of an Emperor who was outraged to discover that a commoner could direct the imperial moves, even in a game!

The board is still an eight-by-eight-square grid, although it is divided in half by a "river." All the pieces can cross the river except the elephants. Pieces move on the intersections of the lines, rather than the spaces. The two middle squares of the first two rows on each side are "fortresses" and the general and mandarins are confined to those spaces.

When the game begins each player's major pieces are aligned along the home row. Beginning in the left corner the order is chariot, horse, elephant, mandarin, general, mandarin, elephant, horse, and chariot. No pieces begin in the second row. In the third row the cannons are set one point in from each edge. In the fourth row the five soldiers are spaced equally—one on each outside point, one on the midline, and the other two on the third point in from each side.

All pieces capture by replacing an opponent's piece when they land on an occupied point (but notice the added requirement for a cannon). Captures are not compulsory.

Generals can move just one point at a time, vertically or horizontally, and they cannot leave the fortress. The generals cannot stand in the same file unless there is another piece between them. The mandarins, like the counselors of shatranj in the Middle East, move one point diagonally in any direction. They, too, are confined to the fortress.

Elephants move two points on any diagonal, but the point in between must be vacant. They cannot cross the river. Horses move in an angle; one point horizontally or vertically and then one point diagonally. The in-between point must be vacant.

Soldiers move one point at a time. On their own side of the board they move only forward. After crossing the river they may also move side-ways. They never move backward and there is no promotion, so reaching the opponent's home row confines the soldier to a side-to-side movement.

Chariots move any number of points in a straight line, horizontally or vertically, as long as the points in between are vacant.

Cannons are the most unusual pieces in this game. They move like chariots, but in order to capture they must jump (or fire) over an intervening piece, which acts as a "screen." They can land as many places as desired beyond the screen. (Note that this means at the beginning of the game the cannons can immediately capture and replace their opposing horses.) They cannot jump over two pieces but may jump over one and capture the next. They can move sideways and backward but can only capture forward (because Chinese cannons could only fire in a forward direction.)

The object of the game is to place the opposing general in checkmate; that is, in a position to be captured from which it cannot escape. The check may be broken by capturing the threatening piece or placing a piece in such a way as to make the threatened capture impossible—this can include removing a screen from a cannon or placing a piece on the midpoint of a horse's move.

Draw or paint a xiangqi board on paper or wood: four rows of eight squares on each side with a row without cells in the middle. Mark the fortresses, the two center squares of the first and second rows on each side. Chinese chessmen are disks, marked with the characters of the various pieces, with each player having pieces of a distinct color. You can make these pieces from wooden disks or modeling dough, and mark them with symbols representing the piece's roles.

⬛ Yet-pang-mang-i

This medieval Korean game is a playing-card variation of a dominos game. Any number of players can play. The object of the game is to make combinations equal to nineteen. The dealer gives one card to each player, which they look at before deciding how much to bet. They place their bets beside their cards, and the dealer matches each bet. Each player then draws one or two cards from the pile. A total of nineteen wins the hand. If no one has nineteen, then the winner is the player with the next best combination: three of the same rank, or the next closest sum to nineteen (a player whose cards number more than nineteen has lost). If more than one player's cards equal the same sum, then the rank of the suits determines the winner.

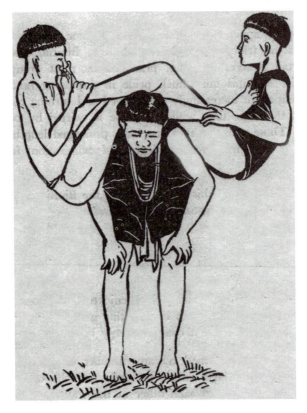

Figure 3.6. Awoli-sheshe, or back riding, was popular in the Himalayas. *Source*: Pugh (1958).

PLAY

▦ Awoli-sheshe

This game was popular with children in Kampur and Nepal. One child bent down on hands and knees, and two others (of about the same weight) lay on the ground with their legs up and over his back (Figure 3.6). Each grabbed the ankles of the other and held on tight. Then the first player stood up (but stayed bent over at the waist) and gave the others a ride as if they were packs on a horse or camel.

▦ Back-riding Duels

In Japan, as probably everywhere, one child would climb up on another's back for a ride. When several pairs of "horses" and "riders" had assembled, they would gallop toward each other, the riders using their feet to try and knock each other off.

⊞ Blind Fishing

The game of a blindfolded player attempting to catch those who can see has always been a source of amusement. In China this game went by the name of blind fishing. While searching the blindfolded player would announce, "tide is high" or "tide is low." When the tide was high, the "fish" clapped their hands, to sound like fish splashing in the water. When the tide was low, the fish were quiet. The fisherman, once he caught someone, had to identify the person before removing the blindfold and passing it to the next fisherman.

⊞ Calah Panjang

Calah panjang is a Malaysian running and chasing game for two teams of six each. The game is played on a grid drawn in the dirt: five parallel lines about twenty yards long and four to five yards apart, with a center line running through them all on the perpendicular. Each chaser is assigned one line to patrol. He or she must remain on that line, ranging back and forth to try and tag any runner that crosses it. The running team tries to run up and down the length of the field, avoiding being tagged by the various chasers. If a runner is tagged, the teams change places. If one runner succeeds in getting the length of the field and back, his team wins.

⊞ Chowdia

Leapfrog was played all over the world. In Kampur, in what is now northeast India, it was called chowdia. Players lined up, crouched on the ground and leaned forward, placing their hands on the ground in front of them. The last player in line took a running start, placing both hands on the backs of each bent-over player and vaulted over him. Upon reaching the front of the line the player crouched down and the next player had a turn.

⊞ Diabolo

This popular toy was not known in Europe during the Middle Ages, but the diabolo, or *tjouk-pang-oul*, had been a standard among jugglers in China from ancient times. By the time Marco Polo made his journey into China, the "devil on two sticks" was a plaything throughout Asia.

During the Ming Dynasty a poem was even written about this toy, the "hollow bamboo bell."

Players held two sticks with a string tied between them in their hands. There were two types of wooden tops: one was a single cone, the other resembled two tops joined at their tips with an axle. Players spun a top up and down the string, tossing it and catching it again. The poem warns the players to "pull the string slowly." Players also played in groups, tossing the spinning tops from one to another. Spinning quickly, the tops made a humming sound. The pitch of the sound depended on the size of the top and the number of holes in it.

▦ Dragon Dance

Dragons in Chinese mythology were good, not evil, and at festivals games and dances celebrated the stories of the dragons. The dragon dance was a form of follow-the-leader. Players lined up, each with a hand on the shoulder of the player in front of him or her. The front person was the "head" of the dragon, and the head tried to catch (tag) the tail. The "tail," or last person in line, tried to escape. Everyone else tried to stay together as the head and tail ducked and weaved to keep the head from catching the tail. When the head caught the tail, the head moved down to become the tail and the next person in line was the new head.

▦ Forcing the City Gates

The name of this game may well recall the days when Mongol raiders from the West and Japanese from the East repeatedly invaded China. Players formed two teams. Each team lined up, hands joined, on opposite sides of the playing area. The captain of one team sent a player to "force the gates" by running as fast as he could against the other line. If he broke through, he returned, bringing with him the two players whose hands he broke through. If he was unable to break the opposing line, he had to join it. Play continued until one team had all the players.

This game is very similar to the American playground game "Red Rover," but the bringing back of the players who let the charger through changes the dynamic. Is it better to target weaker players, thereby increasing the chance of getting through but also perhaps weakening your own line? Also, instead of the opponent choosing who will run, the team captain chooses which player to send.

▦ Hago Abosi

The game of hitting a feathered ball with a paddle, commonly called badminton today, was a woman's game in medieval Japan (Figure 3.7).

羽子戯 ハゴアソビ

Figure 3.7. Women playing hago abosi. *Source*:
Culin (1991).

The *hago ita*, or battledore, was a flat wooden paddle about a foot long
and four inches wide, painted with elaborate designs or the faces of
famous people. The *hago* was a large seed of the *Mokuran*, or soap-berry,
with several small feathers attached at one end. The object of the game
was to keep the hago in the air and pass it back and forth among the
players.

▦ Hana, Hana, Hana, Kuchi

Any number of players can join this silly game from Southeast Asia.
Players divide into teams, and each team chooses a captain. The captain
stands up and says "hana, hana, hana," tapping her nose each time
("hana" means "nose"). The fourth time, however, she says one body
part and touches another. The players on the opposing team have to
imitate what the captain does, not what she says. Any player who makes
a mistake has to drop out. Now the other team captain tries to trick the
players from the first team. The game ends when one team has no players left.

⊞ Keleret

In this game from Singapore, children drew a circle in the dirt as a target. Each child had a *batu keleret*, a flat stone. The children took turns tossing the stones toward the target. When all the stones had been tossed, the half of the group whose kelerets were closest to the target were given piggyback rides by those whose kelerets were further away.

⊞ Ken

In Japan there were many forms of ken, or finger games. Adults and children all played them, sometimes very seriously and for high stakes, sometimes just to determine who would go first in another game or whose turn it was to do some onerous chore.

The most common ken, ishi ken or "stone ken," was the game American's call rock, paper, scissors. A player's fist was the rock (*ishi*), an open hand was paper (*kami*), and the extended index finger and thumb or first two fingers represented scissors (*hasami*). Players faced each other and on a count of three extended their hands simultaneously in one of the three shapes. A stone beat scissors, as scissors cannot cut stone but stone can crush scissors. Scissors beat paper, which it can cut. But paper beat stone, because a paper can wrap a stone. Mushi ken was the same game with different figures. A thumb is the *kebi*, or snake, which ate the index finger, a *kairu* (frog). The frog, in turn, ate the *namekuji*, or slug, represented by the little finger. (How the slug beat the snake is not clear, but it did.)

Kitsanu ken was a more complicated game, played sitting down. It's not clear when it began but it became a fad in Japan during the sixteenth century. The motions were hands beside the head (like pointy ears) representing a fox, *kitsune*; hands on thighs representing the village magistrate, *shoya*; and the index finger and thumb raised in the familiar angle represented *teppo*, the gun. The magistrate was beaten by the fox, which could deceive him, but was not shot by the gun. The gun could shoot the fox, but not the magistrate. The fox deceived the magistrate, but was killed by the gun.

An Englishwoman recorded a Chinese version of the game using all five fingers: the thumb represented the local idol, the index finger a bird, the middle finger a gun, the ring finger a fox, and the little finger an ant. The idol beat the bird (which might be sacrificed to it) and the gun (which might be fired in religious ritual but would not harm the god). The idol and the fox were tied, because foxes were supposed to be on good terms with the gods. The ant, surprisingly, beat the idol because it was a wood chewer and could destroy the image. Guns shot birds and foxes; foxes ate birds; and birds ate ants. Ants tied with both guns and foxes because neither had any effect on the other. These throws could be repeated any number of times, and once concluded, each of the players could move on to play against another.

▦ Kong Keui

In the Orient there were different kinds of jacks played by boys and girls. Boys played this Korean version using five small bits of brick or stone.

In the first round, called "laying eggs," the boy would spread the five stones on the ground. He would toss up the first, then pick up the second and toss it before catching the first. Putting that one down, he would toss the third stone up and then catch the second, and so on through all five. When he succeeded in this he moved on to "setting the eggs," which resembled placing eggs under a brooding hen. He held one hand cupped over the ground, with the stones nearby. Tossing one stone up into the air, the boy tucked one of the stones under his hand, then caught the tossed stone and repeated the process. Finally, in the part of the game called "hatching the eggs," the boy held one stone in the palm of his hand, tossed another up, and used the one in his hand to strike the other three before catching the tossed stone.

In Japan and Singapore "jacks" was a girl's game. They played using seven small cloth packets filled with rice in the place of the stones, but with almost the same moves. Touching any of the packets on the ground other than the one being picked up on that play forfeited the turn.

▦ Kubi Hiki

This two-person tugging game was played in Japan. Players sat cross-legged, facing one another, with a sash tied into a loop and passed around both their necks. At the signal both begin to pull, the object being to pull the other forward past the center point. It is interesting to note that the people of the arctic in North America played almost this identical game.

▦ Loo K'bah Zee

In this game from Burma, children lined up with their hands cupped behind their backs. The last player in line walked up and down the line, pretending to place a small stone into each player's hands. Suddenly she left the stone in one player's hands, and that player jumped out of line. If the players just ahead or behind her caught her as she moved, they pulled her back into the line. If she succeeded in escaping from the line, she took the place of the player hiding the stone.

⊞ Mai-am-tol-ki

Spinning until one is too dizzy to stand is a favorite activity of small children. In Asia this was done as a game. Players drew a circle on the ground. The spinner stood in the circle, crossed his arms and held an ear with one hand. He would spin and his friends would count the turns, until he stepped (or fell) out of the circle. Then the next player would spin.

⊞ Nel-ttoui-ki

What we call a seesaw was a girls' game in the Orient, and was played standing up. Children would roll mats and lay a board across the roll, then one girl would stand on each end of the board. By coordinating their jumping the girls could propel each other quite high off the board. Good balance was essential when coming down!

⊞ Qigong/Wuqinxi

In these Chinese exercises the participants moved through a highly stylized series of movements based on the movements of five different animals: tiger, bear, deer, ape, and bird. This activity dates back at least seven hundred years B.C.E. Combined with an emphasis on breath control and silent focusing of the concentration, the exercises of qigong developed tremendous balance and surprising strength.

The popular and modern exercise method, tai chi, is based on qigong, and many tapes and books of tai chi are available. In tai chi the participant moves from one form into another, while in qigong a few movements are repeated many times. This makes qigong a bit simpler to learn. It also means that some qigong exercises can be done sitting or even lying down. To practice quigong participants should have loose-fitting clothing and bare feet. Breathe deeply and move slowly, turning and shifting your weight from one side of the body to the other.

Here is one simplified set of movements to try:

Sitting or standing in a relaxed and comfortable position, close your eyes. Breathe deeply and slowly through the exercise. Imagine that you are a bird in the early morning. Dawn is just beginning to drive the darkness away. Slowly stretch upward from the top of your head, down your neck, and down your spine. Keep your neck and spine "tall" throughout the exercise (imagine you're hanging from a string above your head). Slowly turn your shoulders first one way, then the other. Slowly lean at the waist, first one way, then the other, then to the front, then back. Now raise your arms (wings) from the shoulders. Slowly straighten your elbows and reach your arms toward the sky, then slowly lower them again. (Breathe!). Repeat this "flapping" motion, slowly, five times. If you are standing, bend your knee and place your foot against the other knee. Repeat the flapping motion. Change feet and flap your wings five more times.

⊞ Syou-pyek-tchi-ki

Rhythmic hand-clapping is a common cooperative game. In Asia these games were played by children and adults. The patterns could be simple or complex, and the accompanying chant may have been related to the motions or just nonsense.

One pattern from Korea was described this way: Standing face to face, players clapped their palms against their thighs, then on their chests. Then each clapped their own hands together in front. Then they clapped each other's hands, and repeated the sequence faster and faster until one missed.

⊞ Syoun-ra-tjap-ki

Korean boys playing this universal game of tag called the one who was chasing *syoun-ra,* "the watchman." A player could avoid being tagged by sitting down on the ground.

⊞ Throwing Fists

This Chinese version of the "how many fingers" game added a layer of complexity that made it endlessly interesting. Three or more players could participate: three, four, or five was most common. Players took turns being the caller. The other players formed a circle, and the caller stood to one side. At the signal, the players "threw their fists," shooting one hand into the center with as many fingers extended as they chose. At the same time the caller announced the winning number, not by just stating a number but by calling out a phrase representing the number. The phrase could be a simple representation of the number ("double sixes," a dice term, would mean twelve), or a line of poetry or other expression with a numeric meaning ("Jack and Jill" would be two, or "the month of May" would be five). Or, if the players agreed in advance, the number could be the number of words in the phrase. If the number matched the number of fingers thrown, the caller won. The game could be played just for fun, but often players put up stakes so the winning callers took home a real prize.

⊞ T'iu Lung Mun

The name of this game is translated as "jumping the dragon's gate." It recalled the days when the gates of a city were closed at night to keep marauders out. Players drew straws to determine which two would be the gate. They sat with their knees slightly bent, legs apart and the soles of their feet together (this is easier to do while leaning back on the hands). The others tried to jump into the space created by their legs, while the "gate" tried to prevent them from doing so. Other players could attempt to distract the "gate" to make it easier for the jumpers.

⊞ Tjye-ki Tcha-ki

Korean men played this shuttlecock-kicking game with a ball made of cloth stuffed with ashes or clay so that it was fairly solid with a long feathered tail. They kicked the ball from one person to another, up and down the street, with the object being to keep the ball in the air. Some writers suggested that the game was developed by shopkeepers to keep their feet warm during the winter!

⊞ Tops

Many different kinds of tops were used in Asia, some for amusement by children, others in competition among adults. Tops were made from conch shells, wood, seed-pods, and even iron.

Hand tops were often made from painted wood, with a bamboo spindle the spinner rolled between the palms of the hands to start the top spinning. Ladies at court in China during the Sung dynasty played with *ch'en-ch'ien*, tops made of ivory. Small tops were made by drilling acorns to pierce with bamboo spindles, which could be spun with two fingers.

Humming and whistling tops made by piercing or carving the surface of the top were very popular in Japan. Top games included spinning tops on a paddle held in the hand, or on a string tied between two uprights or held taut between the hands. For top battles a circle drawn in the dirt or a mat folded into a tray served as the battleground. Each player simultaneously set his or her top spinning. The tops would strike against each other, knocking each other over, off the mat or out of the circle. The one left spinning was the victor. Children and adults would bet on the outcome of top battles.

⊞ Touhu

Touhu, the game of throwing darts into a pot, began as a form of archery competition in feudal China. Later it became a game for the common folk as well. A variety of pots were used for targets, ranging from cooking-pot size to some so tall and narrow that the arrow would just fit into them. These must have been very challenging from a distance.

To play touhu, collect a variety of pots, and make darts from sticks with feathers for fletching. Commercial darts will work but cover the tips with athletic tape to protect the floor. (Foam darts don't throw well because they're not heavy enough.) Mark lines at several distances from the targets for competitors to stand behind while tossing.

⊞ Tsuna Tobi

Jumping rope was a boy's game in medieval Asia. Ropes were made from straw or cotton thread. The best ropes were a combination of the two, coated with wax for durability. Generally each person turned their own rope and jumped, and players competed to see who could jump fastest or the most times without tripping. (The "Chinese jump rope," an elastic loop, is a relatively recent American invention.)

⊞ Tuy

Flower games were common among country children in Asia. In tuy, Chinese children would take a strong grass or flower stem and fold it over, linking it through the folded stem of the opponent. Then they pulled, and whichever child's stem broke first was the loser. Hana sumo, Japansese flower wrestling, might have been better named flower sword-play, as it consisted of swinging and hitting each other's flowers until the heads came off.

⊞ Two-person Walk

The two-person walk was a Chinese cooperative game that made for an entertaining race. Two players stood on a pair of flat boards with leather thongs or strings attached. Holding the strings in their hands they had to step with first one foot and then the other while pulling up on the strings, coordinating their motions so that they and their "skis" walked forward together.

⊞ Uthi Pirithal

In parts of Southeast Asia children used this method for choosing sides for a game. Two leaders went from one player to the next, asking them to choose "mud or stone" (*mann* or *kal* in Tamil). Once all the players had chosen, the "muds" went to one side and the "stones" to the other. Then the leaders took a flat stone, spat on one side, and tossed it into the air. If the wet side landed down, the "muds" went first.

SPORTS

⊞ Archery

Archery in medieval Asia was both a tool of war, for which competitions encouraged training, and an ornate ritual game. The weapons used ranged from the enormously long bows of the Japanese sport-archer to the short, powerful bows used by the Mongol horsemen, so tight that modern athletes can scarcely draw them. (See hypen sa ha ki, lishe, puukhai, and toshi-ya; see the Appendix for suggested methods of constructing bows and arrows.)

⊞ Chiao-ti

In China there are records of chiao-ti (wrestling) tournaments from the second century B.C.E. Early contests featured wrestlers wearing the horns of animals and attempting to gore one another. By the time of the sixth century wrestling contests before the emperor had become monthly events. Art from the period shows wrestlers standing, bent at the waist, and grasping one another around the waist and thighs. The object was to lift the opponent off his feet and throw him to the ground.

⊞ Chikara Kurabe

When we think of Japanese wrestling today we inevitably think of sumo, but modern sumo with its characteristically huge athletes is a relatively recent development. In the seventh and eighth century the Japanese imperial court adopted the notion of the wrestling tournament from the Chinese. Each year the emperor would summon wrestlers from all the provinces to assemble in the capital. Under the direction of one of the princes, the wrestlers were divided into teams and began a series of practice matches. The festival culminated in a tournament before the emperor.

In addition to the thirty-four wrestlers, each side was represented by musicians and dancers who celebrated each victory. The wrestlers faced off, one pair at a time, and those who were victorious on the first day faced each other the second day, until champions were declared on each team. The actual chikara kurabe matches were generally short. Two wrestlers glared at and circled one another in the ring, each watching for the opportunity to grasp the other by the loincloth. Once the move was made, the goal was to throw or twist the opponent to the ground, or to drag him out of the ring. Kicking and hitting with the fists were prohibited. Two referees observed the match and kept score by sticking an arrow into the ground for each victory won. If the match went on too long, the referees would chase the wrestlers out of the ring so the next pair could wrestle.

During the Shogun era as warlords battled across Japan the tournaments died out, and wrestling became an essential skill for soldiers. Not until the sixteenth century did wrestling become a sport once more. Wrestlers were divided into leagues, and rules for play were established. Twelve holds, twelve throws, twelve twists, and twelve lifts were defined as legal; the size and shape of the ring were defined, and the authority of the umpire was given by order of the emperor and vested in one family, where it passed from generation to generation. This was the beginning of modern sumo.

To stage a chikara kurabe tournament, secure an open location where the ground is clear and covered with sand. (You could use wrestling mats in a gym instead.) Each wrestler should have a cloth sash tied loosely around the waist. Only the sash may be grabbed by the opponent. Match wrestlers by weight and strength, and have referees to watch for violations. Each player must try to move the opponent out of the ring or bring him down so his body touches the ground. While trying to pull the opponent over you must keep your balance, so keep both feet planted firmly on the ground and bend your knees.

⠿ Chuiwan

In the Palace Museum at Beijing there is a Ming dynasty painting of the emperor and his nobles playing a game that appears to be almost identical to modern miniature golf! A book written in China in the thirteenth century describes this sport of chuiwan in detail. The game was played on greens, either natural or constructed, with short groomed grass and hazards or traps to be avoided while trying to get the ball into the goal. Ten different types of clubs are described in the book, although it is difficult to conclude from paintings how complex the courses may have been. The imperial course had four greens and a total of ten holes, but since commoners as well as the nobility played the game we can surmise that there must have been some variety of courses. The imperial clubs were made of gold and jade. Commoners no doubt played with clubs made of more ordinary material. For each hole a player had to begin from a designated base, then hit the ball from wherever it landed. The goal was to land the ball in the hole on three strokes.

Some scholars have concluded that the Mongols brought chuiwan back into the Middle East and the Crusaders brought it back to Europe, while others vigorously defend the shepherds and rabbit-holes tradition of Scottish golf (see "colf" in European Sports). Golf is a good example of a game that could have arisen spontaneously in several locations.

For a chuiwan game you will need wooden clubs with small heads and wooden balls. Lay out a course that is relatively flat and not very spread out: this is primarily a putting game, not a driving game. Two or three holes can be in different parts of the same green or grassy area, approached from bases in different directions. (If you are playing on a lawn you can mark circles of string or with lime in place of holes.) Each player plays his own ball.

▦ Cilnem

Mongolian wrestling was a contest of agility and balance as well as strength. Two men faced each other, bent forward at the waist. Each braced his head against the other's shoulder, and they grasped each other's short wrestling jackets. (Legend reported that a woman had once shamed her countrymen by beating them at cilnem, so from that day on wrestling jackets were left open to prevent any woman from sneaking into the competition.) If any part of the body other than the feet touched the ground, that wrestler was eliminated. (In some parts of Mongolia, knocking an opponents' legs from under him was legal, in others it disqualified the wrestler.) Tournaments began with 512 or 1,024 wrestlers who were paired off by ability. Each pair would wrestle, with the winners going on to wrestle again and again over several days until a final champion was determined.

Cilnem tournaments took place on grass. You can improvise a cilnem jacket by putting on a T-shirt and then pulling the front up and over your head, so it rolls across your shoulders.

▦ Horse Racing

The Mongols were renowned for their incredible strength, marksmanship, and equestrian skills. Their small horses (ponies by modern standards) were agile and enduring. Riding across the steppe, in weather more often frozen than not, both horses and horsemen were formidable warriors.

The premier racing event of the Mongols was run across the open steppe for a distance of 30 to 75 miles. The riders would convene at the finish line and ride together to the starting line, establishing the course and noting such obstacles as hills, rivers, and ravines. Once all the horses were behind the starting line the racers gave three rousing shouts of "Giingo!" and they were off. Spectators lined the course, and those at the finish line served as judges. A finish line ritual rewarded the winner with a drink of *airag*, a form of fermented mare's milk, which he or she traditionally shared with the horse. The judges also recognized and lauded the last place finishers, sometimes even composing a poem in their honor.

A dirt-bike race is probably the best adaptation of Mongolian racing you can manage without horses. Choose a course with plenty of natural obstacles and ride it together to make sure everyone knows the layout. You can offer the winner a glass of kefir, which is similar to airag, but don't pour it on the bike! And don't neglect to praise those who persevere and finish even after they've lost.

▦ Hypen Sa Ha Ki

In Korea, archery competitions matched two, three, or four teams of twelve archers each. Teams represented villages or neighborhoods, and carried flags, wore decorative costumes, and were accompanied by fans and musicians to cheer their efforts. The target was a square, with a black spot in its center. Each player shot fifteen arrows, scoring one point for each arrow that struck the target and an additional point for each one that struck within the black spot. Shooting rotated among the teams: each archer took five shots and then an archer from the next team would have a turn. Traditionally the best archers were saved for the last rounds. The losing team paid for a feast for all participants at the end of the match.

▦ Jiju

The Chinese encountered jiju, or polo, during their wars with the Turks during the Tang Dynasty (Figure 3.8). Observing the excellent horsemanship of the Turks, the Chinese adopted polo as part of the training of the cavalry. Polo was also played in India, where it was known as sagol kangjei. Polo was played by teams of seven on each side, riding small horses or ponies. The ball, about three inches in diameter, was made of bamboo root and painted white. Polo sticks were bamboo or wood shafts, about four feet long, with long wooden heads attached at a slightly obtuse angle (like a modern ice-hockey stick). There were no goal posts, but goal lines were marked at each end of the field, which could be anywhere from 200 to 600 yards long. Players had specific positions: two backs who defended the goal line, two wings, a center who moved the ball up the field, and two inners who attempted to score. In Japan a variation of polo developed using sticks with netted ends so the ball could be scooped and thrown.

You can play polo on bicycles or scooters, using field hockey sticks and la-

Figure 3.8. Jiju, or polo, came into Asia with the Mongols. *Source*: Dale (1905).

crosse balls. Or make balls and sticks from wood for a more authentic game. You need a wide flat grassy field for polo. Don't ride across lawns or playing fields when they're wet or you'll tear up the grass.

⊞ Kabbadi

Kabbadi is an ancient game still played today throughout India and Southeast Asia. Playing kabbadi probably started to develop skills useful in self-defense and warfare, but kabbadi has been played just for fun for centuries. Both children and adults play the game. In modern, organized kabbadi the field is 12.5 by 10 meters. Each team puts seven players on the field at a time, substitutions are allowed, and scores may be kept instead of eliminating tagged players.

In the Middle Ages the details of kabbadi were still quite flexible. The field was divided by a line, usually of stones. Players divided into equal teams and lined up on either side of the line, twenty to thirty feet inside their own zone. Team A sent a "raider" into the opposing zone. The raider took a deep breath and ran through the zone, chanting "kabbadi, kabbadi" and tagging as many players as possible before returning to her own zone. She could not draw another breath until crossing the line. If she succeeded, the players she touched were out. Meanwhile, the players on Team B tried to capture the raider, to keep her from returning to her own zone. If she did not get at least a hand or foot back across the line before drawing another breath, she was out. Once the raider was out or safely home, Team B sent a raider into A's zone. The game ended when one team had no players left.

You can mark a kabbadi field on grass or pavement, or use existing basketball court lines to define the playing area.

⊞ Kemari

Kemari was a ball game played by primarily by the well-to-do, but imitated by people of all ages and social classes (Figure 3.9). The kemari ball court was an enclosed garden, about twenty feet square, with the four corners marked by a willow, cherry, pine, and maple trees pruned to be just four feet tall. The ball was six to eight inches in diameter, made of deerskin and stuffed with feathers. Kameri balls are distinctive-looking, rather puffy with a band around the middle.

In keeping with the Japanese emphasis on the value of the collective, kameri was cooperative rather than competitive. Rather than one player trying to outplay the other, all the players competed together to achieve the best possible score. Eight players participated in the formal game, two in each corner of the court. Each player had to kick the ball three times and then pass to another corner, with the object being to keep the ball from hitting the ground. A record from 1208 reports that players achieved 980 hits, dropped the ball, and then proceeded to keep it up for another 2,000 hits. Informal games of kameri could be played by any number of people: frequently two players would play, kicking the ball up three times and then passing it.

The walls are not essential to kemari so you can mark a twenty-foot square on pavement with chalk to play the game. (In fact, a ceremonial kameri game is played today in an open courtyard in Japan.) Make a ball from leather and stuff it with feathers or crumbled newspaper. All players have to develop the

Figure 3.9. Japanese kemari was characterized by elaborate ritual. *Source*: Culin (1919).

skill of keeping the ball aloft with their feet, but within each pair one may be the better passer and the other better at receiving from the adjacent or opposite corner.

▦ Kenjutsu

The development of the curved-blade sword in the second century marked the beginning of the rise of a new class of warriors in Japan, the *bushi*. The feudal bushi lived according to a code of virtues derived from the teachings of Buddhism, Confucian idealism, and Shinto piety. Justice, courage, honor, and loyalty were balanced by benevolence, politeness, and veracity. Over time elaborate traditions of swordfighting and ritual combined to form a discipline known as kenjutsu, which is still practiced today.

The bushi had two swords, a long sword with a blade two feet or longer, and a short sword about a foot long. The *bokken*, a wooden sword, developed during the Middle Ages, added another set of skills to the swordfighter's repertoire. Japanese swords were held with both hands, so swordfighting was done face-to-face, not turned sideways as in Europe.

There were more than 1,700 *ryu*, schools or styles, in Japanese kenjutsu, and learning to use and counter all of them was the work of a lifetime. Athletes would learn and practice *kata*, or forms, and engaged in duels following carefully choreographed steps, which were scored according to form and style.

For a kenjutsu reinactment, make or buy two plastic swords for each contestant, one long and one short. Bushi carried their swords in their sashes, so each contestant will need at least a sash and perhaps a scabbard for the long sword. Plan a series of kata for each pair of contestants, including drawing the swords, facing off, circling, engaging the swords, thrusting and parrying. Remind the contestants that they are being judged on how well they conform to the form, not just whether they manage to land blows on their opponents.

⊞ Kong-tchi-ki

It is a bit surprising, since baseball has become such a fixture of modern Japanese sport, to learn that medieval Japan did not have a bat-and-ball game. The Koreans played this ball game, but it was closer to croquet or even hockey than to baseball. It probably developed as a team version of chuiwan.

Two baselines were drawn at opposite sides of the field, with a dividing line down the middle. Two teams of equal numbers were distributed across the field, with sticks that had a flat paddle at one end. A wooden ball was placed on the centerline. At the signal, players attempted to push the ball across their opponent's goal line, while the opponents, defending their line, attempted to intercept the ball and drive it in the opposite direction.

Kong-tchi-ki teams were small, with just three to five players on a side, so the field did not need to be large. In paintings, the clubs looked like golf clubs, about three feet long with a small flat head.

You can use golf clubs and wooden balls to play a kong-tchi-ki game.

⊞ Lishe

In ancient China the basic skill of archery developed into a military training exercise and then an ornate and elaborate ritual competition for the upper classes. By the medieval era, lishe competitors wore elaborate costumes and went to great lengths of meditation to achieve focus, then invested all their skill in just three shots: one straight ahead, one over the back, and one from a full gallop. Bow strings came from different animals and were related to the rank of the sportsman: lower officials used bowstrings made from bear sinew, while higher-ranking ministers had leopard sinews in their bows. Only the emperor could use a bow strung with the sinew of a tiger. Various competitions specified the precise weight of the bow tension of the string. Targets were just fifteen-by-nine-centimeters square, printed or painted on doeskin, and generally had a series of concentric squares decorated with the faces of animals or other designs.

▦ Pentjak-Silat

According to Sumatran legend, Pentjak-silat was developed by a woman who watched and memorized the movements of a battle between a tiger and a bird. Silat fighting looks like a dance. The fighters' arms and feet are constantly in motion, while their eyes are fixed on their opponents. At the first sign of an opening, the rapid movements of the arms become a hail of blows and kicks at every vulnerable spot on the opponent's body.

More than 150 styles of pentjak-silat have been recorded in recent years, all developed from the ancient forms. The Sumatran form is believed to be most like the ancient pentjak-silat. Combatants crouch very low to the ground, very like the tiger. They inch closer to one another, every muscle taut, ready to pounce at the first opportunity. Students must learn and practice the motions empty-handed before being allowed to use the *tjabang*, a short pronged weapon that is probably the ancestor of the more familiar ninja tsai. As with the other Asian martial arts forms, in competition form is as important or more important than combat.

▦ Puukhai

Under their leader Chingas Khan, Mongol archers were the awe and terror of the Orient, carrying bows so heavy other men could not draw the strings, lofting arrows over distances reported to be six hundred to nine hundred meters. In contests, Mongol archers aimed at rows of small leather rings lying on the ground. Spectators stood nearby to serve as judges, raising their hands and shouting "Puukhai!" when an arrow hit a target.

▦ Taekyon

The form of martial art known today as taekwondo is a descendant of the ancient form taekyon. This was a style of fighting suited to the open fields and rural areas of Korea, characterized by high kicking, flying leaps, and extraordinary balance. Students practiced by kicking at a straw-covered log suspended between two poles, which could be raised as the student's abilities increased. Students learned front (forward) and side kicks as well as the high roundhouse kick.

To develop the skills of taekyon requires many months of stretching, kicking higher and higher, improving your balance, and learning to parry (block) your opponent's kicks with your arms while stepping back to avoid them. If you do stage a taekyon match, be sure to use arm pads and padded helmets! You score points by touching your opponent's body, not by knocking him or her down. Or mount a series of hanging targets at various levels and challenge the competitors to strike some with the hands and others with forward, backward and side kicks. Judges award points for each target successfully struck and deduct points for missing the target, falling after landing a kick, or being hit by a target on the rebound.

▦ Tako-no Kiri-ai

In Japan and Korea kite fighting (tako-no kiri-ai) was a very serious competition. It seems odd to us to combine kites and fighting, but Chinese history reports that kites were originally tools of war. Whistles attached to kites could frighten an enemy or send a signal to an ally. Kites were also used in Asia for fishing and as scarecrows.

Boys and men built beautiful and elaborate kites of paper on bamboo frames. Some types had tails and some had hummers that made sound when the wind blew through them. Silk string was the standard, though cotton cord might be used for children's kites. For kite fighting, the cord would be coated with glue mixed with powdered porcelain or fine sand. When kite strings crossed, the sharp coating quickly cut through the strings.

The traditional season for kite flying differed from place to place, no doubt due to the seasonal winds. When the competition began each player would get his kite aloft and flying well, then begin to challenge others by drawing the kites closer together. Often four or five kites might battle at once. The players would quickly let out and draw in their strings: too much slack, and the kite would fall; but the tauter the string the more easily it was cut. Skillful players could make the battle last for hours when the wind cooperated.

Children watching the battles would often claim the kites that fell from battle.

Asian kites are often very complex compared to the typical American kite. They can be in the shapes of animals, plants, or fantastic creatures. Building a kite combines good science and a good imagination.

To build an Asian kite, you will need bamboo strips, rice paper, and paint. You will need crepe paper or light cloth for the tail and string to fly your kite. (If you cannot find bamboo and rice paper, you can use long thin pieces of sumac or other wood and newspaper.)

Every kite must be balanced in order to fly. Choose a straight piece of bamboo for your center pole. Design a shape that will be exactly the same on each side of the center: butterflies and birds with outstretched wings are good examples. Soak thin strips of bamboo in water until they can be curved without breaking. Shape the strips into the parts of your design: a round circle for a head, an oval for a body, and half-circles or triangles for wings. Tie the strips together wherever they cross, and tie the design to the center pole so that it is balanced on the center. (Hold the two ends of the center pole and see if the kite frame will balance. If not, whittle down the bamboo on the heavier side to even the weight.) Once the frame is balanced, glue the strings holding the joints together so they will not slip. Let the frame dry. Lay the frame over the rice paper and trace the pieces of the design. Leave enough of a margin around each piece to wrap it over the frame when you glue the paper in place. After the glue dries, paint your kite in bright colors. Be careful, as the rice paper will absorb water. Once it dries again, you are ready to add the tail and the string.

A kite tail keeps the kite upright in the air. The larger the kite or the windier the day, the longer the tail of the kite needs to be. Long strips of crepe paper make an easy and attractive kite tail, although cloth is sturdier. If you use short bits of rag tied on to a string, be sure to wrap the string around the rag so it doesn't slide down the tail.

Before you attach the string to your kite, you must make a harness. Tie one string to the center pole above the middle of the kite and another one below the middle. Use a nail to make holes on either side of the center pole so you can thread the string around the pole. Bring these two together about six inches above the center point of the kite and tie them. Now attach the kite string to this knot. (On a very large kite three or four strings attached to the kite to form the harness make for more stable flying.)

Be sure to fly your kite in a place where there are no power lines or trees nearby. An open field or the beach is wonderful, and a school playground is usually a good place. Stand so the wind is pushing against your kite and toss it into the air. Gradually let out the string, so that the kite pulls against it, and it will rise into the air. If the tension on the kite string lessens, pull in some string—a slack string will make the kite fall.

For a kite battle, the kite flyers should stand ten or more feet apart. The kites' strings are supposed to cross paths, not the kite flyers!

▦ Tjoul Tariki

In Korea, tjoul tariki (tug-of-war) was played as an intervillage competition during the celebration of the New Year. The rope was made of bundled straw and was reportedly two feet in diameter at its center. Toward the ends it branched. When the teams competed the men held parts of the thick part of the rope while the women held the branches.

This meant that the women were spread out, giving a much more solid footing at the ends of the rope. It is also said that the women sometimes loaded the hems of their skirts with stones to anchor their teams more effectively!

In China, tug-of-war was played across a span of two parallel lines designated as "river banks." This recalled the origins of the sport in the exercises the navy used to prepare for catching and boarding ships with a *qiangou*, a grappling hook and rope. A red flag tied in the middle of the rope showed the progress of the two sides as they pulled back and forth across the "river."

You can stage a Korean tug-of-war if you braid several ropes together to form a thick rope with many ends.

⊞ Toshi-ya

Japanese warriors and hunters used longbows in ancient times, but in medieval times archery was practiced mostly as a sport. A toshi-ya was an opportunity to demonstrate the archers' skills. The Japanese bow was a very long piece of naturally curved wood, strung with hemp. Japanese bows were unusual in that they were considerably longer than the archer was tall (six to seven feet long), and held so that two-thirds of the bow was above the hands. Archers were required to shoot one thousand arrows each day to stay in training, and practiced with both fixed and moving targets. In the *inouimono* competition, teams of twelve archers on horseback fired whistling arrows with blunted tips at dogs. *Inagashi*, or flight shooting, was a sport where the object was to shoot many arrows, one right after the other, at a distant target. In a temple in Kyoto there is a gallery built for this marathon competition. Archers competed to see who could fire the most arrows in a twenty-four-hour period through a space at the top of the wall in the far end of the gallery: records of more than eight thousand have been recorded.

Simply learning to shoot a seven-foot bow may be challenge enough, but if you want to stage a toshi-ya you will need a long shooting area with a target for the arrows to pass through, and a large number of arrows for each archer. The gallery in Kyoto is more than 300 yards long. Japan stopped the inouimono in the early twentieth century because of concern for the dogs, but perhaps with the new robotic dog toys a humane version of inouimono is possible.

⊞ Tsu Chu

In ancient China tsu chu was a football game for two teams, each guarding six goals! During the Tang Dynasty the number of goals was cut to two, and apparently two versions of the game developed. One was a team game with bamboo uprights as goals at the ends of the field. The two teams attempted to kick the ball down the field and through the opposing goal in a game that was very similar to modern soccer. The other form of tsu chu was a one-on-one version in which the goal was a silk net about a foot across and some thirty feet above the ground. Imagine playing basketball with a thirty-foot net and your feet!

Scholars believe the Japanese kameri ball was derived from the Chinese tsu chu ball, which would make the tsu chu ball about six inches across and light, probably made of leather and stuffed with feathers.

You can make a ball like this and play two-person tsu chu with a basketball hoop for a goal.

⊞ Tuen Ng

Dragon-boat racing (tuen ng) developed as a religious ritual in ancient China. The ancient Chinese had regarded the fifth month (late spring) as a dangerous time when insects could spread disease among people and devastate newly planted crops. They offered sacrifices to the river gods and invoked the blessing of the dragon to bring about a fruitful harvest. During the Warring States period of Chinese history (about four centuries B.C.E.) a poet and government minister named Qu Yuan drowned himself in despair over corruption in his beloved country. According to legend, the people of his province set out in boats to try to find his body before it was consumed by fish. They made *zong zi* (plump rice dumplings) and tossed them into the river to distract the fish. But they never found the body, and some say the ghost of Qu Yuan haunts the river still.

By the year 1000 dragon-boat racing had become a popular sport associated with the spring festivals and honoring the legend of Qu Yuan. Dragon boats were long, heavy boats, anywhere from thirty to one hundred feet long, in which many paddlers sat side by side (modern dragon boats hold up to twenty-four people). The boats were decorated with fierce dragon heads and tails. Before the race a priest dabbed paint on the eyes of the dragons to "wake them up." The boats were propelled with beautifully painted oars. A drummer beat out a rhythm, helping the paddlers to coordinate their efforts. The race course could be along a stretch of river or, in coastal provinces, the paddlers would bring the boats out from shore, turn, and race toward land. A flag marked the end of the course, and in the front of each boat a flag-grabber stood ready to be the one to capture that banner, marking the winning boat. Everyone ate zong zi and cheered for their village or clan to win.

With so many people in each boat, dragon-boat racing was a sport that men and women, old and young could compete in together. It was not without danger, however. Rules allowed racers to ram one another's boats and throw stones at their opponents. In some places a capsized crew would not be rescued, and in an echo of the ancient sacrifices to the river gods, a drowning in the race was considered a good omen for the year to come.

Decorate row boats for a water parade, or for a land version of the dragon boat race, build long wooden "boats" and mount them on wheels. Use sticks with rubber crutch tips as oars to "row" the "boats" in your race. Arm some of the racers with foam balls to throw at their opponents.

▦ Wrestling

Different styles of wrestling existed in Asia, (see chiao-ti, chikara kur-abe, and cilnem).

To stage a wrestling match, find a suitable surface (grass, sand or wrestling mats) to wrestle on. Match wrestlers by weight and experience. Have referees to watch for illegal moves and to declare when a player has been thrown. Most wrestling matches are two-out-of-three sets, with the winners of the first round then wrestling against one another until champions are determined.

▦ Wushu (Kung Fu)

Several legends describe the origins of wushu (kung fu), but all lead back to a monk named Bodhidharma, a young man from India who had traveled to northern China in his quest for enlightenment. There he joined a monastery at Shaolin. Bodhidharma developed a series of exercises to strengthen both the body and the mind. The results were spectacular: although the Shaolin monks were sworn to reverence for life, they were known to be able to kill with their bare hands if placed in a life-or-death situation. Monks trained at the Shaolin monastery founded schools of kung fu throughout China, spreading the techniques and developing new forms.

Kung fu exercises are based on the movements and habits of particular animals. "Monkey" kung fu requires tremendous agility; "Preying Mantis" kung fu rewards strength and speed; and "White Crane" kung fu combines evasive maneuvers with persistent "pecking" at the opponent with the fingers. In each case, students practice imitating the movements of the animal in ritual poses, which are adapted as fighting moves in matches. Kung fu fighters also use a variety of weapons in their matches: in each case the weapon must be handled according to strict moves. A kung fu match is won not simply by knocking down the opponent but by completing the required movements as prescribed: in this way it is like a gymnastics event as well as a fight.

Wushu is the study of kung fu for exercise and sport. Kung fu variations are very popular in the West and there are kung fu schools in many communities. You can also find kung fu exercises in several books. Or design your own forms by observing different animals, and imitating their movements.

Remember that deliberate, slow movements, shifting the weight from one side of the body to the other, and maintaining balance are essential to wushu. For a wushu competition players should have a series of movements to complete. Judges award points based on the degree of control and how closely the player conforms to the standard description.

Here is a series of movements similar to one taught to beginning students:

Begin with the feet together and hands at the sides. Swing the right arm up with the palm facing in. Follow your hand with your eyes. Now do the same motion with the left hand, while at the same time bending your right elbow and dropping your right hand to your left shoulder. Lift your right leg to the side and turn to put your weight on that foot. Keeping your elbows straight, swing your right hand down and bring your left hand up as you turn. Bring your right hand up over your head and bend your wrist so your palm faces up. Now swing your left arm down to your side and reach back, bending the right knee and leaning forward. Step onto the right foot, stand up straight and raise the left knee high, bringing both hands up with the elbows bent, palms facing your face. Step onto the left foot, dropping your hands to your side with the palms facing forward. Now step on your right foot and swing your hands up and out from the shoulders.

Facing left, bring your hands to your waist and make fists. Standing on your left foot, point your right toe and bring the right foot up in front of your left knee, while bringing your fists up to cross in front of your chest and then out to your sides. Hop on the left foot, bringing your right hand down in front of you, and land with your knees bent so your right hand nearly touches the ground. Swing your right hand up over your head while you swing your left hand down so your fist touches your left knee. Lean forward on your left foot, straighten your right leg, and bring your right hand in front of you across your chest. Bring your right fist back to your side while straightening your left arm in front of you, palm up. Step onto your right foot, straightening your left leg behind you so that your left leg and arm form a straight line. Bend the left elbow and bring your hand to your right shoulder; then swing your arm down and back, turning your body and bend your right knee so you are squatting very low, with the left leg and arm extended. Shift your weight to your left foot, step forward and raise your left arm over your head, thrusting your right fist forward. Bring both hands to cross in front of your chest, standing straight on your right foot. Raise your left knee high and bring your hands up with your palms facing your face again.

⊞ EUROPE

At its height the Roman Empire stretched across the continent of Europe to the Atlantic and the North Sea. Roman soldiers conscripted from places like Palestine and North Africa manned outposts on the borders of Scotland and along the Danube River. They built an immense network of roads so well constructed that many are still in use today. Their language, laws, and technology united the people of Europe with those of the Middle East and North Africa. But in the third and fourth centuries those distant borders became difficult to defend. Wave after wave of "barbarians," so-called because their Germanic and Slavic languages sounded like barking to the Romans, moved across the border to settle in the outskirts of the Empire. The emperors aligned themselves with first one and then another of these tribes in an effort to gain defenses for their borders, but the fine points of military alliances had little meaning for the leaders of the Goths, Visigoths, Huns, and Vandals. Bit by bit the Empire crumbled. The unity and stability established by the Roman Empire dissolved. Ostrogoths and Visigoths settled along the Danube. The Visigoths took Gaul (France) and the Saxons took Britain. The Vandals conquered the Iberian Peninsula and North Africa. In 476, Attila the Hun conquered the Italian peninsula and the Dark Ages had begun.

Compared to the Pax Romana, those first centuries of the Middle Ages seemed dark indeed. Much of the preserved knowledge of the ancients was destroyed when cities such as Alexandria and Rome were sacked. A few monks retreated to their monasteries, laboriously copying those ancient manuscripts that remained. For most people, learning took a back seat to survival. Travel and trade were dim memories. Villagers lived their whole lives within a few miles of the places they were born.

Europe was an agricultural society with the calendar defined by planting and harvesting.

Northern Europe, Russia, and Scandinavia, never conquered by Rome, were home to peasant farmers and nomadic Lapps as well as the world-traveling Vikings. The British Isles and the northwestern coast were all Celtic in medieval times. The Norman French conquered England in 1066 and tightened the connections across the channel. In Europe national boundaries developed with languages: the Romantic languages of French, Spanish and Italian in the west, Germanic tongues in the center of the continent, and Slav-speakers in the east.

Gradually alignments and alliances developed and lines of authority were drawn. The feudal system, based on the exchange of land for military service, established a new order in Europe. Ireland, protected by island geography and a fierce reputation, sent missionaries back to the mainland bearing the fruits of their isolated peace. Toward the end of the first millennium the "barbarians" embraced the Catholic faith and pledged fealty to the Pope, who attempted to channel their warrior energies by sending them off to reclaim the Holy Land. Science was reintroduced to Europe by the Muslim invaders from the south. Libraries and universities grew up around the monasteries. Languages stabilized and nations began to form. As the constant warfare subsided, agriculture and trade thrived. Europe enjoyed several centuries of peace and prosperity. And then came the plague.

The plague started in Asia in 1346 and moved west with the Mongol raiders, apparently arriving in the Mediterranean in 1347. The infection, carried by fleas on rats and later mutating into an airborne virus, swept across Europe and wiped out between one-quarter and one-third of the population before 1350. Plague returned in 1360 and 1400, eventually killing about one half the population, completely decimating some towns. Fear and prejudice were perhaps inevitable consequences of a disease that appeared suddenly, causing horrible suffering and gruesome death. Both the Roma people ("gypsies"), recently arrived from India, and those ever-present scapegoats the Jews were accused of causing the plague. Ironically, the reduced population resulted in a better standard of living for those who remained. Wages increased, working conditions improved, and labor-saving technologies were embraced, leading to the Renaissance of the fourteenth and fifteenth centuries.

By the time Gutenberg's development of the moveable-type printing press made the mass manufacturing of books possible, the feudal order had been all but replaced by a new economic class system. Europe's new nation-states were fueled by international trade and exploration and home to universities and cathedrals where art, literature, and philosophy thrived. Europe was well on its way to the cataclysmic conflict between old and new that would erupt in the Reformation, the Age of Enlightenment, and the American and French Revolutions.

The sports and games of medieval Europe developed naturally from the activities of the people. Feudal lords trained for war, and hired skilled soldiers to fight for them: knights who had mastered the intricacies of swordplay and horsemanship, and archers whose skill with longbow or crossbow would decimate enemy infantry. To keep these fighters' skills sharp the nobles encouraged peacetime competitions, offering prizes and honors as well as hiring those who demonstrated excellence in staged combat. Common people were not allowed to participate in these "noble" sports, though they often imitated them. The games and sports of ordinary folks are not as colorful as jousting and fencing, but were more widespread. Rules of games like bandy, colf, and camp varied from place to place in the Middle Ages. As the rules were formalized, many of these common games developed into the popular sports of our own day.

The Church contributed to the development of sports and games in medieval Europe, both by providing the space where many games were played, the churchyard, and by mandating both a weekly Sabbath and a year-round series of festival holidays. These days of recreation imposed by the clerical authority provided the opportunity for community play. Many traditional races, regattas and other sports events are still connected with the feasts: Shrove Tuesday (the day before Lent begins) football games and rope-skipping festivals, Easter Sunday sled-dog races in Lapland, and the beheading of the goose on the feast of St. Martin in Switzerland are just a few.

Europe's winters are long and dark. Board games and gambling provided a welcome diversion. *Tafl* (table) games came south with the Vikings to blend with the dice games left by the Romans. The Moors who came to Spain from North Africa brought a table game from Persia that reenacted battles. Shatranj, or chess, spread rapidly across Europe, and spawned numerous regional variations. In the thirteenth century King Alphonso X of Spain commissioned a book describing dozens of popular games of his era, and called it *Libro del Acedrex*, the "Chess Book."

Checkers was a simpler game than chess. Rithmomachia was much more complicated: the people of Europe had time to develop and play many variations of their favorite games. Toward the end of the era of this book a new craze took hold. The origin of European playing cards has been a subject of much dispute, but their popularity is not.

A couple of items notable for not being included here: Skiing dates back into prehistory in Scandinavia but was a means of transportation, not a sport. There were probably impromptu races, but the first records of skiing purely for pleasure are found in Norway in the 1850s. Pallmall, the forerunner of croquet, is commonly mentioned as medieval but isn't recorded before the 1700s. The Spanish corrida, or bull fight, only dates back to the eighteenth century, although it has precedents in the historical sport of bull-vaulting in ancient Crete and the venationes of the Roman circus.

GAMES

⊞ Acedrex (Chess)

Medieval chess was not very different from the game as we play it today. The *shatranj* board was not checkered, but boards were frequently decorated and by the twelfth-century European boards were more often checkered than not. For acedrex either a checkered or plain eight-by-eight-square board is authentic. Each player had sixteen pieces: eight soldiers, one king, one counselor, two bishops, two knights, and two chariots. As the game changed and moved from India through Persia and into Europe the Indian elephants became bishops. Eventually the counselor would become a queen, and her power was increased tremendously. The chariots became castles, which explains why the modern chess castle can travel so rapidly across the board.

Soldiers moved one space forward at a time and captured by moving one space diagonally. Chariots could move any number of spaces along a row or column. Knights moved in an "L" shape, two spaces horizontally and then one vertically or one horizontally and then two vertically, in any direction, and could leap over other pieces. Bishops moved two spaces on any diagonal and could leap over other pieces, recalling their origins as elephants. The counselor moved one square diagonally, and the king moved one square in any direction. The king could also move like a knight, one time in any game as long as he had not previously been in check. "Check" meant that an opposing piece could on one move reach the space occupied by the king. (Unlike Asian chaturanga, the king was not actually captured.) All pieces captured by landing on a spot occupied by an opposing piece.

To begin the game, pieces were set up as in modern chess, beginning from each player's left home corner: chariot, knight, bishop, king, counselor, bishop, knight, and chariot. The soldiers filled the second row. Soldiers that reached the opponent's home row were promoted, generally to counselor.

As in chess, the object of the game was to put the opposing king into a position where he could not escape capture (checkmate) or where he could not move without moving into check (stalemate). (Stalemate can also mean neither player can checkmate the other.)

To play medieval chess with a modern set you need only remember that the pieces move differently.

⊞ Alquerque

See El qirkat in the Middle East chapter.

⊞ Chess, History of

Chess developed in northern India around 570 c.e., and spread with traders and crusaders throughout the Middle East and into both Europe and Asia. The origins of chess are a subject of great scholarly dispute, and a case can be made for it having begun in China. Even if that is true, the version that became European chess came from India through Persia and the Middle East as chaturanga, and entered Europe as shatranj. (For purposes of clarity in this book, chaturanga has been used to name the original four-player game, which is described in the section on Asia. Shatranj is used for the two-player version as described in the Middle East, and Acedrex is used in Europe. In reality as the game changed the distinctions were never that clear!)

By the year 1100 more than a dozen versions of chess were being played from Korea and Japan to Spain and England. It displaced hafnetafl in Scandinavia and rivaled go in Japan. In addition to the games mentioned above, see gala and grande acedrex in this chapter and xiangqi and shogi in Asian games.

⊞ Cross and Pile

Coin flipping is a game that is older than coins themselves, and one that was popular throughout medieval Europe. It was called cross and pile in England after the marks on the farthing, a coin worth a quarter of a pence. The rules were no different a thousand years ago than they are today: toss the coin into the air and call "pile" or "cross" before it hits the ground. The player who called the toss correctly pockets the coin.

⊞ Dablot Prejjesne

Dablot prejjesne appears to be a combination of alquerque and hafntafl. It was played in Lapland and the traditional designation of the pieces as "tenant farmers" and "Lapp warriors" represented the conflict between the nomadic Lapps and the Finnish farmers who settled in Scandinavia in the late first millennium.

The board was a five-by-six-square grid, thirty squares each divided on both diagonals, for a total of seventy-two points or intersections on which the game was played. Each player had thirty playing pieces—

twenty-eight "farmers" (with pointed hats) or "warriors" (with horned caps), a larger piece known as the Finns landlord or the Lapp king, and a middle-sized piece designated as either the landlord's son or the Lapp prince.

To play Dablot players sit on the short ends of the board. At the beginning of the game each player's smaller pieces are lined up on three rows closest to the player. The son/prince is located on the furthest right point of the player's fourth row, and the landlord/king is on the furthest right point of the center row (so the two chief pieces are at opposite ends of the same row).

All pieces move one point at a time in any direction on to a vacant point. All pieces capture by leaping over an opponent's piece into a vacant point beyond, and if multiple captures are possible they are allowed to continue on the same turn, although capture is not required. Pieces can capture their equal or lesser opposing pieces, but cannot capture a superior piece; thus the king can only be captured by the landlord, and the sons only by the other son or his father.

The game is won if one player immobilizes the other's major piece by surrounding it so it cannot move, or when one player loses so many pieces that he resigns. If both players have single pieces left of equal rank, so that they could simply chase each other around the board indefinitely, they may call the game drawn or agree to "single combat," advance upon each other, so that one will inevitably capture the other. If only the king and the landlord are left the game is a draw.

Dablot prejjesne pieces were generally carved from wood but are easily made with modeling dough. A single point on the top makes the piece a farmer, a notched or two-pointed top represents the warriors. Remember that you need one medium-sized piece and one larger piece for each side along with twenty-eight small pieces each.

⚏ Doblet

This Spanish tables game was played with three dice and only twelve pieces on a side. The game began with two pieces placed on each point of both players' home quarters and they began bearing off immediately according to the roll of the three dice (essentially this is just the end game of nardshir). Any roll a player could not use could be used by his opponent.

⚏ Doublets

In this tables game from Tudor England both players began at the same end of the board and moved toward the other end, side by side.

The game began with pieces already on the board: two each on the first three points and three each on the next three. The players rolled two dice to determine how many places to move. They moved their pieces across the board, bearing off first from points with more than one piece, then any singletons. Rolling doubles entitled the player to another roll (hence the name). Any roll that a player could not use could be used by his opponent.

▦ Fayles

Fayles was a three-dice tables game described in the Alfonso manuscript and so probably played throughout Europe, although its name seems to point to an English origin. When the game began all the pieces were at one end of the board. "Dark," moving counterclockwise, had two pieces in one corner (point a) and thirteen (stacked) on the opposite side in the row at the middle of the board (point s). "Light," moving clockwise, began with two pieces in the other corner (point x) and thirteen opposite dark's thirteen (point f) (see Figure 6.3). For each roll, each of the dice were played separately: a single piece could use all the moves or three pieces could be moved, one according to each die. A piece could not land on a point occupied by two or more opposing pieces, but landing on a point occupied by only one opposing piece knocked that piece back to the starting point.

Normally the game was won by the first player to bear off all her pieces, but if a player rolled a number that he could not use, he lost immediately (failed, hence the name).

▦ Fierges (Draughts)

Fierges was invented in twelfth-century France. It was later called dames or draughts and eventually checkers. The game spread fairly slowly through Europe and was not popular outside France and England until the 1600s. The game was played on the white squares of a checkered chessboard. (The carving or coloring of alternating squares on the chess board appears to have begun as a purely decorative device, but quickly became the standard.) Each player began with twelve pieces (possibly chess pieces in the earliest games, though the substitution of the flat disks used for tables was a simple switch). In each turn the player could move a piece forward diagonally, in a single step. If the place was occupied by an opponent's piece but the space beyond was vacant, the player could "jump" over the opposing piece and capture it, but capturing was not required (the rule of huffing, where the player was forced to capture when possible or forfeit the piece, was introduced in the sixteenth century). A piece which reached the back row of the opponent's side would be promoted or "kinged," and could then move either forward or backward.

Since checkers has hardly changed at all since the twelfth century, a modern set is perfectly acceptable for medieval play. Even the tradition of drawing a tables board on one side of a board and a chess board on the other dates back to medieval times.

▦ Gala

Gala is a chess variation that developed in Germany. It may have come into Europe from the east, as it resembles four-player chaturanga and even Chinese xianqgi more than shatranj and acedrex.

Gala was played on a ten-by-ten-square board that was in effect an eight-by-eight-square board quartered with a cross of two rows and columns inserted between them, rather like the "river" in xiangqi. This line between each quadrant and the cross was called the deflection line. Crossing the deflection line changed the movement of the pieces.

Gala is described as a two-player game, but from the setup of the board it seems likely it was originally a game for four players like chaturanga. It could certainly be played by four players with pieces of four colors. The pieces were set up with a king in each corner and the other pieces aligned on the diagonal, facing the center of the board. In the two-person game, each player controlled the pieces in two quadrants. In front of the king on the player's left, he or she had two bishops; in front of the king on the right, two rooks. In the next row on the left were three rooks and on the right three bishops. Four pawns were lined up in front of each array. For a four-person game each player would begin in one corner.

The pawns moved one square at a time on the diagonal, forward toward the middle of the board. Within the cross or in the opponent's sections of the board, a pawn could move in any direction, but if it returned to one of its player's quadrants it could only move forward again. Pawns were not promoted.

Rooks could move any number of squares horizontally or vertically within the quadrants, and on the diagonal within the cross. Bishops moved any number of spaces diagonally in the quadrants and horizontally or vertically within the cross.

Kings moved one square in any direction, and had an additional, unusual move: a king in one of the four central squares could be moved to any square on the board that was empty at the beginning of the game.

Pawns could not capture until after crossing the deflection line. Other pieces had to cross a deflection line in every capturing move.

When a player was able to capture an opposing king he would say "gala." The other player must defend the king if possible. If not on the next turn it would be captured.

If gala was in fact a four-player game, a player who lost a king would turn her pieces over to her partner to play, as in chaturanga. As a two-person game, one player had to capture both the opposing kings to win. If each player lost one king, the game was drawn.

You can draw or paint a gala board on paper or wood. Mark the deflection lines or make the checkered squares a different color inside the cross. Unless you have a large collection of spare chess pieces, you will probably need to make them from modeling clay. For a two-player game, you will need two kings, five bishops, five rooks, and eight pawns in each color. For a four-player set, two players will have three bishops and two rooks while the other two will have three rooks and two bishops: partners should be arranged so that each partnership has five rooks and five bishops between them.

▦ Grande Acedrex

Grande acedrex is one example of the many unusual variations that developed in chess during the Middle Ages. It was called "Grande" because it was played on a twelve-by-twelve-square grid. It was a game for two players, each of whom controlled an army of twelve pawns, a king, two rooks, and a collection of exotic and mythological animals: a griffon, and pairs of lions, crocodiles, giraffes, and unicorns.

When the game began the figure pieces were aligned on the player's home rows: left-to-right—rook, lion, unicorn, giraffe, crocodile, griffon, king, crocodile, giraffe, unicorn, lion, and rook. The next two rows were empty, and the pawns were lined up across the fourth row (so the distance between the rows of pawns was the same as in acedrex/chess).

Pawns and rooks moved as they do in modern chess. Pawns moved one square at a time in forward direction and captured on the diagonal. Rooks moved any number of spaces, forward or backward vertically or horizontally, and could not jump. Kings moved one space in any direction except on the first move, when a king could jump two squares. The crocodile moved like a modern bishop: any number of spaces forward or backward on the diagonal with no jumping. The unicorn moved like a modern bishop except on its first move, when it moved like a knight: an three-square "L" shape of one or two squares horizontally or vertically, followed by two or one squares at a right angle to the first. The unicorn could not capture on its first move so the final square had to be vacant. The lion moved three squares horizontally or vertically, and could leap over opposing pieces. The giraffe moved one square diagonally and then three horizontally or vertically, and could leap. The grif-

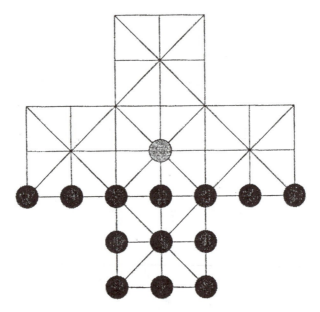

Figure 4.1. In halatafl, later called fox-and-geese, one
player captured pieces while the other attempted to surround the hunter.

fon moved one square diagonally and then had the option of moving
any number of squares vertically or horizontally, but could not leap. All
pieces captured by landing on a square occupied by an opposing piece.
The king could not be captured—the object being to maneuver the king
into a position where it could not escape capture ("checkmate"). If a
player captured all her opponent's pieces except the king, she won by
"baring the king" unless her opponent could capture her last piece on
the next turn.

*To play grande acedrex you will have to paint a twelve-by-twelve-square
board on paper or cardboard and make the various pieces. You can model pieces
from clay, or use wooden disks from a craft store and draw the animals' silhou-
ettes on them.*

⊞ Halatafl

Halatafl was an Icelandic game that spread through northern Europe
with the Vikings and developed into many regional variations of fox-
and-geese (Figure 4.1). The board was a cross, made up of five squares
(one in the center and one on each side). Each square was divided on
the diagonals and in some versions also in quarters. Since the game was

played on the points, or intersections, this board had thirty-three spaces. There was one light-colored piece, the fox, and thirteen dark pieces, the geese. All the pieces moved one space at a time, along the lines in any direction. The fox could capture by leaping over a goose if there is a vacant spot just beyond it. The fox could make multiple captures in the same turn. The object of the game, for the geese, was to pen in the fox by surrounding it so it could not move. The object of the game, for the fox, was to capture so many geese that they could not pen it in. (The geese had a definite advantage.)

The halatafl board has been found scratched in stone in ancient buildings and painted on boards. You can easily draw one on paper for a quick game. Thirteen light-colored and one dark stone make traditional pieces, but checkers, backgammon discs, or even thirteen pennies and one dime will work.

▦ Hasard

This dice game was popular in Europe in the later Middle Ages and became an obsession in the sixteenth and seventeenth centuries, when fortunes were made and lost and great gaming houses were built similar to the gambling casinos of modern times, with banquets and accommodations to entice players. In medieval Europe, however, hasard was still a game played on street corners and in pubs.

Any number could play by laying their money on the center of the table. The caster set the wager by paying the first stake, and could accept or refuse any bet.

The game began with the caster rolling two dice to set the "main." This number had to be from 5 to 9, so if a higher or lower total came up the caster rolled again. Next the caster rolled the two dice to determine the "chance." The chance had to be from 4 to 10. While rolling for the chance the caster could win or lose immediately. He won if he rolled a "nick." There were three nick rolls: duplicating the main, rolling a 12 when the main was a 6 or an 8, or rolling an 11 when the main was a 7 (whence the expression "seven come eleven"). If he rolled a nick, the caster won all the stakes. He lost if he threw an "out." There were four out rolls: a two or a three, called "crabs," were always outs. In addition, rolling a 12 if the main was a 5, 7, or 9; or rolling an 11 if the main was 5, 6, 8, or 9 were outs.

If neither an out nor a nick occurred in setting the chance, the caster continued to throw the dice. If he duplicated the chance, he collected all the stakes on the table. If he duplicated the main, he lost the stakes, which were divided among those who had bet.

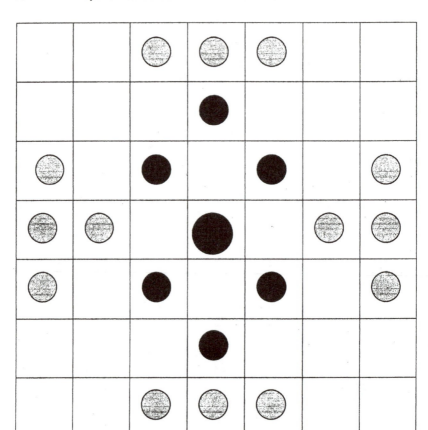

Figure 4.2. In hnefatafl the king and his guards are outnumbered by their attackers.

▦ Hnefatafl

"Tafl" is Norse for table, and there were a variety of Viking "tafl" games. Hnefatafl, "King's table," is perhaps the best known. A hnefatafl board was lined with an equal number of squares in each direction, but the size can vary from seven-by-seven-squares up to nineteen-by-nineteen-squares (always odd). The larger the board, the more pieces each player has to begin the game. (The game can be played on a modern checkers board by placing the pieces on the points instead of the squares.)

Unlike checkers and similar board games, hnefatafl sides are unequal in number. The dark pieces represent the *hnefi*, or king (which is a bigger piece) and a small group of *hunn* (men), his guards (Figure 4.2). A larger number of light-colored hunn represent an invading force. Typically there are as many dark pieces (including the hnefi) as there are spaces in one row on the board, and twice as many invaders as guards. Thus dark has an odd number and light has an even number of pieces.

When the game begins the hnefi is on the center square, or "throne." On some boards this square is raised. The guards surround the hnefi in ranks. The invaders are dispersed evenly around the outside of the board.

Dark moves first. Any piece can move any number of vacant squares, horizontally or vertically. Capture is by surrounding: positioning a piece on either side of an enemy hunn. (But a piece can move between two enemy pieces without being captured.) The hnefi must be surrounded on all four sides to be captured.

The object, for the light-colored invaders, is to capture the hnefi. The object for the hnefi is to escape: if the hnefi reaches an outside square without being captured, dark wins the game.

Try this game on a seven-by-seven-square board first, and once you've mastered it, move up to a larger board. For a the smaller board you'll need six dark hunn and a larger hnefi and fourteen light-colored hunn. Tafl pieces made from glass and carved in wood and stone have been found by archaeologists, but you can make them from modeling clay.

▦ Irish

Irish is one of the many names for the game that developed into modern backgammon. (See nardshir in the Middle East chapter).

▦ Karnöffel

Karnöffel is one of the best-documented early trick-taking card games, although it was clearly not the first game of its kind played in Germany. In 1496 a local bishop condemned the "new" game for turning the natural social order upside down, which would seem to imply that there were other, older games already known that did not include this disruptive feature. Karnöffel also seems to have incorporated the idea of the "trump" suit from trionfi, (discussed later in chapter) and may be the original game where one of the ordinary suits was declared trump in place of the extra cards of the trionfi deck.

Karnöffel is played with a forty-eight-card deck. Traditional German cards had suits of leaves, hearts, bells, and acorns, with the face cards called the *konig*, (king) *ober* (cavalier or knight), and *unter* (jack). Number cards from two through ten fill out the deck for karnöffel (there are no aces). Four people play, with partners sitting opposite each other. Partners are encouraged to discuss the game as it progresses—"table talk" is considered part of the game. A player is sure to let his partner know if he can win a trick so the partner doesn't waste a high card.

The dealer deals five cards to each person, with the first card face up and the rest face down. The lowest of the five exposed cards determines the trump suit for that deal. (If two cards of the same rank are exposed, the first one dealt is the trump.) All players now pick up their cards (including the exposed cards) and examine their hands.

The player to the right of the dealer goes first and play moves counterclockwise. There is no requirement to follow suit, but the highest card in the suit led wins the hand unless there is a trump card played. (The rank in the non-trump suits is the standard order.)

Not all of the cards in the trump suit are trump, and even those which are have particular restrictions—thus the "disruptive" (and complicated!) nature of the game.

The unter of the trump suit is called the karnöffel, and beats all the other cards in the deck. The six of the trump suit ranks next. It is known as the *pope* card. The two of trump, known as the *kaiser*, ranks just below the karnöffel and the pope. Known as *konigstechers* (king-takers), any of these will beat any card of the suit led.

The seven of the trump suit is called the *devil*. If led, it beats any other card except the karnöffel. If it is not led, it is the lowest of its suit (and has no power to trump). The devil cannot be led on the first trick.

The 3 (oberstecher), 4 (unterstecher), and 5 (farbenstecher) of the trump suit beat any numeric card of the suit (*farben*) led. The 4 also beats the unter of that suit and the 3 will beat the unter and the ober (any card except the konig). The other cards of the trump suit (10, 9, 8, and 7 unless it was led) have no special value and do not beat the led suit. In a trick where more than one trump is played, the rank is karnöffel/unter, devil, pope, kaiser, king, 3, ober, 5, 10, 9, 8, 7. The winner of each hand is the team that wins the most tricks (three out of five). Individual cards have no scoring value.

The deal passes to the right. A game can be any multiple of four deals (one hand dealt by each player) with a tiebreaker if the agreed-upon number is reached and two players have won the same number of tricks.

To play karnöffel with a standard American deck of cards, remove the aces. The king is the konig, the queen is the ober, and the jack is the unter.

⊞ Merrels

Merrels or morris games are common throughout Europe, Africa, and the Middle East, and their existence in far-flung parts of the world has been seen by some anthropologists as evidence of early communication and trade between regions.

Variations on merrels were played in Bronze-Age Ireland and by the Vikings, carved into Egyptian temples two millennia B.C.E. and into the steps of a shrine in Ceylon during the first decades C.E. Visitors to Westminster Abbey in London are amused to see the "Nine-Men's Morris" board carved into a stone bench there.

During the Middle Ages a variety of merrels games were popular in Europe. Five, nine, and twelve-men's morris were named for the number of pieces each player had to place on the board.

A simplified version of merrels, sometimes called naughts and crosses, became the game commonly played today on paper with players drawing Os (naughts) and Xs (crosses) in the nine spaces of a cross-hatched board made of four crossed lines.

⊞ Nine-Men's Morris

The nine-men's morris board is three concentric squares. Lines are drawn from the inner to outer square at the midpoint of each side. The game is played on the intersections or points. Each player has nine "men" or "merrels" of a distinct color; pebbles, sticks, or wooden disks are most common.

In the first phase of the game the players take turns placing one piece on the board at a time, trying to gain the most advantageous positions for the second phase. Any time a player is able to place three of his pieces in a row (called a *mill*) he can remove any one of his opponent's pieces from the board.

In phase two, after all the pieces have been placed, players move their pieces, one point at a time, to try and form mills. Each time a player forms a mill she can remove an opponent's piece. (Moving a piece out and then back on the next turn is allowed.) Pieces that are in mills cannot be removed. If a player makes a mill and all the opponent's pieces are in mills there is no capture, but the other player must move on the next turn even if it means breaking a mill.

The game is won by removing all but two of the opponent's pieces (so that he cannot make a mill) or by blocking all the opponent's pieces so he cannot move.

⊞ Ombre

Ombre is one of the earliest card games known in Europe. It was a huge fad in the seventeenth century, but was well established in Spain long before that. At its peak it inspired a unique form of furniture—a three-sided card table.

Ombre is a three-handed game, and "l'ombre" or "man," refers to the single player who plays against his opponents. If four are playing, the dealer for each round sits out. The game is played with a forty-card deck. Spanish card suits were commonly coins and cups (female) and swords and clubs (male).

By the seventeenth century, ombre adopted the notion of trumping from trionfi, but in medieval times it was a simple trick-taking game. Once the cards were dealt, each player bid how many tricks he believed he could capture with the cards in his hand. The winning (highest) bidder then played against the other two, who were allowed to consult over their hands to attempt to block the ombre from making the bid.

The ombre leads the first trick, and the other two must follow suit if possible. As the game progresses, the winner of each trick leads the next.

If the ombre makes the first five tricks, he may declare the hand won, or may choose to continue—but if he goes for the sixth trick, he must take all nine to win the hand, or "vole." If he believes he cannot win, he can surrender before taking the fourth trick. In that case, one of the opponents may choose to continue, taking over the role of ombre and the potential win (the other player then joins the first ombre in the opposition).

Like most card games, ombre is most often played for stakes, and the amount won depends on how decisive the win: simply to win the first five tricks entitles the ombre to collect a single stake from each player, while winning the vole wins him a fivefold payout. Failing to make the bid requires him to pay each of his opponents instead. If one of the opponents wins the game, the ombre pays that player five times the stake.

To play ombre with modern cards, take out the 8s, 9s, and 10s. Red cards are female, with the rank "reversed" from what we consider typical—the ace and deuce ranks just below the face cards, or matadors, and the 7 is the lowest-ranked card. Black cards follow the modern pattern, but aces are low (see playing cards).

▦ Paumecary

This English tables game was played by teams of two or three players, using a half-sized board or just half of a standard twelve-point board. On each turn all the players on one side rolled and played in succession, and then the other team did the same. The game began with no pieces on the board, and players entered according to the roll of two dice. A roll of doubles entitled the player to another roll. Any number of pieces could be on the same point (they could be stacked), and landing on a point occupied by a single opposing piece knocked it out. It had to be re-entered as in the beginning. Once all of a team's pieces were on the board they began bearing them off, and the first team to bear all of its

Figure 4.3. Playing cards, left to right: Chinese myriads, Persian parakeets, German acorns, Trionfi sun. Bottom: Korean general. *Sources*: Adapted from Culin (1896, 1991).

pieces off then began to bear off the other team's pieces, slapping the hands of the opposing players with each piece so removed.

▦ Playing Cards

Playing cards developed first in China before 1000, then traveled along the Silk Road to India and Persia. There is no record of playing cards in Europe before 1370, and fifty years later they were wildly popular from the Mediterranean to the Urals (Figure 4.3).

How playing cards first came into Europe is something of a mystery. The Persian game, as nas, is played with a five-suit deck, and Indian gangifa games have from eight to twelve suits. Both cultures had round cards. The earliest known references to card games in Europe are to a game played in Spain with of a deck of fifty-two cards in four suits, and European cards have always been rectangular.

A set of cards now considered representative of the most likely ancestor of European cards was found in Istanbul, but had been made in Egypt during the Mamluk era. These cards were long and rectangular, and the deck had four suits: swords, polo-sticks, cups, and coins. Each suit had ten number cards and three court cards: a king (*malik*) deputy (*na'ib malik*), and underdeputy (*thani na'ib*). Most scholars today believe that these cards support a theory that cards, called *naipes* in Spanish, first came into Spain from North Africa when both regions were part of the Arabic world.

As playing cards became popular in Europe the four suits developed differently in different countries. The suits Americans think of as typical are the French suits that became the standard in England: hearts, clubs, spades, and diamonds. These were a late development. Medieval Europeans were more likely to play with cards in German suits (hearts, leaves, bells, and acorns), or Italian suits (coins, cups, swords, and clubs). Other variations included batons, shields, and roses.

Originally the straight suits (swords, clubs, batons, and the like) were considered "male" and the round suits (cups, coins, bells, etc.) were "female." In the male suits the rank of the numbered cards is what we think of as typical: ten high, two low. In the female suits, the numbers rank the other way—the two (or deuce) is higher than the three, and so forth. With modern cards you can play the black suits as male and the red suits as female. By the 1400s the counterranking male/female suits had been dropped from most games.

Early card games were mostly matching and trick-taking games. The concept of trump developed originally as a separate suit, the *triumphs*. Within a few years the idea of turning one suit into the trump suit for a given hand or game had taken hold (see karnöffel, ombre, and trionfi).

⊞   Queek

Queek was a game of chance that made use of the new checkered chessboard. Taking a predetermined number of pebbles in hand, players bet on how many dark or light squares would be filled, then cast the pebbles on the board. The player who chose the closest number could win the bet, or play could be repeated for ever-increasing stakes until someone's guess was matched, when the winner would take all the stakes. Alternatively, one pebble could be cast at a time, giving a fifty-fifty chance of winning the bet: light or dark? Every new game introduced new ways to cheat: checkered boards carefully constructed so that one color squares were lower than the other are evidence that some Queek games were rigged.

⊞   Raffle

Raffle was a three-dice game that might be considered the ancestor of the modern slot machine. Players placed stakes on the table and took turns casting the dice. The winner was the first player to have all three dice come up the same way. (Weighted dice were a constant threat, and wise players insisted on alternating whose dice were used.)

⊞ Rithmomachy, or the Philosopher's Game

In twelfth-century France some mathematics scholars invented a new game to be played on a double chessboard. The flat pieces were black on one side, white on the other, and numbered on both sides. One player was "odd" and the other "even," based on the numbers of the round, smallest pieces: 3, 5, 7, and 9 or 2, 4, 6, and 8. These pieces were set up centered on the fourth row from the player, with the smaller numbers on the left. (There were many versions of this game, with pieces starting in different arrangements, but this is the most basic; Figure 4.4.) Behind them were arrayed the second rank of round pieces, valued at the first-ranked numbers squared (odds = 9, 25, 49, and 81, evens = 4, 16, 36, and 64). Beside these (on the first two and last two squares of the third row) came the first triangular pieces, which were equal to the first and second rounds added together: 12, 30, 56, and 90 for the odds side; 6, 20, 42, and 72 for the evens. The second rank of triangles were valued at the base number plus one and then squared, which meant each player's triangles shared some numeric values with the second rank of rounds on the opponent's side: odds were 16, 36, 64, and 100; evens were 9, 25, 49, and 81. These were arrayed behind the rounds. The highest numbered pieces on the board were squares. The first squares, which were placed behind the lower triangles, had the values of the triangles added together: 28, 66, 120, and 190 (see discussion of king below) for the odd player, 15, 45, 91 (see king), and 153 for the even. The second rank of squares was valued by doubling the base number, adding one, and squaring the result: odd had 49, 121, 225, and 361; even had 25, 81, 169, and 289. These began in the first and last two squares of the home row.

On each side one square was replaced with a pyramid, called the king, formed by stacking pieces bearing square numbers. The odd king was built of the squares 64 and 49, the triangles 25 and 36, and the round 16, totaling 190. The even king was made from the squares 25 and 36, the triangles 9 and 16, and the rounds 4 and 1, for a total of 91. Including the pieces that made up the two pyramids, the white player began with 29 pieces: ten rounds, ten triangles, and nine squares, while the black player had 28: nine rounds, ten triangles, and nine squares.

The movement of each piece was determined by the number of sides it had: round pieces moved one space, triangles moved three spaces, and squares moved four spaces. All pieces could move in any direction as long as the spaces being crossed were vacant (no jumping). Pyramids could move in the same way as any of their layers.

There were four ways of capturing in rithmomachia, three of them mathematical. In all cases the capturing piece did not move into the space occupied by the captured piece, but the captured piece was re-

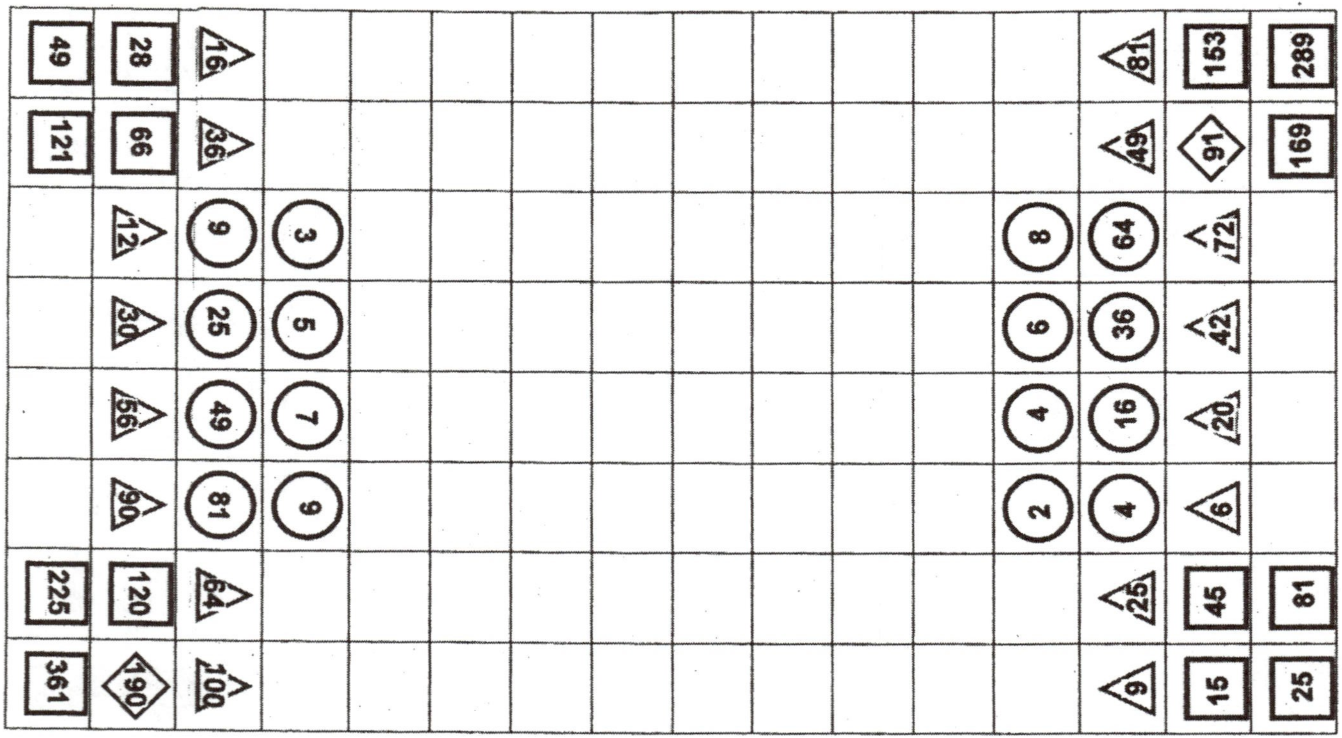

Figure 4.4. The shape of rithmomachia pieces determined their method of capture.

moved. Captured pieces were flipped over and entered from the home row of the player who captured them. Capture by "meeting" (equivalency): If a piece was in position to land on a space occupied by an opposing piece of the same value, it captured that piece. Capture by "assault" (multiplication): If the result of multiplying the value of a piece by the number of vacant spaces between it and another piece equaled the value of the larger piece, the smaller piece captured the larger piece. Capture by "ambuscade" (addition): If two pieces could move on to either side of a piece that equaled the sum of their values, they captured that piece. The only nonmathematical means of capture was the "siege," when a piece was surrounded by enemy pieces on all four sides. Whole pyramids could be captured if their base square was captured by one of the methods above, or individual layers of the pyramid could be captured.

There were a variety of wins, or "victories," possible in rithmomachia, and players agreed in advance whether to play for a "minor" victory, also called a "common" victory, or a "major" or "proper" victory. The simplest common victory (*de corpore*, or "by bodies") was to decide on a number of pieces to be captured, and the first player to capture that number of pieces was the winner. Another common victory was called *de bonis* or "by value" and was given to the first player to capture pieces which added up to a predetermined value. A *de lite* victory was based on capturing pieces totaling both a certain sum and a certain number of digits. Players might instead choose to try for a *de honore* victory, based on both the sum of the value and the total number of pieces captured. Finally, there was the victory, *de honore liteque*—where the victor needed the correct sum, number of digits and number of pieces (not every combination was possible here, requiring advanced planning!).

Major victories added yet another level of mathematical computation to the game for the very advanced player. To achieve these victories the players had to understand arithmetic, geometric, and harmonic progressions, although charts listing the possible combinations were commonly used during games. A player who had captured the opponent's king could then attempt to build a progression on the opponent's side of the board, incorporating at least one of the opponent's pieces in the progression.

Arithmetic progressions are those where the numbers are separated by a constant amount (as 7, 11, 15 are separated by 4). In geometric progressions the relationship between the numbers is one of multiplication rather than addition: 7, 28, 112, for example, with the constant again being 4. A harmonic, or musical progression, is based on ratios: the ratio between the largest and smallest number must equal the ratio between the differences between the middle number and the larger and smaller ones. A "Victoria Magna" was declared when a player managed to build one three-number progression of any type. A "Victoria Major" was accomplished when a player built a four-number sequence which incorporated two progressions—three of the four numbers forming one kind and three of the four another kind. Finally, a "Victoria Excellentisima" was achieved when a four-number sequence included all three kinds of progressions.

You can make rithmomachia pieces from purchased wooden shapes or shapes made from modeling clay. Paint them all one color on one side and the other on the backs, and be sure to put the same numbers on both sides! You need nineteen rounds: 1 through 9, plus two extra 4s and an extra 9, two 16s, and one each of 25, 36, 49, 64, and 81; twenty triangles, two each of 9, 16, 25, and 36, and one each of 6, 12, 20, 30, 42, 49, 56, 64, 72, 81, 90, and 100; and eighteen squares two each of 25 and 49, and one each marked 15, 28, 36, 45, 64, 66, 81, 120, 121, 153, 169, 225, 289, and 361. You may want to tape two chessboards together to make a permanent rithmomachia board.

▦ Sixe-ace

This was a quick, simple dice game for two or four players, played with a tables board and pieces. (The board is really incidental to the game.) Players sat on the long sides of the board, each beginning with six playing pieces lined up on the six points in front of him. Two dice were cast at once but each was played separately. If a one came up, the player paid one piece to the player on his right. If a five was rolled, the player paid one piece into a pool in the middle of the board. If a two was rolled the player took a piece from the pool (if there were any to take). A six allowed the player to bear off one piece. (Threes and fours were disregarded.) A doublet earned the player another roll. Play passed to the right. The first player to clear all his pieces off the board and then roll another six was the winner.

▦ Tables

In medieval Europe there were many games played on a board that today is used almost exclusively for backgammon (Figure 4.5). The game we call backgammon was previously known as "Irish." It was played almost exactly like nardshir, which is described in the section on the Middle East. Scholars believe games played with two dice are descended from nardshir, while those played with three developed from the Roman game tabula (also the source of the English name.) Many of the three-dice games were also played with two dice, with rules such as "assume the third die is a six" or "count the lower die twice." In all cases each die was played separately: one piece could be moved for each die,

Figure 4.5. Many different games were played on a tables board. *Source*: From the Codex Manesse, courtesy Universität Heidelberg.

or a single piece could move, first the number shown by one die and then the number shown by the other.

You can play any of these tables games on a modern backgammon board, since the design of the board has not changed at all in 700 years. If you are not familiar with backgammon, read the directions for nardshir before playing the table games described in this chapter: doblet, fayles, paumercary, and sixe-ace.

▦ Trionfi

The notion that tarot cards are an ancient fortune-telling device is a persistent hoax concocted by French writer Antoine Court de Gébelin in 1781. Tarot cards were invented in Italy in the fourteenth century as an addition to ordinary playing cards for the game trionfi. Before the introduction of "triumph" cards each trick was won by the highest-ranked card played in the suit led. The new, pictorial cards "triumphed" over (or "trumped") any card in the ordinary deck. The early trionfi deck combined an ordinary Italian deck of 56 plain-suited cards (14 each of swords, batons, cups and coins, each having four court cards: king, queen, cavalier, and jack) with 22 triumph cards for a total of 78 cards. Each triumph card had a different picture and rank. The pictures listed here are traditional but there were many regional and even individual variations. Memorizing the sequence of the 22 triumph cards was necessary for the game until the practice of putting numbers or other indicators on cards was introduced in the eighteenth century.

In descending order of rank the triumph cards are:

Angel (representing the Last Judgment; sometimes trumpets were used instead)

World

Sun

Moon

Star

Thunderbolt

Devil (sometimes a ship was substituted for the devil card)

Death

Traitor (the hanged man)

Old Man (sometimes a hermit)

Wheel (of fortune)

Fortitude

Justice

Temperance

Chariot

Love

Pope

Emperor

Popess (Because many people found the pope/popess cards offensive they were often replaced by likenesses of Jupiter and Juno.)

Empress (sometimes the pope/popess and emperor/empress cards were replaced with four matching and equally ranked soldiers.)

Bagatto (con-man)

Matto or Fool (technically the fool has no rank)

If you have a modern tarot deck the cards are probably numbered, and it will be easier to use those ranks if they are different from these. If you are making your own deck, you can use any pictures you like—frequently triumph cards represented local families, guilds and locations.

This game was called taracco in Italy beginning about 1500. Later versions were called tarocchino ("little taracco") and were played without the 2, 3, 4, and 5 cards. By the 1500s there were many different forms of tarocchino games played in Italy and France, but no recorded rules for the earlier game have been found.

Here is a reconstruction of trionfi.

Early trionfi was probably a three-player game, with each player receiving twenty-six cards. With four players, partners sat opposite one another and played as a team. Each player received nineteen cards, which they looked at but did not reveal to the other players. The dealer received the two leftover cards, and had to discard any two cards before play began, saving them to add to his point total in the end. Some three-player versions called for each player to receive twenty-five cards, and the dealer discarded three cards. The deal, and the play, was counterclockwise.

After the deal and discard, if any, players looked at their cards to determine if they were holding any *cricche*, or sequences. Before playing the first trick, each player had the chance to "declare" these combinations to receive points. (Because declaring a sequence means revealing the cards, a player could choose not to do so.)

Cricche were combinations of three and four cards of the same rank:

Table 4.1
Cricche Cards and Points

Card type	Points for 3	Points for 4
Triumphs	18	36
Kings	17	34
Queens	14	28
Horses (Cavaliers)	13	26
Jacks	12	24

Sequences were combinations of cards within suits, with a king plus two court cards as the shortest sequence. A four-card sequence could be king plus three other court cards of a suit or king plus two court cards plus the ace, while a five-card sequence would be all four court cards plus the ace. In the triumph suit, a sequence was called a *grande*. It required the angel and at least two of the next three (world, sun, and moon), to which could be added as many of the other sixteen triumph cards as you had in your hand in consecutive order. Any three-card sequence was worth 10 points, and each additional card was worth 5 points. The points were doubled if a player held three or more sequences.

Having declared or not declared, the player to the right of the dealer opened the first trick, leading any card except the *fool*. Each player followed suit unless he had no cards of the suit led, in which case he could play a triumph card. In each case the highest-ranked card won the trick, and if more than one triumph card was played, the higher-ranked triumph card won.

The fool had no rank. It could be played on any suit, allowing a player to save a more valuable triumph card for later play: in France it was called the *excuse*. Once the fool was played, the next player could play any suit and that suit determined the trick. After the trick, the player who had the fool could exchange it for any card in his or her hand, so it could be played more than once: it had no rank, but lots of power!

The player who won the trick led (played the first card) for the next trick. When the round was finished, each player or team was awarded the points for all the tricks they won and any cricche or sequences declared. Deal passed to the right and the next round was played in the same way.

In scoring, the angel, world, bagatto, fool, and all four kings counted 5 points each. Queens were worth 4 points, cavaliers, 3, and jacks, 2 points each. Number cards were counted by twos, earning one point for two cards (a leftover number card had no value). The team which captured the last trick of the round won 6 bonus points. Points for declarations were added to these scores to determine the points earned in each round. Usually the first team to reach 800 or 1,000 points won the game.

PLAY

▦ Base

Chase-and-capture games, according to many anthropologists, have their origins in prehistoric bride raids, when the young men of one clan would descend upon the village of another and carry off eligible mates. Whatever the case for species-wide memories, it is certainly true that chase-and-catch games are a universal form of play.

In Europe base, or prisoner's base, was a game played by both girls and boys. Players divided into teams and defined the playing area—a street, field, or courtyard. Each team had a tree, pillar, or rock designated as their "base" and another as their "prison." The teams lined up, linking hands, each chain with one player touching the base. One by one the players at the ends of the chains let go and chased each other. If one caught the other, the captive was brought to the prison, and soon chains of players were strung from each prison. Now the runners leaving their bases would try not only to capture new prisoners but also to liberate their teammates by touching the chain of prisoners. Once freed, prisoners ran back to their own bases, where they were safe until they set off again.

▦ Bear-baiting

Bear-baiting was a popular amusement in Europe during the Middle Ages. People would pay for the opportunity to dash in and strike or otherwise tease a chained bear, leaping back before the animal could strike back. The owner of the bear would have it chained to keep it from mauling the baiters, but the risk of being caught by a clawed paw was still very real and apparently part of the game's appeal.

A children's version of this game had two children in the role of the bear and the keeper. The "keeper" held one end of a short rope, with the other end either tied around the "bear's" waist or held in his hand. The others tried to tag the bear without themselves being tagged by the bear or the keeper. A player tagged by the bear or keeper changed places with that player.

▦ Blind-Man's Buff

The game of blindfolding and challenging a player to identify those teasing him was very popular among children in Europe, and was also a flirting game among young people. The player chosen to be "it" could be blindfolded or could simply turn his hood around backward, so the game was sometimes called "hoodman's blind." Usually the other players tested him by holding up some number of fingers to check if he could see. Then the blindfolded player was spun around three times before being challenged to capture another player. While the blindfolded player tried to catch one of his playmates, they "buffeted" him, tagging him, and dashing away to avoid being caught. When the blindfolded player captured another, he generally had to identify her before removing the blindfold. Then the captured player was blindfolded and the game continued.

▦ Boules (Bocce)

A variety of bowling games were popular in Europe. Each player had one or two painted wooden balls about the size of a large apple. The target could be a stake, sometimes called a *mistress*, or another, smaller ball, known as a *jack*. Players took turns rolling their balls at the target, or at other player's balls in an effort to knock them away from the target. Some variations allowed players to drive the jack away with their balls. When all had completed their turns, the player whose ball was closest to the target was the winner of that "end" and received a score of 1. Play continued until one player or team reached the score needed to win, usually 25.

Bocce is the modern form of boules, and bocce sets are readily available today. You can also play boules with the balls of a croquet set. A level grassy area is the best for boules: balls make depressions on sand and can break on pavement. A purpose-made bocce court is 60 by 8 feet, with a raised board edge, and generally has a slight pitch from the walls to the middle to keep the balls from clinging to the wall, but not so great as to make them roll. For medieval boules the dimensions of the court are more flexible, generally a long narrow alley or churchyard served the purpose. If the target is a jack rather than a mistress, the first player begins by tossing the jack, then tosses his first ball as close to it as possible. The winner of each round tosses the jack for the next round.

⊞ Counting-out Rhymes

A counting-out rhyme can serve as a simple game, but these rhymes are more typically used to select which player will be "it" or perhaps go first in another game. All players chant the rhyme, often a series of non-sense words, while pointing to each player in turn. The player who is pointed to on the last syllable is designated as "it." Some scholars have studied the familiar "eenie, meenie, miney mo" and its German and other European counterparts and concluded that they all have their origins quite literally in counting: that they are derivations of the old Norman French "une, duexne, trois . . ."

⊞ Drop the Handkerchief

This ancient children's game was recorded in Roman times and continued throughout centuries in Europe. Some scholars believe it dates back to ancient times when guarding the fire was an important community task. The players sat in a circle, and the player who was "it" walked stealthily around the outside of the circle carrying an object: a handkerchief in most versions, but in Germany it was played with a bag of dried peas and in some places a boiled egg was used. Eventually "it" dropped the object behind a player and raced around the circle. The selected player had to leap up, chase, and tag the runner with the handkerchief before he completed the circle. If the runner returned to the empty space without being tagged, he sat down and the other player continued around the circle as "it."

⊞ Hoops

Hoops such as those used to hold barrels together made terrific playthings, and throughout Europe adults as well as young people enjoyed the challenge of using a stick to try to roll a hoop farther or faster than an opponent. Hoop rolling could also be made more challenging in games where players tried to leap through the hoop as it rolled by. Children also turned hoops and jumped through them like jump ropes, and young people danced circle games in which players held hoops between them and others danced through the hoops, or were caught inside the hoop when the music stopped.

▦ Hopscotch

Jumping and hopping games are probably universal, and early scholars reported that Christians took an ancient game of hopping through a labyrinth and made it into a Christian game by designating the sections as the journey to heaven or the seven levels of heaven. In addition to paths alternating one and two squares, hopscotch paths could be in grids, spirals, circles, and triangles.

Some people believe hopscotch took its name from the roads built by the Roman troops across all of Europe and as far as Scotland. The Romans never did conquer Scotland. Eventually the emperor Hadrian ordered construction of a wall across the island to keep the Scots and Picts out of England. Hundreds of young men from the far-flung lands occupied by the Romans found themselves at the end of the world, guarding the wall. Legend says soldiers passed the dreary hours of guard duty playing games, including one where they hopped on one foot along the road (sometimes while carrying backpacks or other soldiers on their backs).

Medieval hopscotch courts were often as long as one hundred feet. In medieval Europe they were often scratched (or perhaps "scotched") on the stone pavement. Today the path is usually marked with chalk. Players take turns hopping along the path on one foot. Sometimes marked squares show where the player can change feet. In other versions, a player tosses a stone onto the court, and changes feet or turns around in that square.

If hopscotch seems like too simple a game for you, perhaps you'd like to try the version played by adults in medieval England, with a friend mounted on your back!

▦ Hot Cockles

Cockles were shellfish, sold in Britain by street vendors and eaten hot out of the shells, but the only thing this game had in common with hot cockles was sore hands. Players sat on the floor. One, blindfolded, leaned forward with her hands behind her back and put her head into the lap of another. When she called out "hot cockles" the others would slap her hands, and she had to try and guess had who struck her. When the guess was successful, the striker became the target. This game became popular with both boys and girls, while teenagers enjoyed it as an opportunity for flirting.

▦ London Bridge

This English version of the universal "arch-trap" game recalls the destruction of the bridge over the river Thames in London during a Viking invasion in the eleventh century. Two players link their hands and hold them high, while the others form a line and pass underneath. Everyone sings, "London Bridge is falling down, falling down, falling down. London Bridge is falling down, my fair lady." At the end of the verse the "bridge" falls down, capturing whichever player is inside. That player is generally out. The song can go on for many verses, each suggesting that the bridge be rebuilt with various materials, and explaining why they are unsatisfactory.

▦ Obstacle Course Races

Obstacle course races were popular among adults and children across Europe. Some had runners running across swords and among dagger blades sticking out of the soil! Some races required the runner to balance cups of water on his head or carry a partner on his back as he ran.

Lay out an obstacle course with bales of hay and tubs of water to leap over and a row of wooden swords to step between. For an authentic race runners should be barefoot.

▦ Quilles or Kailes

This predecessor of modern bowling was popular throughout Europe. Quilles were wooden pins, wider at the bottom than the top so they would stand on end (Figure 4.6). The quilles were lined up in rows or other patterns at one end of the playing area. Players took turns attempting to knock them over by tossing a stick at them from the other end of the lane. Each pin knocked over earned the player one point. In some variations, there was a kingpin, larger than the others, that was worth ten points if a player succeeded in knocking it over without knocking down any of the others.

Modern bowling pins are designed to be hit at the base, and will not tip over as well when struck on the side. You can cut quilles for your game from lengths of scrap wood or kindling. Sand the bottom of each quille flat so it will stand

Figure 4.6. Tossing a stick to knock over quilles outside a pub. *Source*: By permission of the British Library, Additional Manuscript Ms. 22494, f. 42.

up. Use another stick, eight-to-ten inches long, as the club. Draw a line fifteen feet away from the quilles. Each player in turn stands behind the line and tosses the club (a horizontal spinning motion is most effective) toward the line of quilles.

⊞ Quoits

Quoits were flat stones or metal disks. Players took turns tossing the quoits at a rod stuck into the ground or into a ring, and kept score. The player with the largest number of hits or rings was the winner. By the later Middle Ages players had begun to use horse shoes for quoits, in a game that is basically unchanged to this day. Playing at quoits was frequently prohibited because it was dangerous and because people played quoits instead of practicing archery, but it remained popular.

⊞ Ring-around-a-Rosy

This children's circle game took its song from the horrifying symptoms of the plague that raced from across Asia and Europe in the fourteenth century. The disease was spread by fleas, which sometimes traveled on rats, other times arriving in bundles of cloth or furs with traders. A more virulent form of the plague was transferred directly from person to person by sneezing; mortality rate was nearly 100 percent. One-third to one-half of the population of Europe was wiped out by plague in less than one hundred years. The symptoms of plague were a characteristic rash, the "ring of roses," followed by flu-like symptoms (the sneezing "achoo, achoo") and in a few days with death from blood loss ("we all fall down"). People wore pouches ("pockets") of flower petals around their necks, perhaps as protection, but probably to hide the stench of death. And from this dreadful disease we get the lilting children's rhyme and game:

> Ring-a ring-o-rosies,
> A pocket full o' posies.
> Achoo, achoo,
> We all fall down.

⊞ Round and Round the Village

Variations of this circle game were played all over Europe and in India and the Near East. Some scholars theorize that they are remnants of a prehistoric fertility ritual in which newlyweds walked from house to house to receive blessings and gifts from the others of their community.

Children joined hands to form a circle and sang while the child chosen to be "it" walked around the outside of the circle: "Go round and round the village (repeated three times) as we have done before." On the second verse, "Go in and out the window," the children in the circle raised their linked hands and the circling child went "in and out" around the circle, ducking under each pair of hands, and winding up inside the circle. On the third verse, "Now stand and face your partner" (or lover), the child in the center of the circle chose a partner by facing one of the other children.

Today there are several variations for a verse that runs, "Now follow me to London" (or some other far-off place):

Version one: The chosen child chases the child who is "it" out of the circle and around the outside, trying to catch "it" before the child is able to get around the circle and step into the place of the chosen child. If the chosen child tags the first child, that child is "it" again. If not, the game continues with the second child as "it."

Version two: The chosen child joins hands with the first "it" and they repeat the "in and out the window" action, after which each of them chooses a new partner. In this version the circle gets smaller and smaller as the number of couples grows.

Version three: The two children walk around the outside of the circle again, and end with a bow or a kiss.

▦ Ruzzola

Ruzzola is the Italian name of a game played across central Europe. They were originally played with hard round cheeses, and may in fact have their origins in the transporting of cheese down from Alpine farms to markets and villages.

Players compete as individuals or divide into teams, each with a wooden disk or ruzzola. Some players use a string wrapped around the ruzzola to increase its velocity. The game is to roll the ruzzola along the road, uphill and downhill and around whatever bends there may be. When the ruzzola comes to a stop or rolls off the road, the thrower picks it up and throws it again. The winner is the player or team who rolls the ruzzola the furthest in a predetermined number of throws, or uses the smallest number of throws to cover a predetermined distance: generally the distance from one village to the next.

There is a variation on this game still played in one part of England, where the cheeses are rolled from the top of the hill and runners race behind, trying to beat the cheeses to the bottom of the hill and catch them.

Ruzzola disks are wooden, about five inches across and an inch thick. You may be able to find disks like this at craft or unfinished wood stores. A piece of round firewood cut in slices will provide a number of ruzzola. Sand them well to avoid a palm full of splinters.

⊞ Salt Posts

Salt posts is still played by children today. In North America it is commonly called freeze tag.

In medieval Europe the name "salt posts" recalled the story of Lot in the Bible: Lot's wife was transformed into a pillar of salt when she disobeyed God's instruction not to look back when fleeing her home. Any number of children could play. The one who was "it" tries to tag the others. Those who were tagged had to "turn to salt," remaining absolutely still, unless they were touched by another player. If a player moved after being turned to salt, he or she became "it." Otherwise the last player turned to salt became "it" for the next round.

⊞ Shuttlecock

A shuttlecock was a small ball with a feathered "tail" like that of a cock, or rooster. Shuttlecock was the child's version of tennis, and played in the same way: first by knocking the shuttlecock back and forth with the hands, later adding a net and racquets or paddles, called "battledores." Battledores were originally made of wood and later of animal skin stretched over an open frame, which gave more bounce when striking the shuttlecock. The object of the game was to keep the shuttlecock in the air, and if played competitively, one side scored a point when the other side let it drop to the ground.

To play medieval shuttlecock today you can use a commercial shuttlecock or make a small cloth ball filled with hair, grass, ashes, or sand, with feathers attached to one side. A modern ping-pong racket will be more authentic than a modern badminton racket. To make a skin racket, curve the end of a thin branch and tie it to itself to form a loop on a handle. Stretch thin leather or heavy cloth tightly over the loop and stitch it in place. (If you soak the cloth before you sew it on, it will tighten as it dries.)

⊞ Skating

Ice skates made of bone or wood date back into prehistoric times, and it is hard to distinguish between their use for winter transportation and for pleasure. In the Lowlands, Belgium and Holland, where ice was common and snow was not, it was natural that summer footraces became winter skating competitions. Young people and men of leisure developed techniques of skating on one foot, tracing designs on the ice, and sometimes prizes were awarded to those who completed the most perfect circles and figure-8s.

■ Stoolball

In England stoolball developed into a team sport and eventually into modern cricket. During the Middle Ages it was a casual flirting game. Young women sat on milking stools while young men tossed balls at them. The object for the bowler was to hit the stool. The player on the stool tried to keep the ball from hitting the stool, either with her hands or, later, with a small wooden paddle. If she hit the ball, she would run across the field to another stool (about sixteen feet away) and either sit there or, if the ball had not yet been captured, hit that stool with her bat and run back again. For each time the runner hit a stool with her bat, she won a point. The bowler won points by hitting the stool or, once the ball had been hit, by catching the ball or fielding it and hitting the stool with the ball before the runner reached it. The traditional prize for winning at stoolball was a kiss or cake for each point. A stool ball was about the size of an apple, made of cloth and stuffed with feathers, hair or grass.

To play stoolball you will need two short, preferably three-legged stools, a small wooden paddle and a cloth ball for each pair of players.

■ Sword and Buckler

Sword and buckler was a child's version of the swordfight at tournaments and may have begun as a way of training young pages to fight (Figure 4.7). Holding a wooden sword and shield, two players parried until one landed a blow on the other.

The buckler was a small round shield, with a handle that fit over the hand so that both hands could control the sword. Bucklers were easily carried, sometimes even made with a hook to hang on a belt, so they were used by merchants and travelers for self-defense as well as by soldiers. The practice sword would be about the length of the fighter's leg from hip to ankle.

Sword and buckler players began by approaching each other and issuing a challenge. Each then began to swing the sword, looking for an opening to strike at the opponent's lower body. (Striking at the head and face was prohibited.) As one brought his sword toward the other, the opponent would parry the strike, pushing the sword to the side with the flat of his blade, and then attempt to strike. Footwork was critical: dodging blows was as important as parrying them, yet it was important to keep the feet planted in order to maintain balance and to put force be-

Figure 4.7. Sword and buckler could be used for self-defense or for sport. *Source*: Courtesy of the Historical Armed Combat Association, Houston, TX.

hind one's blows. So fighters learned to pivot from one foot or shift their weight quickly, keeping the knees bent for balance.

The basic offensive moves of the swordfight were swinging the sword down from behind one shoulder or the other, or around from behind one hip or the other, or bringing the sword across in front of the body. There were also two basic thrusting moves, one forward from the waist and one downward. For each swing and thrust the fighter learned an appropriate countermove, or parry. In training the fighters would go through each movement in sequence, though in a duel surprise would help a fighter gain advantage.

To reenact a sword-and-buckler duel you should either use foam swords or pad the wooden swords or the swordfighters. Even an accidental slip with a wooden sword can result in a significant bruise!

⊞ Tilting at Quintains

Tilting began as a form of training for the joust, but quickly was taken up by children as a game. A quintain was a target, often a painted face intended to resemble an enemy warrior. The target was hung on a pole, balanced on a point, or set on rockers so that when it was struck it would spin around or rock and then stand back up. Players would take turns running or riding (on another's back) toward the quintain, carrying a pole for a lance with which they attempted to hit the target. Often the quintain had a swinging arm, so that it could "fight back." By the late Middle Ages adults were playing too, sometimes with human quintains who perched atop tall stools, wearing armor made of woven reeds and wielding poles in their defense. Tilting also entered the tournament as a sport in its own right, with a tiny ring for a target that the knight had to try to pluck and carry off with his lance as he rode by.

To make a quintain, put a stick through the sleeves of an old shirt so it sticks out one to two feet from the "body." Tie a rope around the stick and bring it up through the neck of the shirt. Stuff the shirt with straw and give it a face painted on a sack that has also been stuffed. Now hang the quintain from a pole. It should swing freely when hit. Place the quintain in the "list," your riding arena, and you are ready to begin tilting.

Hang some rings from strings and mount them on poles in other parts of the playing area, so that several different events can take place at the same time.

Jousters may ride on bicycles or scooters as well as on the shoulders of their playmates. The lance, a pole ten to twelve feet long, should be held along the forearm and close to the body. The jouster must ride directly at the quintain and strike it squarely, and get out of the way quickly to avoid being hit back.

▦ Top Races

European children used tops for solitary play and also for races. Whipping tops were most suitable for races. Players set their tops spinning by wrapping the string of the whip around the top and pulling it back quickly as they dropped the top to the ground, then chasing behind the top they whipped the string around the top and pulled it away to keep it moving when it started to slow down.

Medieval parish churches often housed a huge top that was driven around the bounds of the village at least once a year, probably a remnant of some ancient ritual intended to protect those within the circle marked by the spinning top.

▦ Voli i Ovtsy (Fox and Geese)

Children throughout Europe played variations of fox and geese. Like many the familiar nursery stories, the game reflected the constant struggle of farmers to protect their poultry against the foraging of foxes and wolves. This version (voli i ovtsy) from Russia was primarily a winter game. Deep snow made the game more challenging, and winter was the time wild animals were most likely to come into the barnyard in search of food.

Two children were selected to be the fox and the mother goose; all the others were the goslings (or chicks, if the game was fox and hen). The fox stood to one side, the mother goose and goslings on the other, and the game began with a dialogue between the goose and the fox: "Where are you going?" "In search of a meal." "Where will you find it?" "Right here!" (the phrases could vary, but always end with the fox declaring his intention of eating the goslings). Then the goose would cry, "Catch one if you can" or "I'll not let you catch one" and the race was on. The goslings tried to stay linked together, and circled around the goose. The goose tried to keep her arms around the goslings. If they could they kept the last in line surrounded, since that child was the target. Meanwhile the fox dodged and reached and tried to snatch the last child in the line. Any child the fox caught was "carried away," to sit back at the fox's base until the game was over.

SPORTS

⊞ Archery

The bow and arrow was the basic tool of the hunter throughout ancient Europe. By the Middle Ages, Europe was an agricultural society and archery became more of a sport than an activity of daily living.

There were three basic types of medieval bows: the shortbow, the crossbow, and the longbow. The shortbow was the ancient weapon, and still used by men, women, and children for hunting small game such as rabbits, and also for target practice. The crossbow was a mechanical bow with a crank or lever to pull back the string and propel the arrow. Large crossbows required two men to fire them and took several minutes to reload. They were widely used on the continent, but not as sporting devices. Smaller crossbows were used for hunting and sometimes for target shooting by young boys. The longbow developed in the eleventh century in England and was immortalized by the legendary tales of Robin Hood. The longbow was more powerful than the shortbow but was also more expensive, and it required much more skill and strength. England actually had laws requiring the yeomen to practice archery instead of wasting their time on football, in case they should be needed in war! By the last century of our time frame the longbow had become the sport of the noble class.

All three types of bows were used for hunting (see separate entry), target shooting, and roving. Targets included "butts," mounds of peat or earth and straw specially built for the purpose (Figure 4.8). Other, less formal targets included garlands of flowers, dead birds, and stuffed birds or animals made of cloth. These could be hung at various heights and distances or tossed into the air as moving targets. "Shooting at the peg" or "prick" was another popular sport designed to improve the archer's

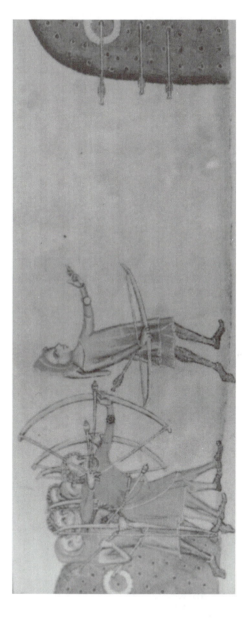

Figure 4.8. Butts were mounds of dirt built as targets for archery. *Source:* By permission of the British Library, Additional Manuscript Ms. 42130, f. 147. v.

accuracy: the peg was a piece of wood stuck into the ground or into the center of a straw-filled target. The archer's task was to split the peg by hitting it with the arrow from various distances.

The popular practice of roving was simply a group shooting expedition. People would gather and troop around the countryside, picking out random targets and challenging one another to hit them. It was the common people's version of the hunt, but the impact of dozens or even hundreds of feet tramping through fields and pastures led to numerous complaints by landowners and the establishment of more and more public butts. In some places roving "trails" were established, with specific targets at various sites around the region, and stops at local pubs where the losers rewarded the winners.

Virtually all these target games were made more interesting by placing bets. The prize could be anything from a few pennies, a chicken for the soup pot, a kiss from the lady fair, a bag of gold, or the hand of a maiden in marriage.

European bows were made from various woods, but yew was the best for longbows: both strong and flexible. Nocks, or notched caps of horn or ivory at the ends of the bow, allowed it to be strung and unstrung quickly: leaving the bow strung at all times gradually would bend the bow and reduce the force propelling the arrow from the string. Bowstrings were made of hemp and beeswax. Longbows were as tall as the archers who carried them and made of several layers of wood. Shortbows could be made from a single piece. Medieval arrow shafts were made from birch, ash, or other light wood. Feathers were cut and bound to the shaft to make it fly straight. Arrowheads could be made of flint but were generally iron.

To stage an archery competition you will need an assortment of bows and arrows. It is probably worth the effort to locate commercially made bows, as making a true longbow or shortbow is not a casual task (but see Appendix for some ideas). Bales of hay can be piled up in the place of butts, and a peg can easily be driven into a bale for shooting at the peg. Be sure to set up in an open area with any spectators behind the archers and well away from the targets. Have archers practice drawing and aiming before letting the arrow fly, to get a feel for the bow.

⊞ Bandy-ball or La Soule et La Crosse

Bandy-ball was a game played in early medieval times with a curved stick for a bat and a small wooden or leather ball. Later in Europe the crook was improved upon with a metal spoon-shaped head. Since the word for "stick" was *creag* or *crick*, some believe this is the ancestor of modern cricket, although it bears a stronger resemblance to the game known in America as field hockey, and the Irish hurling. (The modern sport of bandy is an ice game similar to hockey and still very popular in Scandinavia.) French missionaries to the New World gave their name for the bandy stick to the indigenous game they encountered in North America: lacrosse.

Each team defended a goal, generally just a marked tree or a post in the ground. These were often very far apart: several miles was not uncommon, and a game might be played with one goal in one village square and the other in the next village. The object of the game was to drive the ball past the other team's goal. In rural Europe, bandy-ball was played in open fields, while in cities it was generally confined by the walls of a churchyard or courtyard. Even leather balls could and did break windows, and the tendency of the game to become a violent melee made it a constant target of complaints from church leaders.

Teams pitted one village against another in the country or one guild or parish against another in town. A common variation played the married men of the community against the bachelors. The game was also sometimes played by smaller teams or even one-on-one on a smaller playing area. There was no specific length for a match, which could go on for several days until a pre-agreed-upon score was reached or the festival ended. The only constant rule was that the ball could only be propelled with the stick.

Field hockey sticks are too long for medieval bandy, so to recreate the game you will need to find hurling/camogie hurleys or make creags. The base of a sapling with the crook of a root is the best piece for whittling into a bandy creag. The shaft should be about thirty inches long and the flat crook or head only the size of your open hand. Make a leather ball a bit smaller than your fist, and stuff it with a mixture of sand and straw, unless you have access to horsehair, which is more authentic.

Select a playing area that is fairly open. A level surface without obstacles is safer, but a pasture with hillocks and rocks is more historically accurate! Designate goals at both ends, and begin the game with teams spread out between the midpoint of the field and their own goals. There are no out-of-bounds lines, and no restrictions on who can play in what part of the field. Decide in advance whether to play to a particular score or a fixed length of time.

▦ Caber Tossing and Log Lifting

Every people has had celebrated strong men. In medieval Europe, stone putting and stone lifting were common tests of strength at festivals. The highlanders of Scotland displayed their strength at annual gatherings dating back to the eleventh century when King Malcolm (the same Malcolm depicted in Shakespeare's *Macbeth*) began the competition as a way of keeping his subjects ready for military duty. Unique to the Scots is the activity known as tossing the caber. A caber was a log, stripped of branches and leaves, generally twelve to fifteen feet long and weighing as much as 150 pounds. The caber tossers crouched down to lift the caber, balancing it in both hands, and then heaved it by pushing it up and away with the arms as they stood up (putting the force of the legs into the throw as well). The caber was supposed to flip end-over-end and land pointed straight away from the tosser, so caber contests rewarded not only the one who threw the caber the farthest, but the most accurately.

On the mainland the Celtic Bretons enjoyed a sport called gwernian ar berchem (lifting the log): players lifted a log (by its narrow end) and balanced it in their hands. The winner was the player who held the log upright the longest and with his hands placed the lowest on the log (making it more difficult to balance).

Caber tossing and log lifting are still practiced today at traditional games. A modern adaptation would be to lift and balance or throw a series of saplings, each somewhat heavier than the next.

▦ Camp-ball

Camp was an Anglo-Saxon word for a battle, and camp-ball was a sort of battle over a ball, and the early predecessor of modern football (or what Americans call soccer). Camp-ball was played by teams made up of the whole population of a village or parish. Teams lined up at the center line between two goals, which could be a couple of hundred yards apart at opposite ends of a street, or several miles apart if the game were between villages. The ball was made of leather stuffed with horsehair or, in places, a pig's bladder filled with dried peas. Once the ball was tossed into the air, everyone attempted to catch or control it and kick, throw, and pass it until it could be carried across the opponent's goal.

Needless to say, with rules so vague and so many participants, camp-ball often resembled the battles that gave it its name. Some districts created "camp enclosures" to try to preserve the fun without the danger. Others, like London, attempted to ban camp-ball altogether because of the hazards to passersby. Tempers flared and rivalries between factions were fanned by aggressive play. It was not uncommon for players to die from injuries sustained in the game. The fact that most medieval people wore knives or daggers tucked into their belts for routine chores made the game even more dangerous.

During the fifteenth century "kicking camp" began to be organized, with teams paid to represent guilds and towns. Rules defining numbers of players and forms of play began to control the sport. This evolution into "futeball" was well under way by the time of the Renaissance, but out in the country camp-ball survived into the eighteenth century.

To play camp-ball you need a ball the size of a modern volleyball, but it shouldn't bounce. An underinflated volleyball will do, or you can make a ball from leather and stuff it with crumpled newspaper or dried peas. The playing area should be large and irregular, with a fair number of obstacles for authenticity.

▦ Colf (Bittle-battle and Camboc)

Colf, the direct forerunner of modern golf, apparently began in Europe among shepherds before the fourteenth century. They used the crooked ends of their staffs to hit stones toward distant targets or into rabbit holes. In Germany a fourteenth-century law gave shepherds the right to graze their sheep across a distance defined as: "as far as he can drive a pebble with one strike of the staff." Obviously such a law encouraged driving practice! Bittle-battle and camboc are probably references to the same game in the British Isles: a bittle is a stick with a head attached at the end.

One Dutch colf match was held every year for 500 years in commemoration of the siege of a fort in 1296. Two teams of four players struck a wooden ball along a 4,500 meter course with four goals: from the courthouse to the door kitchen door at the fort, then the door at a local mill, then that of another castle, and finally back to the door of the courthouse. At each stop the teams had to hit their balls through the doors before moving on. At each of the castles, apples were thrown down on their heads as a reminder of the siege! The winners were the team that managed to complete the course with the fewest number of strokes.

In the early fifteenth century students at St. Andrews in Dundee, Scotland, played camboc on the flatlands along the shore where the North Sea had receded some three centuries earlier. They used their canes and a wooden ball, scooped out the sand to make holes, and set up flags to mark the course. To this day golfers flock to St. Andrews to play on the famous "Old Course." By midcentury the game had become so popular that King James II banned it because it was keeping yeoman from archery practice. Apparently the ban had little effect: by the 1600s leather balls stuffed with cowhair were being imported to Scotland in great numbers from Holland, while the Dutch began to buy their clubs from the Scots.

Colf is an easy game to recreate. Any light, straight stick will serve as a club. Cut a round-edged bittle from a soup or soda can with tin snips. (Use a hammer on the cut edge or pound the edge against a stone to dull it.) Nail the bittle to the end of the club. A colf ball was about the same size as a modern golf ball.

Wooden balls of various sizes are available in craft supply stores. Rugged fabric balls made for juggling will also serve for colf. Each player will have a ball, as in golf, and players are grouped in small teams. Lay out the course, choosing a variety of goals into which the ball must be driven: they can be as small as the traditional rabbit hole or as large as a door or archway, and a variety of targets is good. Traditionally some targets may have been defended (as with the apple throwers at the castles) while others provided rewards (usually beer) for the players. Decide whether to have hazards or rewards at any of the targets in your course, and you are ready to play colf.

⚏ Horse Racing

Most horse races were surprisingly short, their courses defined by the design of the city: around the outside of the wall, or from the church to the castle to the river and back. Out-and-back cross-country races from three to ten miles are recorded, but the most popular races were urban affairs that allowed spectators to watch and cheer. If there were many competitors they would run in heats, with the winners of each small group going on to compete against one another until the champion was declared. Several races specifically crowned the horse, rather than the jockey—even if the horse crossed the finish line riderless.

Unless you are an equestrian, bicycles are the best modern adaptation for horse races. If you have BMX riders in your group you can even include some authentic obstacles such as hay bales or small streams. Lay out the course, being sure that all riders are aware of tricky corners or hazardous water crossings. Decorate bike and helmet with colorful pennants or streamers (not so long as to cause a hazard).

⚏ Hunting

In ancient Europe as everywhere, hunting was a skill essential for survival. In the Middle Ages most of Europe was solidly agrarian, and hunting became a recreational sport. Common people hunted rabbits, squirrels, and pigeons in the open countryside. Hunting deer, boars, foxes, and other larger animals was a privilege reserved to the nobility and often leased to the wealthy. The remaining forests of England and large portions of Europe were royal property, and trespassing and poaching were serious crimes. (Robin Hood was an outlaw because he denied the king's monopoly on game.) Parks, or chases, were enclosed private hunting areas.

Ordinary people hunted with dogs and ferrets to flush out their prey, and short bows and clubs to kill them. The wealthy hunted on horseback, using trained hawks and falcons for birds and small animals, and highly trained hounds for larger game. Hunting horns enabled hunters to communicate through the woods and across miles of countryside.

Buying, breeding, and training the hunting animals was a tremendous expense. All these animals were bedecked in the colors of their owners: hoods for the birds, jeweled collars for the dogs, and saddle blankets on the horses. Hunting retinues included the hunters' wives and children as well as servants to tend the animals and prepare the game. Once the harts, deer, boars, or foxes had been flushed out and run to ground, the hunters used both short and long bows and spears to kill them. Game animals were skinned and butchered in the field, their heads brought back as trophies, and the meat for feasting and putting away for the winter, but the hunt was more about sport than about food.

▦ Jousting

Tournaments, or tourneys, developed as a way for knights to practice their military skills during peacetimes. Around the year 1000 they were raucous, dangerous affairs, sometimes as violent and deadly as the battles they imitated. Dozens of knights charged at one another in the field, first attempting to knock each other from their horses with lances, then meeting in hand-to-hand combat with swords and maces. In the later Middle Ages jousting began to supplant tourneying. Jousts were more structured, and just two or four knights rode at one another at a time. Costumes for both men and horses became more and more elaborate. Shields were painted with heralds that represented the lords whose knights carried them. Rules began to direct the conflict, and the victory might be declared by a panel of ladies rather than by the death of the vanquished. At the height of the chivalric movement the size of the "list" was defined (sixty-by-forty paces, with walls at least seven feet high). They were laid out so that the sun wouldn't obstruct vision, stands were built for spectators, and those invited to participate had to submit to inspections of their armor and weapons. Three rounds were fought with each weapon: on horseback with lances, on foot with swords and shields, and finally with axes and knives.

▦ Jumping

High jumping was part of the Celtic games in the eleventh century. Scandinavian legend tells of contests involving jumping across streams and rivers. At festivals across Europe both high jumping and long jumping were popular competitions.

For a standing long jump, the starting line was a plank. The jumper stood behind the plank and jumped over it on to soft (even muddy, by the time several people had jumped) ground, and the prize went to the one who jumped the furthest. Records show that competitions frequently combined a standing jump with other feats. First the athlete jumped over the plank with both feet, then ran a few yards and jumped again (a running long jump) and then finished by hopping, first on one foot and then the other, skipping and a final jump (the origin of the expression "a hop, skip, and jump").

High jumping and pole vaulting were also common competitions, carried out not very differently than today: two poles in the ground held a rod over which the contestants leapt. Each player took his turn running and jumping or vaulting over the rod. Anyone who knocked the rod down was eliminated, and after everyone had jumped, the rod was raised and everyone tried again until finally one was the champion. In Holland jumpers competed in a local variation of the pole vault: jumping across canals!

⊞ Palio (Races)

A palio was a race, named for the prize of a bolt of cloth awarded to the winner at some races in Italy. Prizes for medieval races varied, from a simple handkerchief or badge of honor to more substantial articles of clothing and sums of money. Often the prize would be displayed at the finish line of the race.

It was common for an army laying siege to a town to run races around the walls. This was a sort of psychological warfare, taunting those inside for their helplessness. It also served to keep the knights and foot soldiers fit during what could be months of encampment. Many traditional races that have been held annually for centuries are memorials of such sieges.

⊞ Pelota (Pallone; Kaatsen)

When the Spanish first reached the New World in the 1500s and observed the locals playing ball, they dubbed the game *pelota*, their word for the craze that had swept Europe in the previous century. They also brought home rubber, which revolutionized pelota and gave birth to the present-day game pallone elastico (the term *pelota* now refers to the game Americans call jai alai). Today the medieval game, pallone al bracciale, or arm ball, survives only in a few traditional festivals and at recreations.

Pelota was played with a ball made from a pig's bladder, covered with leather and then inflated. Kaatsen, the version of the game played in the Frisians (now Belgium and the Netherlands), was played with a similar ball stuffed with feathers. Both balls were medium-sized, about six inches in diameter. They were relatively light and did rebound, although not as efficiently as rubber. Players struck the ball with their fists and forearms, which were covered with a glove or guard somewhat reminiscent of a knight's mace; in the Italian game the bracciale was actually spiked. The game was played on a long, narrow court roughly 60 by 20 yards, with a wall along one of the long sides of the court and a line dividing the court in half the short way. Teams were small: three to six on a side. The serving team hit the ball off the wall so that it would rebound into the opposing court. If it crossed the baseline at the narrow end of the court, the server scored a point. The defending team attempted to return the ball. They scored a point and won the serve if the ball crossed the serving team's baseline.

If a ball rolled out of bounds opposite the wall or was stopped (but not returned) by a player before it crossed the baseline, a *caccia* or "chase" was marked at that point. The chase became a "potential" point. Teams switched ends if there were two chases on the court or if there was one chase and either team needed just one score to win. If the next volley ended with the ball again rolling out or dying on the court, the player whose chase was closer to the baseline won the point. (If either team managed to score a real point first, then the chase was cancelled.)

Pallone scoring was the same as tennis: fifteen for the first two points, ten for the third, and the fourth point won the game, except that the win had to be by two. Kaatsen scoring was a bit simpler: Two points for each score, and again a two-score margin was needed to win.

To play arm ball today each player will need a protective covering for the forearm. In Eastern Europe these were made from hollowed-out gourds, so you might try cooking and scooping out the insides of some large butternut squashes and then letting the shells dry. Leather wraps laced up the forearm will probably be simpler.

Stitch a leather ball (see Appendix) and stuff it with feathers for Kaatsen or, for pallone, insert and inflate a small balloon before closing the last seam. Mark the midline, baselines and boundaries with chalk on the ground beside a long windowless wall (the outside of a school gymnasium is a likely spot).

▦ Roth Cleas (Hammer Throw)

Javelin throwing dates back to the prehistoric use of spears, and throwing the discus was an Olympic sport in ancient Greece, but hammer throwing (noth cleas) seems to have developed in the British Isles as a purely competitive exercise. In Ireland men threw a cartwheel, and in Scotland a stone attached to a wooden handle was the chosen weight. The heavy sledgehammer of the village blacksmith seems to have been used for a while, as it gave the sport its modern name, although the hammer of modern track-and-field competition, a round weight on the end of a steel wire, bears no resemblance to that tool.

The athlete stood in a marked circle, first swinging the weight and then turning his body around in place while holding the weight at the ends of his arms, so that centrifugal force lifted the weight and pulled it away from the body. When he achieved his best speed he let go of the hammer, which could fly a great distance. The potential for injury and broken windows in this sport was huge!

A good hammer for adapting roth cleas is a rubber mallet, available from automotive supply stores. Be sure to set up in a safe area where no spectators are in danger! A baseball diamond with a backstop is a good place to compete.

⊞   Rowing

Like so many medieval sports, rowing was an ordinary work activity turned into a competition. Regattas, or rowing competitions, were included in many local festivals. A few noted regattas have continued from the Middle Ages to the modern era, and many more were restored during the nineteenth century. In Italy, the "Regatta of the Four Republics" recalls the ancient rivalries among Venice, Pisa, Almafi and Genoa. Oslo, Amsterdam, London, and Zagreb also hosted regattas that drew competitors from many cities.

The rowboats of the medieval era were shallow crafts with wide, flat bottoms designed for hauling cargo up and down rivers and canals. The seats were fixed in place and the boats could be either rowed with long oars and pushed (or punted) with poles. In a regatta the boat and the rowers would be decorated with the colors of the team's sponsoring noble or guild. Although modern rowing craft have changed dramatically, the act of rowing was the same: the rowers faced the stern, where a coxswain sat to steer, watching the course and calling or chanting to help the rowers maintain a rhythm.

Another popular feature of the medieval regatta was water jousting. Boats rowed toward one another in imitation of horses in a tourney, and one person in each boat was armed with a wooden lance and attempted to knock their opponent out of the boat.

If you want to stage a regatta on dry land, you can build "boats" that are shallow boxes mounted on wheels (use casters that spin 360 degrees for the best results). Make holes in the sides for the "oars" or use oarlocks to hold the oars. Your oars will be for pushing, not rowing, so keep them just long enough to reach the ground at about a 20- to 30-degree angle and put rubber crutch tips on them.

▦ Rounders

Rounders was played by people of all ages in medieval England, and survives there to this day as a children's game. It is generally considered the ancestor of modern baseball. Rounders combined elements of handball (pelota), which was usually played off the wall of the church, with prisoner's base, in which various spots were sometimes designated "sanctuaries" where the player could not be tagged. In rounders, players set up a circle of sticks (generally four or five) in a field, and marked out a base (a good-sized box or circle, as in prisoner's base, not a small spot as in baseball) at one point just inside the circle. The stakes became the sanctuaries. Players divided into two equal teams. Players on the team that was "in" stood in the base and hit the ball with a small stick. The "outs" were fielders, and one was the "feeder" or bowler. The feeder tossed the ball to the first batter. If the batter hit it, she ran around the circle. If she returned safely to the base before the ball was returned, she scored a rounder for her team. The outs, meanwhile, attempted to field the ball and hit the runner with it while she was running: if they succeeded, she was "out," and had to sit out until ransomed or until the inning was over. However the runner could not be put out while touching a boundary stake, and could choose to stop at one if she did not think she could get back to base, running again on the next hit.

Each batter got three tries to hit the ball. On the third toss she had to run even if she missed the ball, and the out team tried to hit her before she reached the first boundary stick.

If a batted ball was caught in the air, the "inning" was over and the teams changed sides. The outs could also put out the whole side by bouncing the ball in the base when there was no player in there, which was called "crowning" the base. (This almost inevitably happened when the last player left on the "in" side hit the ball.) A complete rounder could be used either to score a point or to ransom a teammate who was out.

A "dead" tennis ball and a flat paddle such as a ping-pong paddle can be used to play rounders. For a more authentic game make a leather ball stuffed with feathers and cut a long narrow paddle (like a small cricket bat) from a piece of wood.

▦ Running

A medieval footrace could be run for almost any distance, from the castle to the church or from the market to the river. By the late Middle Ages both short (about four hundred feet) and longer (about ten thousand feet) races were commonly run at festivals. Runners competed in classes that included old men, children, and women. Nobility generally would not compete against common people, and in most European cities Jews were only allowed to compete against one another. Separate races were also held for women and children.

■ Stone Lifting and Putting

The discus of the Greek Olympics doesn't seem to have remained popular in Europe, but throwing stones as a show of strength was very common. By the 1450s a festival in Zurich recorded specific events: throwing three different stones, weighing 15, 30, and 50 pounds. In Breton the competitors threw a millstone weighing more than 40 pounds. The rules generally allowed stone putters to run several steps and turn around once or twice to add force to their throws. Because of the weight, the stone is more "pushed" than thrown.

Many heroes of European legend were reported to have thrown or lifted stones of great weight. In the Basque region there is still a competition of stone lifting called *arrija soketa*, which consists of lifting very heavy stones as many times as possible in a fixed period of time: the player who lifts the heaviest weight the most frequently is the winner.

Stone lifting and putting are as easy (or as hard) today as in medieval times. Since the minimum weight of a modern shotput is 16 pounds for men and nearly 10 pounds for women, 6-to-10-pound stones would be reasonable for stone putting. The court should be an open area with clear sight lines and preferably a barrier between the thrower and the spectators: a baseball field with a backstop is good.

■ Swimming

The Romans had built public baths in most of the cities of Europe, and the Puritan insistence on hiding the body didn't develop until after the Reformation, so medieval Europeans enjoyed bathing during the summer months. Manuscript illuminations show children learning to swim at what appears to be a very young age, though drowning was a common cause of death. For the seafaring Scandinavians, swimming was a life skill and competitions were common. Boys indulged in "water wrestling," trying to hold the opponent under water under he gave up (still widely practiced if frowned upon today). Swimmers also competed for speed over distances, swimming out from shore around a marked point (a float tethered to an anchoring stone) and back. Diving competitions included diving for depth and to see who could remain under water the longest.

▦ Swordplay

Swords were the primary weapons of medieval European warfare. A knight named his sword and kept it with him at all times. Whether a battle began on horseback or on foot, most often it was the sword that delivered the final deathblow. The changing technology of swords and armor divided the Middle Ages, and the introduction of gunpowder put an end to the role of the knight in armor. Swordfighting joined archery as more sport than a technique of war, and modern fencing techniques developed quickly.

The light swords, the rapier and the epee of modern fencing, did not develop until the Renaissance. The swords of medieval Europe were broad and heavy. Most blades had blunt ends and sharpened edges; they were slicing weapons, not thrusting ones. Many had handles designed for swinging the blade with both hands. Shields were carried while riding, but for the most part discarded in hand-to-hand combat. In battle or tournament, chain mail and plate armor protected the body against the slicing blow of the blade. A small shield, called a buckler, was sometimes used in dueling. It was designed to be held over the wrist so that both hands were still free to wield the sword.

Constant training and practice (Figure 4.9) were needed to maintain the upper body and arm strength required for sword fighting, and there are many records of men being injured or killed in peacetime by "playing at swords." Sword training was serious work. Schools taught various methods of parrying, and illustrated texts explained the exercises. Fighters faced off, swinging the sword back to give force to the blows and aiming blows at the opponent's lower body (raising the arms exposed the fighter's own torso). Once an enemy was on the ground the finishing blow might be dealt at the head or neck, but that was not the target of the swordfight itself.

The sword-and-buckler, described in the section of this chapter on Play, provides a modern adaptation of medieval swordplay.

▦ Tennis

Tennis apparently began in France as a handball game, possibly in the enclosed courtyards of monasteries and stately homes. (Some scholars believe it may have been brought home by crusaders or modeled on racquet games of the Middle East.) Common people played too, calling their version the "long game" because the teams of four or five played in streets and alleys (see also pelota). Eventually two distinct games developed, both called tennis. "Real" tennis was a racquet game played in a specially designed court, and so available only to the wealthy. Field or

Figure 4.9. Swordsmen training with a variety of exercises. *Source*: Courtesy of the Historical Armed Combat Association, Houston, TX.

lawn tennis as it developed in the 1700s could be played by anyone. Both games kept the original scoring method, based on French currency: a denier was worth fifteen sous. A game played without any stake was played "for love," which became the name of a score of zero. In addition to the concept of the chase (explained under pelota), court tennis included a variety of rules based on the idiosyncrasies of the court.

Tennis balls were leather and hard, stuffed with wool or hair. Only at the end of the fifteenth century did slightly softer rag balls come into play. (Once the Spanish brought rubber back from the New World the game changed tremendously.) Courts for tennis were about seventy by seventeen feet, often though not always with one flat wall and three sloping roofs, perhaps in imitation of those monastic courtyards. A woven rope net with weights to hold it in place was stretched across midcourt, where a line divided the space in the earlier game.

People who play "real tennis" today have to travel far to find real courts, so the medieval common people's pelota remains the better option for recreating this game.

⊞ Wrestling

The native wrestling of northern Europe was simple and immensely popular; by far the most popular spectator sport of the Middle Ages. Combatants faced off, grabbing each other by a scarf, hood, or modified tunic worn around the shoulders, and grappled until one managed to get the other onto the ground. There were a number of local variations, and, of course, the proponents of one form believed it was vastly superior to any other.

Festival days often featured wrestling matches, and each town or neighborhood had a champion to represent them. Guilds or nobles would put up a prize, often a ram, and betting among the spectators was rampant, so the amounts riding on the contests were often considerable. Riots are recorded as following a number of London wrestling matches in the thirteenth and fourteenth centuries.

The match itself was self-directing: participants sat in a circle around a sandy pit or pile of sawdust. The challenger circled the group until one or another of the participants spoke, accepting the challenge (if no one did, the unchallenged victor claimed the prize). In the Celtic style prevalent in northern Europe wrestlers stood, leaning into each other shoulder against shoulder, gripping each other across the back, and were allowed to use their legs to attempt to hook the other's legs out from under him. In southern Europe, Greco-Roman wrestling remained the standard. Wrestlers grasped each other by the arms or around the body and tried to force the opponent down so that his shoulders touched the ground. A wrestler won the match by throwing his opponent three times.

⊞ LATIN AMERICA

In modern usage and for the purposes of this book, Latin America refers to Central America (or North America from the Rio Grande to the Isthmus of Panama) and South America, places where today the primary languages are Latinate, mostly Spanish and Portuguese. We have also included the islands of the Caribbean in this chapter.

Latin America was not "Latin" at all during the Middle Ages, as the Spanish did not arrive in the New World until the 1500s. But all the peoples of the Western Hemisphere were immigrants, having come into North America from Asia across a land bridge in the distant past. Those who had settled in South America were not directly impacted by the Ice Age that shaped North America, and there are evidences of civilizations in South America that date back fourteen thousand years.

Central and South America were populated by people from several different language groups. Geography and climate shaped the history of the region.

In South America, numerous small tribes of hunter gatherers lived in the rain forests and grassland regions. Agricultural societies were established in the grasslands. Nomadic herders roamed the high Andes. There was limited contact among these people. Thick rain forests and towering mountains divided the people of South America. Huari and Tiahuanacao were powerful cities, but their influence did not extend more than a few hundred miles. The Inca, who would build a far-flung empire centered in what is now Peru, were just coming to power at the end of the Middle Ages.

Central America had fewer natural obstacles. The land that is now Mexico, Honduras, and Guatemala, called Mesoamerica by anthropologists, was resettled a number of times by people coming south across the Rio Grande. The Mayan people moved south across Central America about two thousand years B.C.E., gradually displacing the urban dwelling, pyramid-building Olmecs. The Maya were primarily farmers, and subject to the vagaries of weather. Recent archaeology reveals that malnutrition was a constant reality and starvation a constant threat. Teotihuacán, center of the Mayan empire at the height of their power, was a city of more than a quarter-million people in 450; a phenomenal concentration of consumption of resources in an era without overland transportation. It fell to invaders before 900. Then the Toltecs established their center at Tula, further south. Toward the end of the period covered in this book, another group of people, the Aztecs, or Mexica, began their conquest of Central America. Typically they would arrive at a town and send word to the leader demanding food. If the leader agreed to pay tribute, he would be allowed to remain as the governor. If not, the Aztecs would attack.

Almost all of the people of Central and South America had reputations of great ferocity. Their creation story told them that the gods had spilled their blood to create human beings, and their religion required them to repay the gods in kind. They routinely cut themselves as an ongoing offering to the gods. One missionary described players in a ball game who scratched and cut their legs and arms while playing, never taking their eyes off the ball. Even the Spanish friar described this activity as "contemplative." Among Aztec priests this bloodletting was a daily responsibility.

Human sacrifice was central to the religions of the Mesoamerican peoples. Sacrifices were made for special occasions such as coronations, on festival days, and for particular needs such as rain or before a battle. The people chosen for the sacrifice were sometimes captives from other cities and sometimes selected from among the local people. Frequently the people chosen for sacrifice were indulged and feted for months before the ritual slaughter. Many victims were children. The Aztecs believed that the tears of child victims brought rain, and the more they cried before dying, the more rain would fall.

The Aztec sacrifices are best known to us because of the reports of the Spanish. They reported lines of victims being marched up the pyramids to the altars where their hearts were cut out of them to be fed to the gods and their bodies rolled down the stairs. Then their heads were cut off and placed on display. In the Andes, victims were sometimes buried alive or placed into the craters of volcanoes. In recent years, discoveries of the frozen remains of child victims have revealed new details about the lives of these people.

One of the mysteries of the region is what happened to the remains of the victims. One would expect to find huge collections of bones near the temples. Archaeological and anthropological evidence indicates most groups practiced some form of ritual cannibalism. (This is a matter of great controversy, and it should be noted that among many peoples the eating of one's own dead was considered a way of honoring them, so not every case of cannibalism involved conquest.) Since starvation was a very real threat, some scholars have suggested that sacrificial victims supplemented the food supply. Others point out that the Aztecs, at least, had a sophisticated diet supplemented by protein sources we might not recognize (pond scum, for example) that were nevertheless substantial.

The ball game, which dates back to the Olmecs, was closely linked with religious beliefs and ritual sacrifices. In mythology the gods played against each other to determine the fate of the people. Among the Aztecs and the Maya, preselected victims were often required to play the game before being sacrificed. It is also possible that some games were played to determine which people would be sacrificed (and it is not necessarily clear whether it was the victors or the losers who were killed, since being sacrificed was considered an honor). The Toltecs conquered the Maya in about 1000 C.E. It is an indication of the significant role of the ball game in both cultures that this conquest is recorded in stone friezes at the Great Ball Court at Chichén Itzá (Figure 5.1).

What we know of the histories of the people of Central and South America comes from oral histories collected by anthropologists and the written chronicles kept by the Maya and the Aztecs. These chronicles were recorded in pictures and hieroglyphics on long, multifolded sheets of paper made from bark. The chronicles included detailed information about the rituals and lives of the people, although decoding the material provides plenty of opportunity for controversy and scholarly disagreements.

Fifty years after this book's time frame, Spanish conquistadors stepped off their ships and began to explore Central and South America. They were awed by the displays of power and wealth, the huge metropolis of Tenochtitlán, and the gold that seemed to be everywhere. Along with the Conquistadors who arrived in South America in 1519 came many Catholic missionaries. They were horrified at the constant round of human sacrifice, the bloodletting, and the worship of many gods.

The blood offerings the Aztecs and Maya made to their gods confirmed everything the Catholic Spanish believed about pagan religions. Some of the conquerors believed the indigenous people were not fully human and therefore felt no compunction about killing or enslaving them. (The Catholic Church officially condemned this position in 1537.) Others undoubtedly used religion as an excuse for overrunning the local population. Some truly believed they were rescuing the people from subjection to an evil blood cult, not a difficult conclusion to understand when you read their descriptions of the Aztec rituals.

Figure 5.1. Ball courts like this one at Copan have been found all over Central America. *Source:* Stephen L. Whittington, Hudson Museum, University of Maine. Used by permission.

The missionaries both destroyed and preserved the heritage of the peoples they encountered. On the one hand, they burned artifacts and banned activities in their efforts to rescue the people from their religious heritage, with its emphasis on bloodletting and death. On the other hand, some of them were meticulous recorders of the stories they heard and the activities they witnessed. They copied the codices with the same care that centuries of monks had given to illuminated manuscripts in Europe.

Because the local games and sports were so closely intertwined with the stories and worship of the gods, the Spanish attempted to eradicate them. Even patolli, a board game, was condemned, because the players bet heavily on the outcomes and invoked the gods to help them win (see Figure 5.2). Xochipelli, the cheerful figure so popular today, was the Aztec god of games.

It is likely that the Indians played other games of which we have no records. Stone tops have been found in many archaeological sites in what is now South America. The indentation about one-third of the way down from the top leads scholars to believe they were spun with a string. Clay marbles have also been found, so it is reasonable to believe that they were used in the same sorts of games as in other places. Children in Central and South America, surrounded by rubber balls, almost certainly played the nearly universal game of bouncing a ball off the wall, though no one thought it merited recording.

The Spanish were astounded at the rubber balls used by the South Americans. They had never seen anything so elastic, and the excitement in their descriptions of the bouncing ball is almost childlike. They had come in search of gold, but went home bearing other, more important contributions, among them maize (corn) and rubber. European sports would never be the same.

Some descriptions make it sound like "the ball game" was a single game played throughout Central and South America. Certainly the formal game had characteristics that were seen throughout the region. It was played on a long narrow court, divided by a centerline. Players tried to keep the ball in the air without using their hands, and scored points when the ball died in their opponent's court. From there the descriptions generally move on to the connections between the games and human sacrifices.

In reality, these sports varied tremendously from one people to the next. Catching and tossing the ball with the hands was nearly always prohibited, but some versions had players striking the ball with their heads, others with their backs, and others with knees, hips, fists, and even paddles. Some people played with a ball as big as a basketball, others used a ball as small as a tennis ball. Some balls were made of solid rubber, others were hollow made by wrapping strips of rubber around a mold, or dipping a mold into the liquid rubber. When the rubber hardened, the mold would be removed. To say that they are all the same game is the equivalent of saying that soccer, basketball, and football are all the same game because they all involve trying to get a ball through an opponent's goal!

GAMES

▦ Mosquito

In rain forests, people made string from the fibers of the pissava plant and used it to weave bags, hammocks, and all sorts of nets. They also played string games. This is a very simple string trick. It requires a piece of string about six feet long, bound or knotted to form a loop.

To play this game, hang the string around your thumbs. Turn your left hand toward you and twist your wrist so you pick up both strings around the back of your hand. With your right little finger, pick up both strings where they come between the left thumb and forefinger, and pull your hands apart. Now use your left little finger to pick up both strings from the palm of your right hand and pull your hands apart again. Use your right fingers or your teeth to pull the strings from the back of your left hand over your fingers. You have a cross between your hands; the loops on your little fingers are the mosquito's long legs, those on your thumbs are its wings, and the twist in the middle is its body. Quick-smack it (by clapping your hands together). As you extend your hands again, let the loops drop from your little fingers. Oh dear—it got away!

▦ Patolli

Patolli is a Mesoamerican game so similar to South Asian pachisi that many anthropologists considered it evidence of a precolonial contact between the peoples of the Old and New Worlds (Figure 5.2).

The game was a passion of the Aztecs, who enjoyed both playing and watching and bet heavily on the outcome. The missionaries who arrived with the conquistadores considered the game a curse to be eradicated, because the players would frequently invoke various gods for good fortune as they rolled the dice. In addition players' losses could be so great that they sometimes sold themselves and their families into slavery.

Despite the banning and burning of gaming materials, patolli survived and is still played in some regions of Central America to this day. Patolli is usually played by two or four players, but early records indicate the pieces could be divided among even larger numbers. The board, marked in liquid rubber on a straw mat, is in the shape of a St. Andrew's cross (two perpendicular bars of equal length). The bars are divided horizontally into sixteen segments and lengthwise into two, so that there are four-

Figure 5.2. Patolli players invoked the god Xochipelli when roll-ing beans. *Source*: Culin (1896), courtesy of the Brooklyn Museum of Art.

teen squares in each of the four arms and four squares form the center of the cross. The corners of the third segment from the end of each arm are darkened, so that there are eight marked spaces on the board.

Four or five beans serve as dice. Each has a hole drilled on one side. The playing pieces are twelve small stones, six painted red and six blue. (So two players begin with six each, three begin with four each, four begin with three each, or six begin with two each.) In medieval times, players often had their own dice and playing pieces that they carried with them.

After deciding on the stakes and placing stakes in a pool, players toss the dice to determine the order of play. Rolling the beans between the hands, players used to chant and call upon the god of games and gam-bling, Macuilxochitl, for luck, then toss the beans on to the mat. One step or space is awarded for each bean that falls with the marked side up (doubled if they all turned up).

On the first turn a player moves a piece into the central square and then proceeds along one arm. (Each player can decide whether to move clockwise or counterclockwise, but all of one player's pieces have to move in the same direction.) On subsequent turns the players can move one piece for the total number of spaces rolled or divide the roll between two or more pieces. Pieces move around the board, out one arm and back and then into the next, until they are borne off by arriving back at the space next to the one where they entered. Landing in one of the rounded end spaces wins another turn. Landing in one of the marked spaces loses a turn.

No piece can move into an occupied space. If a player has only one possible move, he has to use it, even if it is to his disadvantage. If a player can not move at all he or she has to pay a forfeit, which is added to the pool.

The first player to remove all the pieces from the board wins the pool. There is one other way to win: the board game equivalent of the ball-through-the-ring victory of the Aztec ball game (see Ulamaliztli). In medieval times, if one of the counting beans landed on end and remained upright, it was considered a powerful omen, and the player who tossed the bean won the game and all the stakes immediately.

You can draw a patolli board on paper or on a straw mat (such as a placemat or piece of a window shade). Find and paint six small stones as described. Red or black beans make the best dice. Use the tip of a knife or a nail file to "drill" a small hole in one side of each bean.

▧ Pulac (Bul)

Pulac is played by the Ketchi people in the Guatemalan highlands to this day. There is no reason to believe that it was not played by their Mayan ancestors.

Ten to fifteen ears of corn are laid in a row, with the tips pointed in alternating directions. The game is played on the spaces between the ears: the trail. The pieces, or warriors, march along the trail from their own "village" or end to the "village" of the enemy/opponent.

Each player has five flat warrior disks, cut from a small branch and colored or marked to distinguish the pieces. Split sticks or corncobs serve as dice. Four sticks are tossed together. For each flat or darkened side that falls facing up the player moves one place. Pieces enter from the near end of the row and exit from the far end. If only two are playing, a player may choose to enter a new piece on the next turn or to move a piece already on the trail. If many people are playing, each can have only one warrior on the trail at a time; so new pieces are only put into play when a piece has been taken captive.

Two pieces of the same color cannot occupy the same place. If a piece lands on a place occupied by an enemy piece, the enemy is captured, but not removed from the board. The capturing warrior is placed on top of the captive piece, and takes the captive along as it moves. If an opposing piece lands on the place occupied by the warrior and its captive, it tops the stack and takes both pieces along with it, thus the stacks can grow and the directions of the pieces can change several times as the game progresses. When a warrior (and any captives it may have) reaches the far side of the trail, opposing pieces are removed from the game while the warrior and its "rescued" compatriots are re-entered from their own end. The game is over when one player has lost all of his or her pieces.

Figure 5.3. Stewart Culin believed this drawing represented a divination game similar to sholiwe. *Source*: Culin (1896). Courtesy of The Board of Trustees of the National Museums & Galleries on Merseyside.

It's easy to make an authentic pulac game. Use the ornamental dried corn that people hang on their doors in fall for the board. Cut disks from a branch and mark the tops of the disks with crosses or dots to distinguish one player's pieces from the other. Saw a dried corncob in half lengthwise and crosswise for the dice, or use any small sticks cut down so one side is flat.

⊞ Sholiwe

In the much-reproduced codex *Fejérváry-Mayer*, there is a picture of the god of divination holding three arrows and an *atlatl* seated at the center of an outline of four trapezoids and four loops, each marked with a series of dots. The noted American game scholar Stewart Culin believed that the picture was actually a reproduction of a game board representing the four points of the compass (Figure 5.3). If so, it would have been a game very much like sholiwe, an appropriate frame for the god of divination.

Cane dice or arrow dice were used both in religious rituals and divinations and for amusement in what is now Mexico and the southwestern United States. Sholiwe could be either played as a game for entertainment and betting or as a ritual for ascertaining what the future might hold.

To play sholiwe, four players (or priests, if the game was being played for religious purposes) represented the four points of the compass. North represented winter and the god of war and was designated by yellow. West was blue, and represented water and fertility. South was red, fire, and summer. East was white, representing Earth and seeds. North and East were considered masculine, and South and West were feminine.

When sholiwe was played for religious reasons the results would be interpreted according to the symbolic representations as answers to the question asked before the game: if North won the battle would be successful, or if West won the rains would be good.

The board was laid out on a buffalo robe, arranged so the head faced east, and the players sat at the four feet of the robe: yellow on the northeast corner, blue on the northwest, red on the southwest, and white on the southeast. Above the board was hung a deerskin stretched over a hoop like a drum.

The round sholiwe board followed the same design as the zohn ali board (see North America chapter), pointing to their common ancestry, although sholiwe is a more complex game. An opening pointed in each of the four directions, and a line was traced from one opening to the next, marked with forty dots or grains of corn, colored to match the player who sat on that side. Each player was represented on the board by a splint, and each had a supply of counters in his own color. Each player also had four arrow shafts or canes, one in each color but each set distinctively marked.

To cast the dice a player held the cane of his own color across his fingers and stacked the other three dice perpendicular to it with their bases against his palm. He then tossed the dice up so they hit the deerskin and bounced down onto the board. The value of the toss was more complex than in zohn ali. In addition to moving the pieces around the board, points from the tosses were tallied with counters (explained below).

The cane in the player's own color was counted separately from the other three. If the player's own colored cane landed on top of the other three, he moved four spaces and earned another toss. If the other three canes fell split side down, the player earned five spaces, two up was worth three and one up was worth one. If the other three canes landed split sides up, he moved ten points and earned a second additional throw.

Starting from the compass point he represented, each player moved his splint counterclockwise around the circle according to the number of points earned. In addition a running tally for each pair (masculine vs. feminine) was kept with the counters. If a player landed on a place occupied by one of the other team's pieces, that player had to start over, and the capturing player won the team's counters. The game ended when the first player completed the circuit and exit by his own compass point, and the winners were the team with the largest number of points accumulated.

You can make sholiwe canes from bamboo or sugarcane, split lengthwise and painted. Use corn kernels for counters to keep track of the points, and painted bamboo splints or craft sticks for playing pieces. Paint the board (four arcs of forty dots each with an opening at each of the compass points) in the four colors on paper or cloth. For an authentic game you'll need to stretch a piece of leather or fabric over a hoop and hang it above the board, but you can toss the split canes up and let them fall onto the board without the skin.

⚏ Totoloque

This game for two, three, or four players was also called totolospi, but is a completely different game from the game referred to by that name in the North American Games chapter.

Boards for totoloque have been found inscribed in sandstone in the desert southwest of the United States and northern Mexico (Figure 5.4). They could easily be scratched on a stone surface or even traced in the sand. The perimeter of the board was a rectangle, marked off in sets of four lines each with a circle between each set of four, one circle at each corner, one in the middle of each end and two along each side of the rectangle. The trail began in the middle of the board and followed a line, sometimes straight and sometimes curved or coiled like a snake, to join the perimeter at the middle of one of the ends of the rectangle. This central line was usually three sets of four spaces. The game was played with three stick or cane dice, each painted red on the flat side, and a stone marker for each player.

Players cast the dice to see who would go first. To begin each player put his marker in the center circle. The stick dice were dropped on end, or struck against a stone disk held in the player's hand. If they all fell white (round) side up the player moved two spaces and threw again. If the sticks fell all red side up the player moved one space and threw again. If the dice were mixed, play passed to the next player.

If a player landed on an occupied place, the player who was there first

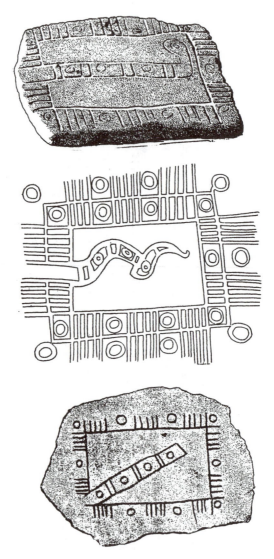

Figure 5.4. Totoloque boards could be simple or ornate. *Source*: Culin (1975).

was "killed" and had to start over. Landing in one of the circles earned the player another turn. The first player to complete the circuit and return to the starting point was the winner.

To play totoloque, draw the board on paper or paint it on wood. Make stick dice by splitting bamboo or sugarcane, or paint craft sticks on one side for dice. Markers can be painted stones or disks made from modeling dough.

▦ Tuknanavuhpi

Shoshone children scratched the tuknanavuhpi board in the sand for playing while minding animals or keeping crows out of the corn. The board had sixteen squares (four rows of four) and each square was divided on both diagonals (with an "x"). The two-person game was played on the intersections, or points, and captured pieces were kept in the squares.

The playing pieces, called animals, could be corn kernels, bits of charcoal, pebbles, or sticks, as long as the players could tell their pieces apart. The game started with all the pieces on the board: each player had three rows of pieces plus two on the center row. The point in the middle of the board was empty. The player who went first moved into the empty space, and the other player captured the piece by jumping over it. Pieces could move in any direction and jump over and capture any adjacent piece with a vacant space beyond it. Multiple jumps were allowed. Once a row had been emptied it was closed, that is, no other piece could be placed in it. This had the effect of shrinking the board as the game progressed.

Draw a tuknanavuhpi board on paper and play with differently colored kernels of corn for pieces.

▦ Uluki

This unusual activity was part game, part socialization ritual, and part economic activity. The Kalapalo, a Carib-speaking people who lived in the rain forest of the Amazon, practiced uluki within the family, around the village or even between villages. The rules were the same in each case. All members of the group were required to participate in the uluki. In a village uluki, the group gathered and moved from house to house. A village leader supervised the uluki, which, to ensure fair play, began at his house. The head of the household invited the group in, and was asked to bring out anything the family had to trade. Anyone in the group who wanted the objects offered could negotiate for an object, take it home, and bring back the exchange. Ideally both parties agreed on the exchange, but even if the owner of the first object believed the trade was unfair, no complaining was allowed. The values taught by the game were that the community was more important than the individual and harmony was more important than possessions. Children's uluki were supervised by an elder from the community, but the children did their own trading with their own possessions. Uluki between villages were supervised by elders from both communities.

Uluki would be an interesting game to play among classrooms. Each group should decide in advance what objects will be traded, and what things the group hopes to obtain.

▦ Wak Pel Pul

This Mayan target game was made with six sticks. They stood on end, having been cut so that branches growing opposite each other provided a "foot." The sticks were marked according to their point value, one through six. One through five were stood in a circle with six in the middle, and then players took turns tossing cocoa beans at the sticks to knock them over and accumulate points. Any number of players could participate, and the first to reach an agreed-upon total score won the game.

Cut sticks as described above from pruned branches, or make targets from corrugated cardboard: cut nine rectangular "sticks" about six inches long and an inch wide. Cut half of these in half to make three-inch long "feet." Cut a notch about one-half-inch deep in the bottom of each of the sticks and the middle of the side of each of the feet. Line up the notches and slide a foot onto each stick. You may need to adjust them slightly to make them stand up. Mark each stick with lines or small notches to represent its value. Use black beans to knock the sticks over.

▦ Wash'kasi

This Aztec game is a simpler version of sholiwe and similar to toto-loque, a reminder that the peoples of southwestern North America and those of Central America had extensive contact.

The board for wash'kasi was a square, ten spaces on a side, repre-senting the four directions. If the board was traced in sand a flat stone was placed in the center of the square for striking the dice. The "dice" were four sticks or blocks of wood, painted on one side. These were held in a bundle and then smacked against the stone and allowed to fall. If all four fall colored side up, the player moved ten spaces. Three up and one down was worth three spaces, two up and two down was worth two. A throw with all colored sides down was worth six.

Up to four players entered their pieces on their own right-hand corner and moved counterclockwise around the circuit. Probably each player had two or three pieces. The goal was to be the first to get all ones pieces all the way around and out again. The game was sometimes played by two players who moved in opposite directions around the board, which would be an interesting variation to try.

Trace the wash'kasi board on a flat stone with chalk. Make four dice from small blocks of wood, about three one-half inch, each painted on one side. Use small stones for playing pieces, and mark the tops with crosses, dots, or lines to distinguish one player from the other.

PLAY

▦ Acoorie in a Pen

Macoosi children in the Atlantic coastal area of what is now Guyana and Suriname played a number of imitative games. In this one, the players stood in a circle, linking their arms around each other's necks. One child, the "acoorie," hid inside the circle, which represented a pen. Another child was the jaguar, who tried to snatch the acoorie out of the pen. The pen, of course, was alive, and the children circled round and round while the jaguar tried to reach in and grab the acoorie.

▦ Bag Attacks

The severe Aztec view of life did not provide many opportunities for lighthearted play, nor many chances for young men and women to get to know one another. In this odd game, played on one day during the month of Tititl, boys and young men armed themselves with net bags filled with shredded paper and reeds, which they hid under their cloaks. They ran the streets, surrounding and whacking women and girls with shouts of "have a bag, lady!" Some women armed themselves with sticks and branches to fight off their attackers. Others, reportedly, stood and wept. At least one scholar has concluded that this attention was not unwanted, however, and that the more young men a woman attracted, the more popular she must have been.

Buffeting one another with cloth bags full of paper and leaves sounds a great deal like a modern pillow fight!

▦ Basket Game

At the southern tip of South America, Yahgan children played a game where one player dragged a basket on a string across the ground. All the other players chased the basket and threw small spears into it. This game developed the same skill needed for spearfishing, the Yahgan's main source of food.

▦ Chogirali

This Tarahumare target game from northern Mexico could be played with arrows or sticks. First an arrow was shot to land about fifty yards ahead of the players. This arrow became the *chogira*, or target. Two players now took turns shooting arrows at the target. The arrow that came the closest to the target scored one point, four if it was within four-fingers' breadth of the target. If an arrow landed across the target, it was worth four points; if it landed touching the target but not across it, it was worth two. If both players managed to get arrows across the target, neither scored any points. The first to reach twelve points won the game. When played with thrown sticks instead of arrows the game was scored in the same way.

You can play with sticks or see the Appendix for notes on bows and arrows.

⊞ Follow/Tug the Leader

Both children and adults in the Caribbean islands played follow the leader. The players formed a line, each with hands wrapped around the waist of the player in front. Together they moved through the village, each following the leader as in the familiar game today, except that at any moment those at the back of the line might begin to move in the opposite direction, pulling the front of the line with them, while those at the front of the line planted their feet and tried to remain in place. Or, those at the front might suddenly move backward, bowling over the people behind them.

⊞ Hawk Attack

This game was common in South America. It looks very much like the "Fox and Geese" games played by children in northern Europe (see voli i ovtsy). In this game one person was the "hawk." The rest formed a line, with the first person in line being the hen and the rest her chicks. The hawk walked backward, facing the hen, and the hen followed with all the chicks behind until suddenly the hawk swooped, racing around the line to snatch the very last chick. All the other chicks ducked down while the last one raced up the other side of the line. If the chick could reach the head of the line before being captured, she became the hen and the game resumed. If the hawk captured the chick, she was "out" and became a spectator. The game continued until all the chicks had been captured.

⊞ Kaikoosi

In this Caribbean game three players were "it," representing a jaguar and her cubs. They hid while the rest formed a line, each placing his hands on the shoulders of the child ahead of him. The line moved through the village, swaying and chanting "there is no jaguar here to-day" (*kaikoosi bramha celeribè*). The jaguar leapt out from her hiding place, running on both feet and one hand, with the other hand serving as the tail and the two cubs, doing the same motion, trailing behind. The jaguar had to try to capture (tag) the last person in the line before the front of the line could turn and come back to chase her off. If she succeeded she took the captive to her "lair," which is to say, to the sideline, and then hid again while the line regrouped.

▦ Kalaka

The Yahgan people, who lived in the southern tip of South America on Tierra del Fuego, did not have rubber, but they still played a version of the circle game so common in South America. An unusual feature of the Yahgan version was that the players used their hands. Men and women played the game together, standing in a circle and hitting the ball straight up into the air with an open hand. The object was to keep the ball in the air and inside the circle. The Yahgan had two balls, a smaller, softball-sized ball made of an albatross web stuffed with feathers, and a larger inflated ball that was a seal stomach. Neither ball would have been round, making the game more challenging.

You can play kalaka with a small balloon.

▦ Mojo Circle Game

This less-competitive version of the Mojo rubber ball game (see nucaepotò) probably served to develop the players' skills in ball handling. Young people played the game with a very light, inflated ball, while adults would play with the same solid, heavy ball used in the competitive game.

Eight or more players stood in a circle, about fifteen feet across for the heavy ball, and further apart for the lighter ball. Players passed the ball from one to another, using only their knees, lower legs and feet to strike the ball, and the object of the game was to keep the ball from touching the ground.

Use a small beach ball for the light version of this game, and an underinflated basketball for the heavy version.

▦ Palma

Children from what is now Bolivia played this game with a bone and some stones. A line was drawn on the ground, at least fifteen yards long. Shorter lines were drawn across it about every three feet. The bone was stuck into the ground at one end of the line, and players took turns trying to hit that target with a stone, beginning from the closest mark and then moving back one mark at a time. In order to win the player had to strike the target from each mark in turn. If he missed, the next player tried, and when his turn came again he had to start over from at the closest mark.

You can play palma with a stick for a target, or draw the line on pavement with chalk and use a larger stone or a can filled with sand as a target.

⊞   Polkirich (Tops)

Tops were common playthings for Mayan children and among children and adults in the Andes and upper Amazon. Both wooden and stone tops have been found by archaeologists. A whipping top was made from a length of branch, sharpened to a point at one end. A cord wrapped around the top and pulled sharply set it spinning, and with practice the player could learn to whip the top to keep it moving.

One player would put up a stake: a toy or a treat. They drew a circle on the ground, placed the prize in the middle and then spun their tops to see who would win. As in Europe and Oceania, the game could be to see whose top would spin the longest, or to see if one top would knock the other over or out of the circle.

⊞   Ring Game

In this nameless Caribbean Arawak children's game the players formed a circle with arms linked around each others' waists. One player was the captive and stood in the center of the circle. As the circle of children turned around him, the captive tried to break through the circle to escape.

⊞   Stilts

Stilts can be useful tools for crossing streams or getting a better view of the landscape, and their added height makes them a favorite addition to many fantastic costumes. The Mayan festivals included dancers on stilts. The challenge of learning to balance and maneuver made stilt walking a great game as well, and many of the peoples of Central America enjoyed racing on stilts for recreation. Some stilts were made from forked saplings, so that the stilt walker could hold the top of the stilt for stability. Others were strapped to the feet like very tall sandals.

⠿ Tankalawa

Sandstone disks and corncobs were the essential pieces for this game, which will sound very familiar to anyone who has been to a country fair. The cob was stood on end on one disk, with another disk placed on top of it. The prize, which might be a bead or other small valuable or an edible treat, was balanced on the disk. Players stood a short distance away and tossed disks to try and knock over the cob. The one who succeeded claimed the prize. In the Amazon the same game was played with a bamboo stick set into the ground instead of the corn cob.

⠿ To Kybairu

To kybairu was an adult tickling game among the Guayaki, who lived in the rain forest of what is now Paraguay. The object of the game was to capture the *proaa*, a large bean. Each player in turn would hold the bean, grasping it in her fist or under her arm, and then all the others would tickle her until she let go of the bean. The person who captured it would then become the recipient of the tickling.

This game was a sort of courting ritual among the normally very restrained Guayaki, so children did not play. To kybairu condoned and encouraged physical contact in an open, entirely public situation. A man or woman could indicate interest in another person by relinquishing the bean to the chosen one, and indeed many partnerships were formed at these gatherings.

⠿ Uike

The Witoto played this circle ball game with a rubber ball about six inches in diameter. The ball was tossed into the air and the first player to touch the ball had to strike it with his right knee. The next player had to bounce the ball off his left knee, and so forth, alternating sides and keeping the ball in the air at all times, without using the hands. Other groups allowed the use of hands to hit (but not catch) the ball, as well as lifting it with the tops of the feet.

⠿ Weapons Practice

Was it play, or training for the hunt? No doubt it was both. Young Yanomamö boys in the Amazon rain forest would capture a lizard and tie it to a stake in the village, then practice shooting it with small bows and arrows. Yagua youths practiced their aim with blowguns by shooting at targets made from gourds. Spears, darts and slingshots were weapons and hunting tools, but they also made for great competitions: determining who could shoot furthest and hit the smallest target at the greatest distance brought prestige and bragging rights while developing the skills that would put meat in the stewpot.

Rain-forest women made string by rolling the fibers of the palm leaves between their hands or against their legs. These strings could be woven into nets, bags, and hammocks, wound into ropes and cords, or used to string bows and slingshots. Arrows were made from various woods, some stronger, some lighter, each with its own value in the hunt. Rain-forest hunters made use of botanical poisons to bring down game animals, but the poison-bearing tips were removable, and children practiced with arrows just sharp enough to pierce their targets. Spears often had metal tips, too, and were heavy enough to penetrate the hide of an animal. Youngsters could develop their skills with "toy" spears made to match their size. Blowguns, made from hollow reeds, could be used to fire poison darts or sharpened sticks or clay pellets.

SPORTS

⊞ Batey

Like all the people of Mesoamerica, the Arawakan people of the Antilles in the Caribbean played the ball game, but their island isolation led to some interesting variations in the game. Most Caribbean villages had one main ball court in the central plaza of the village and several smaller courts on the outskirts of the village.

The courts were about three times as long as they were wide, with smaller courts about sixty by twenty feet and larger ones as much as two hundred by six hundred feet reported. A centerline marked on the ground divided the court. Low mounds of dirt or sometimes walls along the sidelines incorporated seats for spectators. Teams ranged from ten to thirty players, depending on the size of the court, with the two sides always equal.

Both men and women, young and old, played the game, but teams were not mixed, and while women might play against teams of either maidens or youths it seems that men played only against other men.

The batey ball was about four to six inches in diameter, made of kneaded rubber so that it was heavy but spongy. Men struck the ball with their shoulders if it was high or their hips if it was low, though use of the head and elbows was also allowed. Women used their knees and closed fists to direct the ball, but could not use an open hand.

One player bounced or threw the ball to the opposing team to begin the game. As the teams volleyed, the ball could bounce or touch the ground, but if it began to roll it was dead and the opposing side scored a point. A team could also score by driving the ball over their opponent's goal line. If the ball went out of bounds on a sideline the team that put it into play served again. The first team to reach an agreed-upon score was the winner.

A soft-foam indoor soccer ball is about the right size and bounce for a batey ball, although a slightly underinflated four-square ball would work as well. Divide the group into teams, "youths" (men) against "maidens" (women). Teams should be of equal size, and you will probably want to substitute players as the game goes on. Remember, youths hit the ball with their shoulders and hips, maidens with fists and knees.

⊞ Buriti Race

The Xavante people of the Amazon rain forest in what is now Brazil ran this relay race on a prearranged circular route. The buriti is a tree, and the racers ran while carrying a section of buriti log, about two feet long and weighing well over one hundred pounds. The runner carries the log balanced on his shoulder, holding it with both hands. Two teams with equal numbers of runners run the race. The first runners take off from the starting line carrying the buriti logs, and their teammates run along with them. When the first runner is tired he rolls the log onto the shoulder of his teammate and then continues running with the team. The first team to return the log to the starting point is triumphant.

You can run a buriti race on an ordinary track or lay out a route around an open field or playground. Divide the group into teams of four or five, and be sure there is enough room for the teams to run together. You will need two pieces of firewood of about the same weight, one log for each team. Try to find round wood, not split. Dry wood is lighter than green wood, and softwoods such as pine are much lighter than hardwoods like oak and maple. A two-foot piece of dry oak, six inches in diameter, will weigh about thirty pounds and is probably as heavy as you would want to try. You could have races in several different weight classes if you have a variety of logs available.

⊞ Chaah

This Maya ball game is perhaps the best known of the ball court games because of the large number of courts which have been excavated in Guatemala and Honduras, and the description of the game in the writings of the later conquistadores (Figure 5.5). It shared many characteristics with the games played further south and to the north, but had some unique characteristics as well.

The court for chaah was formed of a narrow "alley," from 36 to 90

Figure 5.5. Among the Aztecs and Maya the chaah ball game was played by professional athletes. *Source*: William P. Palmer III Collection, Hudson Museum, University of Maine. Photo by Tom Wilkins. Used by permission.

feet long and 15 to 25 feet wide, with broad endcourts that ran perpendicular to the alley, forming an "I" shape or, in a few cases, a "T" shape. These endcourts were tricky as the ball could become trapped there, so the job of a backcourt player was to keep the ball from caroming into those corners. Mounds or ridges with long, low benches ran along the sides of this alley, and sometimes rose to form towering stands for spectators above the court. Stone markers in the walls indicate the centerline and probably also zones of the court. In the Mexican game, the centerline markers were stone rings that also served as goals.

While informal games in villages were probably open to anyone, the formal games at the Maya ball courts were played by young men who were professional ballplayers. They had their own equipment, including not only balls, rings, and markers for the court, but also elaborate protective equipment. The most striking piece of equipment was a sort of corset or belt that hung around the player's middle and protected the hips. A leather kilt, kneepads, arm pads or long gloves, and a head net or helmet completed the outfit. In paintings and sculptures the players are often shown wearing yokes made of stone, and carrying stone *achas*, or paddles, in their belts. These objects have been found in excavations and have caused scholars to wonder how such heavy equipment could have aided in play. Some interesting theories have been developed, but recent archaeological work suggests that these may in fact have been trophies awarded to victorious players and worn ceremonially, not while actually playing the game.

The ball used for chaah was relatively small, about half the size of a person's head. Based on the protective equipment worn by the players, scholars believe it was solid rubber.

One or two players represented each side in the game. There were often disputes over whose ball would be used, but generally the home team provided the ball (which had been ritually imbued with magic properties before the game) and served first. When a team scored they gained the serve and in some cases the serving team used their own ball, so that the ball could change several times in the course of the game. Players propelled the ball by striking it with the heavy belt. Players leapt into the air or dropped to one knee in order to position themselves for this maneuver. As in the other ball games, a player scored a point when his opponent was unable to return the ball. Typically a game was played for best two-out-of-three score, after which new players would take their places on the court.

To play chaah you will need to improvise the belt. One possible substitute is a partially inflated inner tube. Another is a nylon stocking stuffed with crumpled newspaper. Curve this around the player's body just above the hips and tie or stitch the ends together. In either case the belt should hang from a harness over the shoulders, which you can make by cutting an old T-shirt so that four strips hang from the shoulders. Tie these around the belt and pull it on over the player's head. A softball is a good substitute for a chaah ball.

A chaah court with its walls and endcourts will not be easy to recreate unless you are ready to undertake a substantial building project! One possibility in some gymnasiums is to pull out the bleachers in the center of the gym and leave those at the ends folded up against the walls, forming a narrower alley with wider backcourts. Outdoors you can mark the outline of the court with cones.

Figure 5.6. Shell divers and fishermen from South America may have reached Easter Island, 2,500 miles away, in rafts made of bundled reeds and balsa wood. *Source*: William P. Palmer III Collection, Hudson Museum, University of Maine. Photo by Tom Wilkins. Used by permission.

Diving and Rafting

Along the coast of Peru diving for shells was both an important economic activity and a recreational competition. Chimu divers paddled reed rafts, long bundles of totora reeds tapering to a point, out to the shellfish beds. From these rafts they dived deep beneath the waves to bring up shells. Divers competed to see who could hold their breath the longest and raced their rafts out and back to see who was the swiftest paddler.

Some reed rafts were single bundles that the rafter paddled while lying along the length of the raft. Others, made from two bundles, allowed the rafter to sit and paddle with the feet. Still larger boats were built with balsa logs and sails.

One of history's fascinating mysteries concerns these rafts, which were also used by the people of Easter Island, far off the coast of South America (Figure 5.6). When European explorers first landed on Easter Island in 1722, they learned from the people living there that the island had been settled twice, by two distinctively different groups of people. For more than two centuries anthropologists speculated and argued about who those people might have been, and where they came from. Sir Peter Buck, an anthropologist from New Zealand, was the best-known proponent of the Polynesian theory. He demonstrated that wayfaring canoes from Melanesia and New Zealand could have traveled to Easter Island via the various smaller islands of Polynesia. But the how to explain the fact that Easter Islanders were cultivating sweet potatoes, bottle gourds, and most important, totora reeds, all native to South America, 2,300 miles away across the open Pacific? The famous Norwegian explorer Thor Heyerdahl believed he had found the answer in an ancient Peruvian story of a ruler named Kon Tiki, who after losing a battle took to the sea with some of his followers in rafts. Years before, Heyerdahl had been told by people in Polynesia that their ancestors had come across the sea from the East with a king named Tiki. To prove his theory that Kon Tiki and the Polynesian Tiki were the same figure, Heyerdahl built a raft and sailed west from Peru, landing in Polynesia 101 days later. Heyerdahl observed that this did not prove the legend, but it did prove it was possible Amerindians had sailed to Polynesia. Perhaps tiny Easter Island was indeed settled from both directions, completing the circle of the migratory journeys of people in the ancient world.

You won't want to paddle a raft thousands of miles out to sea, but you can make a raft from bundles of reeds if you live near wetlands. Or take two dozen foam "noodles" and lash them together into two thick bundles. Bind the fronts of the bundles together (interweaving the ends) to form the "prow" of your raft, and lash the backs of the bundles to the ends of a one-inch board about two feet long. You should be able to sit on the board and paddle the raft with your feet!

⊞ Ifagaka

The atlatl is a method of launching a dart that was abandoned in much of the world when the bow and arrow developed, probably because bows give the archer more precision than atlatls. In Central America and much of South America, however, the atlatl continued to be the launcher of choice, and Native Americans developed this technology to a very high degree. They used tips of precise weight and also added weights to the shafts of the darts in order to give them more control over the flight. They even found a way to "silence" the dart with a stone flange. Aztec warriors used atlatls with deadly effect against the conquistadors, who were shocked to discover that the atlatl darts could fly 200 yards and pierce a Spanish soldier's plate armor.

Atlatls are sometimes called "spear-throwers," but the atlatl dart is flexible, more like a long arrow than a spear. Generally the darts were at least three feet long, and the atlatl was about one-third as long as the "spear."

In the lowlands of what is now Brazil the isolated Kalapalo people continued the tradition of a "spear-throwing" competition into the twentieth century, providing a glimpse of what such an event might have been like in the Middle Ages. The ifagaka ritual began in local villages and culminated in an intervillage competition where the champions of each village faced off. The mock battle served to release aggression and ultimately solidified the bonds between villages. It was also an opportunity for young women to observe and compare the men of the neighboring villages, from whom they would select a husband, sometimes before the feast was over.

In the first, local rounds, a stuffed effigy was erected in the center of each village and proclaimed to be the representative of the village that would host the ifagaka. (In the host village it represented the guests.) Each day the men of the village practiced their demonstration dance, in which they declared their prowess and displayed their weapons. At the end of the dance each one threw his dart at the effigy, shouting some insult about an individual from the other village. On the day of the ifagaka, all the people gathered at the host village. Representatives of each village performed their dances and hurled their spears at the effigy in the host village, again shouting the insults. Of course those being insulted could hear the remarks, and the atmosphere quickly became aggressive. Village elders watched from the sidelines and intervened if the violence became too real. The groups danced again, and then broke into two lines that charged each other in mock attack.

At a signal from the elders, the groups divided again, and the actual atlatl contest began. Two barriers made of bundles of poles were erected at each end of the playing area. The men paired off according to ability (one village sending out its champion against the another's champion, its number two against theirs and so forth). In turn each competitor took his atlatl and launched his dart at his opponent, who tried to leap behind his barrier before being hit. (The darts for the competition were blunt-tipped and aimed at the thigh, so a hit was painful but not dangerous.) After all the players had their turn, the champions of the villages competed again, but without the barriers. Finally the ceremonial darts and atlatls were ceremonially burned, and the feast began.

To recreate an ifagaka, make an effigy by stuffing some old clothes with straw. Use tipped atlatl darts to practice on the effigies, but put foam balls or blocks on the tips if you throw them at each other! (See the Appendix for ideas about making atlatls and darts.)

▦ Matana-ariti

The Paressi lived in the high country of what is now Bolivia and western Brazil. This, the Paressi version of the rubber-ball game, was played with a hollow, inflated ball about nine inches in diameter. The court was very simple, a clear level space—often the central square of the village, with houses on both sides. The goal lines could be marked or they could be simply the ends of the square.

Teams were equal, with eight or ten players on a side, sometimes more. A single referee watched the game and kept score.

Players, who wore no protective clothing or equipment, could only strike the ball with their heads. At the beginning of the game the ball was placed in the middle of the court, and the servers threw themselves down on their chests and butted at the ball with their heads, attempting to toss it into the air. After a few strikes the ball would be high enough to be passed and volleyed from head to head. Each team attempted to get the ball over their opponents' goal line, scoring a point.

If the ball went out of bounds it was tossed back into play by a spectator. After a goal the ball was served from the center of the court again.

A playground ball makes an excellent mataná-arití ball, and a sandy or grassy court, although not authentic, is best for the player's bodies. Allowing the referee to begin the game by tossing the ball into the air at center court will also prevent some crashing.

⊞ Nucaepotò

The Mojo people lived in what is now Bolivia. More than one source has reported that the solid rubber ball used by the Mojo to play nucaepotò weighed twenty-five pounds. Scholars find this difficult to believe, as much lighter balls used in other regions resulted in injury and even death on occasion; nevertheless it is safe to assume that the ball was very heavy. There were reports of both players and spectators being killed by the ball. (The Mojo also played an informal game with a hollow ball that weighed less than a half-pound, described under play).

Two teams, equal in number, stood facing each other with a space of about twenty-four feet separating them. The game took place in stages. In the first stage, players used only the lower leg and foot to propel the ball, dropping to one knee and striking the ball with the other leg. Some players bandaged the leg for protection, while others did not, and considered the resultant swelling a badge of honor.

As the ball game progressed the teams moved back, so that the space between them increased. In the second stage of the game, the players began to propel the ball with their heads. In this stage of the game the ball was allowed to bounce off the ground once before being struck again.

If a team failed to return the ball their opponents scored a point. Play probably continued until one team reached an agreed-upon total.

Play nucaepotò with a basketball on a grassy field. Mark a centerline with lime or chalk. (A basketball isn't as heavy as a nucaepotò ball, which is safer for the legs and heads of the players!)

▦　Otomac Ball Game

North of the Amazon in the grasslands of what is now Venezuela the Otomac people played an interesting version of the ball game. Men and women played it together, but with slightly different rules. The game began with twelve players on a side, and new players joined the game over the course of the day. The game was played recreationally on a daily basis within villages, but also competitively between villages on special occasions. Every village had a court specially built for the game.

The ball used by the Otomac was a very elastic solid rubber ball with good bounce that weighed about two pounds and was probably about six inches in diameter. Men propelled the ball only with their right shoulders and, in some variations, their heads. Women used a racket shaped like a short-handled canoe paddle, about two feet long and nearly a foot across its widest part. If a player touched the ball illegally, their team lost a point.

Each player covered a specific portion of the court, running and jumping to return the volley. A team scored one point when the other side failed to return the ball. As long as the ball was moving, it was in play, and the nearest player might dive to try and propel the ball back into the air if it touched the ground.

After each point the players rotated positions, and substitutes could come in.

To recreate the Otomac game the biggest challenge may be to find a ball of the right size and weight. A volleyball or a four-square ball makes a decent substitute. You can cut paddles from one-inch boards. Tape the handles to make them easier to hold and avoid splinters. The court should be a level area about thirty feet wide and sixty feet long (about the size of a standard volleyball court).

▦　Palitún

The Mapuche people lived in the southern part of South America, in what is now Chile and Argentina. Because rubber trees do not grow that far south, the Mapuche did not play the rubber-ball game. The favored sport of the Mapuche was palitún, or as the Spanish called it, chueca, a hockey-style game played with a leather ball. It was a game very similar to the "shinny" games played in North America. Palitún, also sometimes called palín, is stilled played in Mapuche communities today.

The palitún field was a large open space, long and relatively narrow (about three hundred by thirty yards). Players divided into teams of equal size but no specific number. Palitún sticks had a crook at the end. They could be made from the root end of a sapling or by curving a stick while it was green and tying it in that position while it dried. The ball was stitched of leather and stuffed with hair or grass. A game began with teams spread out on each side of the centerline, with the ball in the middle of the field. The object of the game was to drive the ball across the opposing team's endline.

To play palitún you will need a large, level area. It can be grass or dirt. Make sticks as described above or cut down old hockey sticks so the blade is about five inches long and the handle reaches about to the player's hip from the ground. You can make an authentic ball from leather or stuff an old tennis ball with grass or shredded paper. The centerline and endlines of the field may be marked or their locations can be shown with stakes at the sides of the field. (Sidelines are not generally marked and there is no "out-of-bounds" rule.)

⊞ Quecholli

For ordinary people hunting was work, not recreation, but the nobility of the Aztecs, and probably the Maya and Toltecs before them, had hunting preserves where animals were kept for their hunting pleasure. They hunted with blowpipes, shooting clay pellets, as well as arrows, spears and nets (Figure 5.7). Once a year, on the tenth day of the month, sacred to the god of hunting and the god of war, Aztec warriors gathered for a ritual hunting party called quecholli. They built shelters on the mountain Zacatepetl, where they spent the evening in song and drinking. In the morning they lined up "like a rope" to drive animals and birds together and form a ring around them; then each leapt forward to try and kill the best game. The emperor awarded prizes to those who brought down a deer or coyote, and provided a feast for all the hunters at the end of the day.

Blowpipes were generally made from bamboo or other reeds, and you can easily make one the same way. A straw will work if no reed is available. To project a pellet with a blowpipe you simply place the object in the pipe and blow into it, as anyone who has ever shot a spitball can attest. However, to shoot a dart with a blowpipe you must have something that fills the pipe. In the rain forests a bit of fur or plant fiber would be placed in the pipe and pushed back by the dart. A bit of a cotton ball will serve. You can make darts from twigs, with the bark peeled just a bit on the back to serve as fletching.

⊞ Rarajipari

The Tarahumare of northern Mexico were such accomplished runners that their name for themselves, *raramuri*, means "runners." In addition to long-distance racing, the Tahahumare excelled at the kickball race (rarajipari), which was played by most of the Southwest and Central American peoples.

Figure 5.7. A hunter brings down birds with his blowpipe. Darts and dead birds fall around him. *Source*: William P. Palmer III Collection, Hudson Museum, University of Maine. Photo by Tom Wilkins. Used by permission.

The ball race combined long-distance running with something resembling the urban street game of kick-the-can. The ball was sometimes a stitched buckskin ball, about the size of a tennis ball, but often a cylinder of bone or wood was used. The kick was carefully built into the running step: without breaking stride the runner would position the foot behind the ball, lift it, and project it through the air forty feet or more at a time. This skill was developed by years of practicing, and toddlers could be seen kicking sticks around the village while youngsters kicked their way home from the fields.

The racecourse generally ran from the village out to a distant point and back; twenty-five miles was a standard distance. The course was marked with stakes or blazes, and judges were stationed along the route to be sure the rules were observed.

Players sometimes competed one-on-one, but most often teams of a half-dozen runners would compete, with players alternating kicking and sprinting. Races began with the leader of each team at the starting line and teammates slightly further ahead. Once the ball had been kicked they all took off after it, and the one closest to where it landed would launch it forward again. Accuracy was as important as speed. A ball that landed far off the track or became lodged in a hole or tangled in the grass could quickly put the leading team behind. Players could not touch the ball with their hands, but were allowed to use a stick to dislodge a stuck ball.

In the women's version of the ball race, runners drove the ball along with a forked stick. Another variation was played with a small hoop, which the women would pick up and toss with a stick as they ran.

A dirt path that crosses open fields and through some woods, with a fair amount of uphill and downhill sections would be an authentic racecourse, but a trail marked with signs winding around a park or schoolyard will do. Make some leather balls, about three inches in diameter, and fill them with sawdust. If the ball is a bit flattened it will be easier to scoop up and toss. Some hoops twisted from vines to be tossed with sticks would also be authentic, and it might be interesting to see which version of the game participants prefer.

⊞ Taratoo

Deep in the Amazon rain forest, in what is now Brazil, the Warua people used this mock battle to resolve disputes without bloodshed. If the people of one village had a complaint against those of another village, their chieftains would meet to agree upon a date and place for the taratoo, and determine what penalty would be paid by the losing side. The date would be noted by marking a tree with a notch for each day to pass before the encounter.

During the interim, every man and boy in each village would prepare a shield. The shields were made of lightweight wood interwoven with palms, and decorated with colored tassels made of dyed plant fibers. On the appointed day the villagers would paint themselves festively with colored clay and march to the field, carrying their shields, and line up face to face with those from the opposite village. Each would select an opponent of about the same age and size. In the first phase of the contest the players stamped their feet and shook their shields, alternating between shaking the shields at one another and lifting them over their heads, all the while shouting *saki saki saki*. At a signal from the chieftains the two lines turned sharply and marched away from each other, still shaking the shields and shouting. At a second signal the two lines reformed, and the players pressed their shields up against their opponent's shields and began to push. The object was to push the opponent out of the line, and if possible to push him over. The cycle of marching and shaking, marching, and pushing was repeated over and over until one side conceded defeat and agreed to pay the penalty.

Make taratoo shields from several layers of corrugated cardboard. (Glue the layers so the "grain" of the cardboard in each layer is perpendicular to the layer above and below it.) Make two handles on the back by passing several lengths of twine through two pairs of holes in the shield, leaving loops in the back for the hands. Decorate the shields to make them both fierce and festive.

⊞ Toki

The early Spanish explorers described this headball game, played by the Chane people in what is now Paraguay and Bolivia, as "Indian tennis." Tennis had become wildly popular in Spain just a few years earlier. The toki ball was a small (tennis-sized) solid ball, made by rolling strips of rubber together. It was fairly light and very bouncy. The court was simply a few lines sketched in the dirt of the level street.

Teams had about twenty players (although smaller community games could be played by as few as three on a side). Players arranged themselves according to height, with the tallest in the back row and the front row crouching, the better to strike the ball. The server bounced the ball off the ground, after which the ball could only be struck with the forehead. Moving the ball with any other part of the body cost the team a point. Players dove recklessly to the ground to keep the ball in play, as a point was scored each time a team let the volley end.

Each team brought corncobs or kernels, which were used to count points, and the game continued all day. At dusk the team with the larger score enjoyed free drinks and the opportunity to jeer at the losing side, who went home empty but resolved to triumph at the next game.

An ordinary rubber ball will do nicely for a game of toki.

⊞ Ulamaliztli

Among the Aztecs who conquered Central America in the thirteenth century, the ball-court game reached its ritual pinnacle. While informal ball games continued as amusements of ordinary people, ulamaliztli was the work of professionals and the play of nobility. No game could begin until the deities had been installed in their niches in the court, and any game could be read as an oracle, a message from the gods. In addition the game was used to settle disputes between nobles and as a prelude to the sacrifice of prisoners. Temples and altars were constructed as integral parts of the ball court. A desperate man might wager his total debt on the outcome of a game: if he won, his debt would be cleared, but if he lost, he'd be sacrificed to the gods. Mythology asserted that the gods themselves played the game and by it determined victors and victims. The game was so intertwined with the religion of the Aztecs that the

Spanish conquerors, determined to free the local people from what they perceived as idolatry, had the ball courts destroyed, though the game continued to be played.

Like the chaah courts of the Maya, Aztec courts had a long narrow alley with high walls and two endcourts perpendicular to the alley with lower walls. Many of the courts, particularly in the north, had two stone rings set into the walls at the centercourt line, facing the players. Each ring had a hole in the center just bigger than the diameter of the ball (four to six inches). Some other courts were reported to have a hole in the ground at centercourt of a similar dimension. Although archaeologists have not found any such courts, it is possible that these small holes would not have survived the intervening centuries.

Players were not as heavily protected as among the Maya, wearing a simple leather girdle and deerskin skirt over the hips and thighs. Players' hands were generally protected with thick gloves. Teams were evenly matched, with two or three players being the norm for professional games: one in the alley and one or two in the backcourt. Nobles frequently played one on one.

A referee determined, probably by lot, which team had the opening serve. Professionals used only their hips and knees to strike the ball, and a point would be awarded to the opposing team if any other part of the body was used. Amateur players had a bit more leeway, but never used their hands. The ball was solid and heavy, although extremely bouncy: a player struck in the stomach with the ball often died, and players routinely had to have their bruises lanced to allow the collected blood to escape.

Points were scored by getting the ball over the opponent's end wall or when a team failed to return the ball before it stopped moving. In addition a player could score by driving the ball toward his opponent in such a way as to cause him to hit the ball with a prohibited part of the body. The game was played to a previously agreed-upon number of points, unless a player accomplished the rare feat of putting the ball through the stone ring or into the circle in the court. This score instantly won the game for that player's team, and in addition entitled him to the cloaks of all the spectators, or at least those supporting the losing team— a rule that resulted in a chaotic rush for the doors when it occurred!

The suggestions for recreating a chaah court can be used for ulamaliztli, too. Make side rings by cutting holes just a bit larger than your ball in corrugated cardboard or lightweight wood, and mount them on the side walls of your court. (If the gym has hoops for crosscourt basketball you can just designate them as the goals.) A four-square ball is about the right size for ulamaliztli, and happily quite a bit lighter. A plastic playground ball can be used if basketball hoops are serving as goals.

⊞ Wrestling

Different forms of wrestling were practiced in different parts of South and Central America. In the Amazon wrestling was an important social practice, and men visiting other villages were expected to wrestle each of the male residents as a way of establishing their friendly intentions. The men also wrestled whenever they got together for funerals, weddings, or other occasions. On these occasions the wrestlers would be matched according to their size, experience and skill. The village champions wrestled first, and then the other men. Finally teenagers and boys wrestled against one another and against their elders, to develop their skills. The wrestling styles of the different rain-forest tribes were somewhat similar, and village elders would agree in advance what the rules of the match would be. Normally the two wrestlers faced each other, bent at the waist, and on the signal grasped each other around the chest. The object was to bring the opponent down, usually so that the back, shoulders, or nape of the neck touched the ground. Just one throw determined the winner of a match.

In the mountains there is some evidence that people wrestled from a seated position. Wrestlers began sitting or kneeling side by side, facing in opposite directions. At the signal each leaned over to grasp the opponent around the waist or shoulders. The object was to pull the opponent forward off the ground.

For wrestling you need an open area, either grassy or matted. Players should agree in advance on the rules to be used. Kicking, tripping, and any kind of scratching are, of course, prohibited. Players pair off according to weight and skill, and referees watch for illegal or unsafe moves.

⊞ Xocotl Climb

During the Aztec "feast of the Dead" the men and boys of the city of Tenochtitlan formed a line and danced a serpent dance through the streets until they arrived at the xocotl tree: a tall log which had been erected in the temple courtyard, decorated and laced with ropes. At the top of the tree stood a little dough figure, dressed in a festive paper costume. A ring of warriors, wielding pine rods, guarded the tree. The serpent dance dissolved into a sea of bodies, as the men plunged toward the tree, dodging or taking the beatings of the warriors, and began to climb. As many as twenty men might cling to the same rope, and all around the tree men and boys climbed, higher and higher until one finally reached the top and grabbed the dough figure. The victor crumbled the figure, sprinkling the pieces on the throng below. When everyone had climbed down, the tree was knocked to the ground and the victor escorted to the temple to be rewarded.

Given the importance of this annual ritual, it is very likely that tree and rope climbing were among the activities boys and young men practiced during their leisure time, perfecting the skills that might someday lead to their grasping the dough xocotl from its lofty post.

If you have access to a playground or gym with climbing ropes or a climbing structure, you can practice this Aztec climbing battle. You can make a xocotl figure from refrigerator biscuit dough and dress it in a paper costume. Decide who will guard and who will climb—there should be at least twice as many climbers as guards. Arm the guarding team with foam sticks (the "noodles" sold for swimming toys are good). The attacking team approaches, each one with hands on the shoulders of the person ahead, and circles the xocotl's stronghold, closing in until the first warrior guard swings a stick. Then the attacking team breaks up and the clamoring begins.

⬛ MIDDLE EAST

The part of the world we call the Middle East was, during the period of this book, predominantly governed by the Byzantine and then the Ottoman empires. The region had been united by Alexander the Great and then absorbed into the Roman Empire. After the fall of Rome the power center shifted east toward Persia. The religion of Islam further united the people of this far-flung region, creating a culture that stretched from North Africa to the Indian subcontinent, a bigger territory than we tend to think of as the Middle East today.

Local sheiks and sultans exercised supreme power, but always under the watchful eye of the caliphs and imans, religious leaders who were regarded as successors to Mohammed and therefore as authentic spokesmen of Allah. Caliphs were often succeeded by their sons or nephews, forming dynasties as powerful as any secular monarchy in Europe or Asia. The Abbasids in Baghdad and the Mamluk in Egypt dominated the region during the Middle Ages.

In this land of nomads and traders, geography was less important than religion, and ethnicity was defined by language, not nationality. Even today, Arabs are by definition those whose mother tongue is Arabic, regardless of their race, religion, or national origin. As Islam spread throughout this region, so did Arabic, so that most people spoke their ancestral language (such as Urdu, Farsi or Persian) along with Arabic. With few exceptions the activities described in this section were played throughout the region during the medieval era.

It is impossible to discuss the sports of the Middle East without reference to the sporting traditions of the ancient world. The Greek olympics and the Roman arena did not suddenly disappear with the fall of

Rome and the destruction of the Temple at Olympus. The circus and the hippodrome remained important in the lives of people in the Middle East into the ninth century. In addition to competing in officially sanctioned events, professional athletes traveled the countryside, competing against local amateurs.

In the land that three world religions called "Holy," religion shaped everything, including sports. The Greeks and Romans had celebrated the feasts of their gods with games. As the emperors claimed divine status, they added to the list of festivals. By the time the empire split in two, more than half the days of the year were designated public holidays. The tradition of "bread and circuses" served to keep the idle occupied and divert the energy and attention of the masses. The huge spectacles provided an opportunity for the emperor-gods to reveal their glory and shower their subjects with gifts ranging from sweets to farms. But the emperors who were most enamored of the games, Nero and Domition, were also the most fervent persecutors of the Christians, and thousands of arrested Christians became victims for the brutal animal displays. Roman gladiatorial contests had gradually replaced racing and wrestling as the focus of public games. In Rome, senses had been dulled by constant exposure to the violence. In the Middle East, the concept of watching men kill each other for sport was still a horror.

No wonder that when Christianity became the dominant faith, the games fell into disfavor. Even while still the persecuted minority, Christians had condemned the cruelty of the gladiator games and excommunicated anyone who attended them. After the emperor Constantine became a Christian, he began to limit and reform the games. But it was the cost of the spectacles that ultimately ended them.

Some Christian theologians condemned sports altogether. In addition to the orgy of violence, they cited the pagan rituals at the races and the fact that Greek athletes competed nude. Those who defended athletic exercises did not have to look far for their arguments. Beginning with St. Paul, Christian writers had used athletic competition as a metaphor for the struggle of the Christian life. Christian scholars cited St. Paul's remarks about footraces, shadowboxing, and wrestling to show that sports were not contrary to Christianity. Christian bishops encouraged games and provided places for people to play. Much of what we know about sports in the early part of the Middle Ages was recorded by bishops in this region.

Another religious tradition had an even greater effect on recreational activities in the Middle East. After the life of the Prophet Mohammed in the sixth century and the rapid spread of Islam, the history of sports and games in the Middle East is difficult to trace. While Christianity had disapproved of gambling, the Koran prohibited it, and any games associated with chance were included in this ban. Mohammed specifically forbade the playing of maysir, the "arrow game," because of the way it degraded those who became heavily involved in it, sometimes losing their belongings, their wives, and their freedom. Early on, the imans interpreted that prohibition very broadly, condemning as maysir every game except chess. They even included specifically the apparently harmless games of children such as jackstones.

The imans discouraged play of any kind except for small children and slaves. Play was considered worthless, a waste of time better spent on prayer and study. As Islam spread, the influence of these teachings was broadly felt, reducing both the variety of games played in the region and the willingness of writers to record them. Islamic clerics also prohibited sports except as training for war. The preparation for the jihad was an obligation of every person. Thus horse racing and archery were specifically encouraged, but elephant and donkey racing were prohibited as useless. Betting on the outcomes of races and fights had been the primary involvement of the spectators, so the prohibition on gambling effectively limited the participation of nonathletes in sports.

Finally, Islam prohibited animal fighting as cruel but it proved impossible to eradicate (as indeed it still is today). Most popular and widely practiced was cock fighting, in which roosters were trained to fight against each other. Ram fighting was popular, and dog fighting was also common. The early Abbasid nobility spent enormous sums buying, training, and maintaining animals for fighting, although these contests were not lawful under Islamic *sharia*. One ninth-century caliph (spiritual head) attempted to ban all animal fighting and ordered the slaughter of all the animals in the royal zoo, but the suspension of the fights was apparently temporary.

Greek athletes had competed nude, oiling and dusting their skin before the competition. Christianity frowned upon public nudity, and Islam prohibited it, so during the Abbasid period athletes wore the tubban and sudra, a sort of shortened trousers and waistcoat. These may be the origin of the wrestling uniforms worn by the Mongols, who in the twelfth century conquered most of the Middle East as well as all of Russia and a large part of Asia.

GAMES

▦ Al'zahr

Al'zahr, or jazara, is the Arabic word for dice, and gave its name to the European gambling game hasard (see entry).

Dice had their origins in the use of astragals among the ancients. Astragals are knucklebones, usually from sheep. When tossed or rolled they generally land on one flat side or the other, but they may land with the curved side up or down, and, rarely, standing on one end. By giving each possible position a point value, ancient people created an instant counting (or gambling) game with the bones. The most common position, on the flat side, was worth just one point. Curved side up was worth two or three points, and curved side down worth three or four points. Standing on end earned the player six points.

From the astragal it was a short step to six-sided dice: simply whittling down the rounded top of the knucklebone and marking each side with pips for points. Dice were common in the Middle East, roundly condemned by the clerics but constantly popular.

Another variation on the astragal game assigned values to different combinations of positions. This game was most often played with four bones, and the most valuable combination was to have one bone land in each position.

▦   As Nas

As nas was a five-handed card game played in Persia (Iran today). Although the earliest written records of the game come from the seventeenth century, we have examples of playing cards suited to the game from the medieval time, so it seems reasonable to conclude that as nas or a very similar game was played during the period.

As nas was played with a five-suited deck. The most common suits in Persian cards were cups, coins, swords, and staffs or polo-sticks. Other, more unusual suits included slaves, shells, fans, or harps and crowns. Numbers were not written on the cards, and elaborate background decoration sometimes makes it difficult to count the number of cups, swords, or other objects in the picture! The backs of the cards were plain.

Persian decks typically included ten number cards, a king and a vizir, so a five-suited deck would have sixty cards. Some decks included two other, lower officials as well, which would bring the total to seventy. Islam's ban on representation of the human figure eliminated court cards, so decks from Muslim regions had only number cards. As nas does not require court cards. The seventeenth-century accounts of the game refer to a twenty-five-card deck: a single court card and four numeric cards in each suit, suggesting that the game was simplified over the years to make it faster and to make the cards easier to hold. A deck containing any multiple of five will work for as nas.

Each player was dealt two cards, which they examined. Beginning with the player at the dealer's left, each player might choose to play (by paying a stake into the pot) or to drop out. After each had made a choice, the dealer dealt two more cards to each and the process was repeated.

Finally the dealer gave each remaining player a single card to complete their hands.

Players now showed their hands, and the player with the best combination won the hand and the pot.

The best combination possible was five cards of the same suit. Next would come five of the same rank, one from each suit. In decreasing order of value would come four of the same rank, three of one rank and two of another, three of one rank, and finally two of one rank.

You can adapt an ordinary deck of cards to play as nas by using the six through ten of each suit and making a fifth "court" suit with an ace and jack through king. For a more interesting game make a set of cards from posterboard. Choose five suits and design a simple drawing for each. If you include court cards, the king card should show the king seated under a canopy with at least one of the symbols in the picture. The vizir is always riding—usually on horseback but sometimes on a camel, an elephant, or even a tiger. Again, be sure the symbol of the suit is also in the picture: the king may be holding a cup or being presented with a sword, for example.

⊞ Atlanbaj

This game from Palestine was played on an eight-by-eight-square grid, painted on a board. Each player had sixteen pieces, generally light and dark disks or stones. When the game began the pieces filled in the second and third row on each side. Pieces moved one space at a time, forward or side to side (not diagonally). They captured by leaping over an enemy piece into an adjacent vacant square, and one piece could make multiple captures in the same turn. When a piece reached the eighth row, it became a king. Now it could move horizontally or vertically any number of vacant spaces, and capture any piece in its line of motion even if there were vacant spaces between it and the piece it was capturing. This made the king a very powerful piece. The winner was the first to capture all the opposing pieces (the game was also won if one player had only a king and the other had just one piece left).

⊞ Buqayri

Buqayri was a simple guessing game from Abbasid Iraq. One player made a pile of sand and, holding an object in one hand, buried both hands in the sand. The other player had to guess which hand was holding the object. In fiyal, a variation on this game, the player hid the object in one of two piles of sand. The other player had to guess which pile hid the prize.

⊞ Byzantine Chess

Byzantine chess was one of the many variants that developed from shatranj as it spread in the Middle Ages. This unusual game was popular in Byzantium (now Istanbul) around the turn of the first millennium.

The sixty-four squares of the shatranj board are here realigned in a circle: four circular rows, sixteen columns; like a dartboard with the bull's eye missing. The pieces are the same as in shatranj: each player has a shah (king) and counselor, two elephants, two horsemen, two chariots and eight foot soldiers. The pieces were lined up on opposite sides of the circle, with the shah and counselor side by side in the inside row, the two elephants next to them in the second row, the horsemen in the third row, and the chariots in the outside row, flanked with a column of footsoldiers on each side. Shahs moved one space in any direction and chariots could move in and out or around the circle any number of vacant spaces. Counselors moved one space on any diagonal and elephants moved two diagonal spaces in any direction. The foot soldiers moved a single space at a time, in their own rows away from their superior pieces. All pieces captured by replacing a piece. In addition, if two of a player's foot soldiers in the same row met each other coming around the circle they were both removed from the board.

The object of the game was to get the shah in a position where he could not escape capture. A player could also win by reducing the opponent to "bare king," having no other pieces on the board.

⊞ Dittar Pradesh

This Pakistani game was the simplest form of gambling, a lottery. Sixteen cowrie shells served as the dice, and any number could play. Players paid stakes into a pool and chose a number, 1 through 16. The caster shook the cowries and cast them on the ground. However many fell mouths up determined the winning number, and the player who called that number collected the stakes and became the caster for the next round. If no one called the number that came up, the pot grew richer as players bet again and the new stakes were added to the old.

⊞ El qirkat

El qirkat, or Alquerque, came into Europe with the Moors, but the game dates back at least to the second millennium B.C.E. in Egypt (Figure 6.1).

The el qirkat board was a four-by-four-square grid with each quarter divided by two diagonal lines. As the game was played on the points,

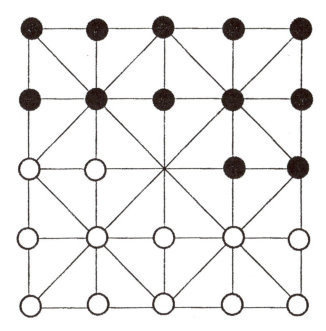

Figure 6.1. El qirkat began with just a single empty spot on the board.

or intersections, this made a twenty-five-position board. Each player had twelve pieces; generally just disks of distinct colors. When the game began each player's pieces were aligned along the two home rows and the two points to the player's left of the vacant point of the center row. Pieces moved one point at a time, in any direction along a line. If a piece was adjacent to an opponent's piece and the next point was vacant, the player was required to capture by leaping over the opponent's piece to capture it. If the piece that made the capture was then in danger of capture it could move again, in any direction, including to capture another piece. The winner was the player who captured all of the opponent's pieces.

⊞ Ganjifa

The playing cards of India and Persia were miniature works of art. Cards were made from layers of paper, recycled from its original uses and glued together with gum, then cut (usually into circles), painted and lacquered. Each court card, painstakingly designed and painted, was a fabulously detailed scene of court life. Even some of the number cards represented hours of careful labor, showing eight beautiful slave girls or ten ferocious lions, for example.

Persian ganjifa decks had ninety-six cards, eight suits of twelve each.

Most scholars believe this represented a doubling of the four suits in the Mamluk Egyptian cards, which were probably the ancestor of both Indo-Persian and European playing cards (see entry in European games). One very early document (a love poem) lists the suits as slaves, crowns, swords, gold coins, harps, documents (or scrolls), silver coins, and stores (or trading). Other suits often seen included polo sticks, jinn (genies), arrows, and various animals such as lions and bulls. Each suit had two court cards, a *shah*, or *mir* (king), and a *wazir* (minister). Half of the suits were "strong" and ranked ten as the highest number card. The other half were "weak" and the ace was the highest ranked number card. This distinction was generally shown by the color of the cards. The shah was always shown seated on a cushion or under a canopy, holding or receiving the symbol of his suit (so the king of documents might be shown reading a scroll, the king of stores inspecting merchandise, etc.) The wazir was always riding—sometimes a horse, sometimes an elephant, sometimes a fantastic creature.

Most of the games played with ganjifa cards have vanished into the past, the rules never written, and the knowledge of them dying with the old ways of life. The game described here is a simplified version of a ganjifa game.

The basic ganjifa game was a simple trick-taking game. On every turn each player contributed a card and the player who played the highest-ranking card took the trick. There were no trumps, no obligation to follow suit, and one rule which eliminated most of the finesse tricks associated with modern card games: a player holding the highest outstanding card in any suit (the *hukm*) was required to lead it. In fact, specific rules determined most leads. But the game was in fact anything but simple, for success depended on knowing and remembering exactly what had been played—which of the ninety-six cards had fallen, and which remained.

Ganjifa games were for three players, and the whole deck was dealt out at once, so each player began with thirty-two cards. Generally players sorted their cards and placed their low cards in a pile rather than trying to hold all their cards in their hands. The player holding the highest shah card had the first lead, and lead that card along with any low card, which was called the throne. The other players played two cards each from their "worthless" piles, knowing that the high shah card would win both tricks. Then the first player led again.

In the first phase of the game, the rules were designed to prevent a player from running through a single suit capturing trick after trick. Instead the player with the lead was required to play any *dukkals* in her hand. A dukkal was any sequence of cards beginning with the hukm, and including as many cards in sequence as were in her hand except the lowest one. Since each of these cards was, in its turn, a winning card, the other players simply added a matching number of cards from their worthless pile to complete the multiple trick. Failure to play a dukkal resulted in all the cards in the dukkal being "burnt" or losing the ability to take tricks.

Next, the player with the lead had to check to see if she had a *deni*, which was the wazir without the shah. If so, she was required to "give the deni," by playing a low card from that suit, allowing the player who held the matching shah to win the trick and the lead. Next, if she did not have a deni, the player had two options. She might choose to give up the lead at once by playing a *talafa*, a low card in any other suit for which she did not hold the hukm. Then the player who had the hukm would have the lead. Her other choice was to lead all the hukm in her hand at once. This was called an *utari*. Having collected all those tricks, the player then turned the rest of her hand (which by definition contained no winning cards) face down, and the other two players agreed on a card at random to be led to the next trick.

The same rules applied to any player who had the lead, until each player had had and lost the lead at least once. By that point in the game, the number of cards in play had been cut significantly. In the second phase of the game, players were still required to lead dukkals and give deni as before, but when playing a talafa the player could play any card face down and name the suit she was calling (thus forcing out the hukm of a suit and creating a new hukm in her hand). In the second phase of the game the hukm were played one at a time, not simultaneously. As cards were played and taken any card might become the hukm for its suit. Low cards could become winners, and high cards could go to waste if the holder was not able to retake the lead.

On the last trick the card led was called the *akheri*. Generally it was the hukm for that suit, but if it was not, the player who beat it was said to have "killed the akheri." If both players beat the akheri it was called *rangeri*.

The game was won by the player who took the most tricks. Capturing more cards than what the player began with gave the holder an increasing advantage, because in subsequent rounds, players who finished the game with fewer cards than they began with were required to pay the winners however many cards they won by: that is, if one player finished with 36 cards (12 tricks) and the others with 30 (10 tricks) each, then each of the losers owed the winner 2 cards at the start of the next round. In practice they passed the winner 2 cards before they had looked at them, and the winner, having sorted his or her cards, returned to them 2 cards from a worthless pile so that the hands remained even. A loser who beat the akheri in the previous round did not have to pay the forfeit.

Figure 6.2. Kawakib was sometimes called the zodiac game: each piece represented a different celestial body and each section of the board represented a different sign of the zodiac. *Source*: Morencos (1977). Copyright Patrimonio Nacional.

⊞ Kawakib

This complex gambling game was popular among the Persians and played for a while in Spain. The board was a circle of seven concentric rings, representing the Moon, Mercury, Venus, the Sun, Mars, Jupiter, and Saturn, the celestial bodies of the Ptolemic solar system. The whole circle was divided into twelve equal sections, each representing one of the signs ("houses") of the zodiac (Figure 6.2). Within each ring, each section was divided into as many spaces as it was numbered from the center (so that the first, or Moon, ring had one space in each house, the second [Mercury] had two, etc.).

Seven players each controlled seven pieces, one in each planetary ring, beginning from the left-most section of that planet's "favorite" house. (Saturn starts in Aquarius, Jupiter in Sagittarius, Mars in Scorpio, the Sun in Leo, Venus in Taurus, Mercury in Virgo, and the Moon in Cancer. (No pieces began in Aries, Gemini, Cancer, Pisces, or Capricorn, and in the Alphonso X manuscript (see the introduction to Europe) the board pictured had only seven zodiacal sections.) The game was played with a seven-sided die along with two regular dice: the seven-sided die determined which piece a player moved, and the regular dice determined how many places were moved. (So, as an example, a player who rolled a 4 on the long die and a 5/2 on the regular dice moved his "sun" piece seven spaces around the fourth ring.)

Virtually every move resulted in money being paid and received, based on the relationships between the planets. If a player entered a sign controlled by another planet ("in conjunction") he paid that player 12, and 72 to the player controlling the house "in opposition" (directly across from the sign entered). He won 24 from the players whose signs were "in sextile" (at a 60-degree angle) to the house he had entered (2 ahead or behind). He won 36 from a player controlling the signs three houses distant ("in trine," a 120-degree angle) and paid 36 to a player whose sign was "in quadrature," a 90-degree angle or four houses distant. (Note that all the payments were multiples of 12, in keeping with the astronomical theme, but could easily be 1 through 6 for ease of counting.)

To play kawakib you will need to draw or paint the board on paper or cardboard, collect or make a set of playing pieces (seven for each player, generally colored in accordance with the zodiacal sign's symbols) and, most challenging, create a seven-sided die. You may find it helpful to make a pattern from a piece of card stock for this. Draw a rectangle four by two inches. Divide it on its long sides into eight one-half inch segments. By folding along those lines, then overlapping and gluing the two end panels, you will have a column with seven equal sides. Use it to mark the ends of a dowel for cutting, or as a mold for modeling clay. Paint the seven sides with the colors and numbers of the different "planets" in the game.

⊞ Mancala

Mancala is the Arabic term for the game known as wari, oware, and adi in northern Africa (see the general description under Africa). By the medieval era the two-rank version of the game was popular throughout the Middle East.

The mancala board was two rows, each with six cups or depressions. There were sometimes two extra cups or storehouses, one for each player to store pieces in. (Many Muslim writers speak of a children's game called "fourteen," which may refer to the mancala board.)

To begin the game players set up the board by placing four pieces in each cup. To choose who would go first, one player hid a seed in one fist and held both fists in front. The other player guessed which hand held the seed. If the guess was correct, she went first. If not, the seed-holder did.

The first player picked up the seeds from one cup in the closest row, and beginning at the cup to the left of the one emptied, dropped one seed into each cup around the board, one seed per cup, until his hand was empty. If the last cup held more than three seeds, the player picked them all up and continued the turn. On any turn if the play came back around to the cup being emptied, players skipped over that one (so that it stayed empty).

If the last cup reached had two or three seeds in it (after the final seed was dropped), the player captured all those pieces and put them into a store. If the cup just before the one ended in had two or three seeds in it, those were captured as well, and so on back to the end of the opponent's row.

If the final seed dropped into an empty cup, or after the captures were completed, the turn passed to the other player.

The object of the game was to capture the most pieces. Play continued until one player won by capturing twenty-five pieces (more than half) or the player whose turn it was had no pieces in his row (in which case all the pieces on the other side went to his opponent). The game was a tie if each player had twenty-four pieces or the pieces kept moving around the board with no more captures being possible.

To play mancala you need forty-eight playing pieces. Depending on the size of the cups, marbles, pebbles, seeds, or small coins will work. You should be able to fit at least twelve pieces in one cup. An empty egg carton makes a serviceable beginner's mancala board, but shallower, wider cups are easier to scoop from.

⊞ Maysir

Maysir was a gambling game that was very popular among pre-Islamic Arabs. It was specifically condemned by the Prophet, so strongly that some of the commentators used the name of the game, maysir, to refer to any prohibited gambling activity. Still some Arabs continued to play the game, justifying it by making it a source of alms for the poor.

The game was originally based on casting arrows as lots. The prize was a camel, slaughtered, and divided into ten parts. (In some old stories there are ten camels, instead.) Ten arrows were cast, seven marked and three blanks. Each of the marked arrows represented a share of the camel: one notch was fadd and worth one share; two notches, tau'am, was worth two; kakib, three; hils, four; nafiz, five; musfah, six; and mu'alla, seven. Players chose which arrow to play, and paid according to its value (the mu'alla cost the most to play). One player might pay to play more than one arrow, or one arrow could represent a team of players who pooled their resources to bet.

The arrows were placed into a quiver, called a *ribahah*, with a small opening in its top. This was held by the *hurdah*, a nonplayer of certain honesty. He shook the ribahah and then shook out or drew out an arrow. The player of that arrow won the first section of the camel. If it was a blank it was returned to the ribahah. The hurdah continued, shaking out arrows until the total of the shares marked on the arrows drawn equaled ten (this could be as few as two arrows, or as many as four if the 1, 2, 3, and 4 were drawn). Those whose arrows were drawn collected their share of the camel meat, and those whose arrows were not drawn paid for the camel, the cost prorated according to the shares they had purchased. In addition, if the shares drawn equaled more than ten, the losers had to compensate the winners for whatever shares they were not able to collect.

It was considered a sign of extreme stinginess for a wealthy person to refuse to play maysir, and great generosity to give one's winnings to the poor. In Islamic times a version of the game developed in which the camel was divided into ten unequal pieces. The players of the winning arrows collected particular sections based on their value, so that there would always be at least three, perhaps more, sections to be distributed to the poor.

You can play maysir with ten dowels for arrows, and a quiver made from the can that potato chips or tennis balls come in. Play for a bag of mini-chocolate bars or some other prize that can be easily divided into ten shares.

⊞ Nardshir

Nardshir was the Persian version of a game that dates back to the time of the Pharaohs and is still played around the world today (Figure 6.3). It was known as irish in Europe and today we call it backgammon, but in the Middle East it was nard or nardshir, from the Arabic words for "battle" and "wooden table." Since Islam prohibited gambling, there were supposed to be no stakes in nardshir, a rule which was mostly ignored.

Two players sat opposite each other and moved their pieces in opposite directions around the board. The board had four quadrants, each with six lines or points, usually long triangles. Each player had fifteen pieces, either light or dark colored disks. According to Islamic tradition the twelve points represented the twelve months and the thirty men are the days of the month.

The object of the game was to remove the pieces from the board ("bearing off") while preventing the opponent from doing the same, and the first to remove all fifteen pieces was the winner. No pieces could be taken off the board until all of a player's pieces were in the home quadrant.

When the game began, each player's pieces were placed on the board

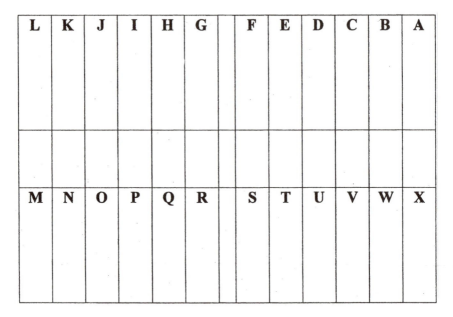

L	K	J	I	H	G	F	E	D	C	B	A
M	N	O	P	Q	R	S	T	U	V	W	X

Figure 6.3. Letters are assigned to the sections of the nardshir board when describing games.

with two in the near right corner and six in the near left corner. On the opposite side of the board, three pieces were on the fifth point from the left and six on the sixth point from the right. Since each player moved counterclockwise, this meant each began with two pieces as far as possible from their goal, and six already in the home quadrant.

Play was determined by rolling two dice. Each number on each die was played separately, so a player could move one piece according to one die and another according to the other, or one piece might move first one number and then the next. (Although this resulted in a move of the total, it was considered two separate moves, so the piece had to be able to land on the end point of one or the other numbers.)

To begin the game each player rolled a single die and the player with the higher total moved, using the two numbers just rolled.

A piece could land on any vacant point or any point occupied by up to four pieces of its own color. If a piece landed on a point occupied by a single one of the opponent's pieces (a "blot"), that piece was knocked off the board. No piece could land on a point occupied by two or more of the opponent's pieces, and no more than five pieces of the same color could occupy one point.

When a piece was knocked off the board, it had to be re-entered "from the bar" (the line across the middle of the board) into the far quadrant (the opponent's home board). It could only enter by the roll of a number that would allow it to land in that board. Thus a player could block re-entry of pieces by filling as many points as possible in the opponent's home board with two or more pieces.

Pentalpha

Pentalpha was a Greek solitaire game played on a board that was a five-pointed star, drawn so that the lines created a pentagon in the center. This made ten points, or intersections: one at the end of each point of the star and one at each corner of the pentagon. The player had nine pebbles, and the object of the game was to get them all onto the board.

Each pebble was placed in the same way: it was entered on one point, then moved along a line to a second point and again to a third point, where it was placed. The second point did not have be vacant (the piece can jump) but the entry and final points for each pebble had to be vacant, and the three points had to be in a straight line.

Draw a pentalpha board and collect some pebbles to give it a try. It can be done!

Qirq

Qirq was the merrels game played in Palestine and the Arabic world (see Merrels entry in Europe). Both three-man and nine-man versions were played. The board for three-man qirq was a square divided into quarters. The nine-man board was three concentric squares, divided by lines from the midpoint of the sides of the center square to the midpoint of the sides of the outer square.

As with the European game, the object of qirq was to build *mills* or three-in-a-row lines. Players began by placing their merrels on the board, then moving them, one space at a time from point to point along the lines, to create mills. Completing a mill entitled the player to remove an opposing piece from the board, but pieces that were in mills could be captured, unless there were no other pieces available. The game was won if one player had only two pieces left, since he then could not make mills.

Shatranj

This direct predecessor of chess developed from the game invented in India in the 600s. It spread rapidly and developed through a number of variations into the chess we know today. (For details, see Chess entry in Europe.)

Shatranj was played on an eight-by-eight-square grid, the squares not colored. Each player had sixteen pieces: eight soldiers, one king and one counselor, two elephants, two knights, and two chariots. As the game changed and moved into Europe the counselors became queens, elephants became bishops and chariots became castles, which explains why the modern chess castle can travel so rapidly across the board.

Pieces were set up as in modern chess. Beginning from each player's left home corner the order was chariot, knight, elephant, king, counselor, elephant, knight, and chariot. The soldiers filled the second row.

Soldiers moved one space forward at a time and captured on the diagonal. All other pieces captured by landing on a spot occupied by an opposing piece. Chariots could move any number of spaces in any direction along a row or column. Knights moved in an "L" shape, two spaces and then one or one and then two, in any direction, and could leap over other pieces. Elephants moved two spaces on any diagonal and could leap over other pieces. Counselors moved one square diagonally, and kings moved one square in any direction. The king could also move like a knight, one time in any game, but not if he had been previously in check. "Check" meant that an opposing piece could on one move reach the space occupied by the king.

As in chess, the object of Shatranj was to put the opposing king into a position where he could not escape capture (checkmate) or where he could not move without moving into check (stalemate). (Stalemate could also mean neither player could checkmate the other.)

Soldiers that reached the opponent's home row might be promoted, always to the piece that had begun the game in that square, and only if that piece had been captured. Thus no one could have more than one counselor or two elephants, and no promotion could be made on the king's square.

You can play shatranj with modern chess pieces if you remember that the pieces move differently. For a more authentic game you may choose to make playing pieces from modeling dough. A noncheckered board is simple to make on a piece of wood or cardboard.

⊞ Siga

This Egyptian game is believed to be very ancient, and remained popular throughout the medieval period. The board was a grid, five-by-five, seven-by-seven, or nine-by-nine squares. It could be etched in stone or scratched on a board, or the spaces could be scooped in the sand for an impromptu game. Each player had twelve pieces, called *kelb* (dogs). Pellets of goat or camel dung, pebbles, sticks, beans, and broken bits of pottery were all used as playing pieces.

In the first stage of siga, players took turns placing their kelb on the board, two at a time. Traditionally the first pieces were placed in the squares in the middle of the outside edges, one player placing his or her pieces north and south and the other east and west. The remaining pieces were placed randomly, leaving the center square vacant. No captures took place during this part of the game.

Once all the pieces were on the board, players began moving and capturing. A piece could move horizontally or vertically and forward or back, but not diagonally. The first move was always made into the vacant central square. Captures were made by surrounding an opposing piece on two sides, but moving your own piece between two opposing pieces did not cause it to be captured. The center square was a sanctuary—no piece could be captured there.

If a player had no possible move the opposing player moved again, choosing a move that would open a space for his opponent. The game was over when one player had only a single piece left.

▦ Sulahai

This game from Pakistan was a gambling game with two parts. Four players sat at the four points of the compass. Each was assigned four numbers, beginning to count counterclockwise from west, so west had 1, 5, 9, and 13, south had 2, 6, 10, and 14, east had 3, 7, 11, and 15, and north had 4, 8, 12, and 16. The caster shook sixteen cowrie shells and predicted what number he would cast, then rolled the cowries out on the ground. The count was how many fell mouth up. If the caster's prediction proved true, each of the other players paid the caster a stake, but the player assigned that number paid two stakes. The caster then rolled again. If the prediction proved false, the caster had to pay one stake to each player, and two to the player assigned the number that came up. The holder of the winning number became the caster for the next round. If the caster rolled one of his own numbers, the other players paid him a double stake, even if it was not the number he had called. If the caster rolled a zero, meaning no cowries fell mouth up, it was considered a sign that the game should not continue.

You can buy cowrie shells at craft stores, or play this game with any small objects that have an "up" side and a "down" side.

▦ Tab (or Kioz)

This Egyptian game of lots, or rods, was prohibited to Moslems but popular throughout the Arab world from Persia to North Africa. The board was four rows wide and could have anywhere from seven to twenty-nine cells across. Each player began with one piece (called a *kelb*, or dog) in each of his home row cells, and moved back and forth: left to right in the home row, right to left in the second, left to right in the third, and then right to left in the top row. Landing in a cell occupied by an opposing piece captured that piece, and the winner was the player who captured all the opposing pieces (or who had the most captives when the game ended by agreement).

The number of places moved was determined by the casting of the rods, which were black on one side and white on the other. One white side up was called tab, and was worth one space. Each kelb had to be moved the first time by a throw of a tab, and all tabs had to be used to move new pieces until all had been moved at least once. For two, three, or four white faces the player moved any piece already on the board that many spaces. No white faces equaled a six. A player continued to roll and move until rolling a two or a three, which ended the turn.

In the second row and beyond, *kilab* (plural of *kelb*) could be stacked and moved as a single piece, an *eggeh*, or king. The eggeh could be dismantled again only by throwing a tab to move a single piece.

Single kelb could be moved back across the second or third row rather than advancing to the fourth row. Once in the fourth row the pieces were dead, unless the player had no other pieces to move.

Kioz, or the walnut game, frequently condemned by the commentators, was a children's version of tab, played with nuts on a board of four rows and twenty-two holes. The kelb, being round, could not be stacked, and a roll of one was called *kioz*.

PLAY

▦ Aporrhaxis

This familiar game was played from Roman times on in the Middle East. The player tossed a ball into the air and then attempted to keep it aloft by hitting it with the hands, feet, knees, and probably elbows. As the player developed skill it is likely that a particular sequence of hits was required: first one hand and then the other, then each elbow, then the knees, and then the feet, but this is difficult to prove from the evidence. If more than one person played, dropping the ball ended the turn.

Pictures show aporrahaxis being played with balls the size of apples or softballs as well as with larger balls similar to a modern soccer ball. The smaller balls were made of skin stuffed with feathers and did not bounce (rubber was unknown). The larger balls were inflated pig or sheep bladders and would have rebounded when hit.

You can make a ball like the smaller balls of leather or use balls made for

juggling. A small beach ball is probably the closest equivalent availabe today to
the larger aporrhaxis ball.

⊞ Astragals

Astragals, or sheep's knucklebones, are mentioned in ancient texts and shown on pottery from the Greek and Byzantine era. By the Middle Ages they had already developed into six-sided dice (see ah'zahr), but they also continued to be used by children for "jackstones" games.

The object of the astragal game is to pick up the bones in a particular order or with certain hand motions before catching another bone tossed into the air. Tossing up one bone, the player had to pick up one bone, catch the falling bone, pass the single bone to the other hand and then repeat the process until all the bones were picked up. Next the player repeated the sequence, picking up two bones at a time, then three, four, and five. The game could be made more complex by requiring the player to move the bones from one place to another or to clap or tap the ground before picking up the bones.

⊞ Azm Waddah

Azm waddah was a game for playing in the dark of night. The only item necessary was a white bone. Players divided themselves into two teams. One person threw the bone as far as he could into the darkness outside of the camp or village. Immediately all the players took off in that direction, hunting for the bone with their hands and feet. The player who found the bone was rewarded with a ride back on the shoulders of the other team.

⊞ Bayd

In this Arabic game, sometimes called "egg jousting," children held hard-boiled eggs in their hands and tried to strike one another's eggs. The player whose egg cracked first was the loser, and the winner got to eat the cracked egg.

No changes are necessary to play this game today!

⊞ Bayga

Bayga was a children's race game. A piece of cloth placed on a fence-post was the goal. Each pair of players represented a horse and rider. The "horse" stood in front and held his hands behind him as the reins. The "rider" stood behind him and hung onto his hands. At the signal all the pairs of players ran toward the finish line. To win, the "rider" had to capture the cloth.

⊞ Boules

Boules was a ball game similar to bocce (See Europe). The rules in the Middle East were just slightly different from the versions played in Europe. This version was recorded in Byzantium. The playing area was a flat surface of hard-packed dirt or pavement. The target could be as simple as a designated stone or tree. Players were divided into two teams, and each player had three wooden balls. The first player tossed a ball at the target. Since that was the only ball on the court, it was the closest to the target regardless of where it fell, so that player's turn ended. The second player tried to position a ball closer to the target than the first. She might either toss her ball closer or use one of her balls to strike the other player's ball and move it away from the target. Once she had a ball closer to the target than the opponent's, her turn ended and the next player on the starting team tossed. If a player used up all three balls without successfully landing closest to the target, that turn ended. When all players on both teams had completed their turns, the team with the ball closest to the target received a point for each ball they had landed closer than any of their opponent's balls. The second team went first for the next round, and play continued until one team reached a score of fifteen.

⊞ Dabkeh

Dabkeh was a line dance, generally danced by men and boys in Asia Minor and Palestine. There were many regional variations of the dance. Often men held handkerchiefs in their hands and danced with their little fingers linked and hands above their heads. Sometimes the men danced with their arms over each other's shoulders, and only the leader at the end of the line held the handkerchief high. In any case the dancers had to watch and follow the leader, who could improvise on the basic form of the dance, adding steps, stomping, hopping, and turning as the dance repeated and accelerated.

Here is a simple beginning to a dabkeh. The line stepped (usually eight steps) first to the left, then to the right. Next turning to face right, the dancers stepped sideways, taking a deep step with the front foot, then bringing the back foot to meet it, and stomped the back foot, repeating that step forward, then back, and turning to face left, did the same. Next they might repeat the steps while turning the body from one side to the other while moving first to the left, then the right.

Dara

Dara was the Arabic name of the familiar "what have I got in my hand?" game. One child held an object behind the back and challenged the others to guess what it might be, or which hand it was in. The player who guessed correctly became the next one to hide an object.

Fanzaj

Fanzaj was one of several circle games played by women and girls in what is now Pakistan. Eight to ten people formed a circle (facing one another) and linked hands. First the circle turned in one direction, then in the other. Then the players ran into the center, raising their hands in the air, and then back out until their hands and arms were outstretched. Now the leader let go with one hand, turned and moved back along the line of players, weaving under one pair of outstretched arms and then back through the next, with the whole line following. When she reached the end of the line they closed the circle and danced in and out again. Then the next girl in line broke free and weaved through the line.

Hora

Most Westerners only know the hora as a dance for wedding receptions, but in the Middle East there were and still are many different hora circle dances that celebrated different aspects of community life.

The most familiar lyrics are from Hebrew:

> Havah nagila, (Gather together),
> havah nagila,
> havah nagila,
> ve-nisme-cha! (Let us rejoice!).
>
> Havah ne-ranena, (Lift up your voices),
> havah ne-ranena,
> havah ne-ranena,
> ve-nisme-cha! (Let us rejoice!).

Dancers formed a circle, facing center, with hands linked or arms around one another's shoulders. (In many Middle Eastern cultures women only danced with women and men with men, so there were separate circles.) The circle turned first in one direction, then in the other. Dancers stepped on the left foot, crossed the right foot behind the left and stepped on to it, then stepped to the left on the left foot again. Next the dancers kicked first the right foot, then the left across the body. This motion was repeated around the circle and then in the other direction, around and around until the dancers were exhausted.

⊞ Junabi

Junabi was generally a children's game although adults might sometimes join in. One team of players hid a basket, and the others tried to find it.

⊞ Khasa-wa-zaka

Guessing games are universally popular. This version comes from the eastern part of the Middle East, the land known today as Punjab. In this guessing game each player began with a small handful of beans. Players paired up. The first player in each pair put some beans in one hand and held it out in front of his opponent, asking "odd or even?" The other player guessed, and then the first player opened his or her hand to show the correct answer. If the guess was wrong, the guesser had to give the questioner a bean to make it correct. Now the roles reversed. After each player in a pair had been both questioner and guesser, the players changed partners and played again. Play could continue until one player had no beans left, or for an agreed-upon length of time. Then everyone counted and the player with the most beans was the winner.

⊞ Khatra

Khatra was played during the Abbasid era in Arabia. To play khatra children would braid a whip out of rags. The players divided into teams. One player held the whip, and tried to hit the members of the opposing team with it. They in turn tried to get the whip away while the child's teammates tried to defend him or her. The child holding the whip could toss it to another player. If a member of the opposing team caught it, they won the game and were treated to a ride on the backs of the losers.

⊞ La'b al-dabb

La'b al-dabb, or the lizard game, was a Bedouin guessing game with at least two variations. In the first version, a player drew a lizard in the sand, and then covered one portion of the lizard with his hand. The other player, blindfolded or with her back turned, had to try and guess which part of the lizard's body was covered. In the second version the blindfolded player was told to touch a particular part of the lizard's body. If she was successful, she would have the next turn to name the spot to be touched.

⊞ La'b al-rumh

La'b al-rumh, the lance game, or stick fight, was a popular amusement for children and adults in Persia. Each player would arm himself with a rod or stick held against the side as if carrying a lance. On the other arm the players had shields, and the game was simply one of running and parrying blows.

You can use wooden or foam sticks and shields made from corrugated cardboard to play la'b al-rumh.

⊞ Madahi

Madahi, or masadi, were round stones used for children's games. Players tried to roll their madahi into a hole. They could also hit the madahi of the other players to knock them away from the hole. The loser had to give the winner a ride on his back. (A version of this game played with walnuts was condemned as a gambling game because the winner got to eat the walnuts.)

You will need marbles, stones or walnuts to play this game. For version two, each players' stones need to be marked so you can tell whose they are.

Version one: Draw a circle five feet in diameter in the dirt and dig a small hole in the center of the circle. Each player rolls one stone toward the hole. If it drops in, he gets to keep it. If it misses, he leaves it. The next player whose stone drops into the hole captures all the stones left in the ring.

Version two: Draw a circle and dig a hole as above. Each player puts an equal number of stones into the circle. Players take turns trying to knock their own stones into the hole, or knocking the other players' stones away. The first player to get all her own stones into the hole wins the game.

⊞ Oonch Neech

Oonch Neech is a tag game still played in Pakistan. One child was "it" and attempted to tag the others. A player was safe from being tagged if he could get up off the ground: climbing a tree, getting on a chair, jumping on to a rock, or any other object provided sanctuary.

⊞ Phaininda

In the public baths and at the beach people enjoyed playing various games with colorful balls. Some were inflated and presumably floated and others were stuffed (and presumably did not). Phaininda appears to have been a type of team dodgeball: players attempted to pass the ball back and forth to their teammates and keep it away from their opponents, but also attempted to hit their opponents with the ball.

A beach ball is perfect for phaininda, but any large ball will do. Divide players into two teams. Teams line up facing each other to begin the game. Throw the ball into the air. Each team tries to capture the ball. When you have the ball you can try to hit an opposing player with the ball or pass it to a teammate. When you do not have the ball, you try to intercept passes without being hit. If you are hit with the ball, you are out. If you can catch the ball you get possession and try to hit players from the other team. A team wins when all the players on the other side are out.

▦   Sadw

This Arab walnut-pitching game was consistently condemned by commentators on the Koran as an example of a gambling game, but it was apparently very popular anyway! Players dug a hole in the sand and, from a distance, tossed walnuts into the hole. If the winner claimed and ate the walnuts, the game was considered a gambling game and prohibited. The game was considered more acceptable if played with small stones instead, presumably because they couldn't be eaten.

Version one: *Players take turns tossing the nuts toward the hole. Whenever a player lands a nut in the hole, all the other players must pay her one nut.*

Version two: *The game begins with one nut in the hole. The first player tries to toss a nut from the starting line, about ten feet away. If he hits the nut in the hole, he has another shot. If he misses, he leaves the nut where it fell and the next player has a turn. The first player to hit the nut in the hole three times claims all the nuts on the ground (including those in the hole).*

▦   Samaja

Samaja appears to have been a sort of Persian blind-man's bluff, played by adults at masquerades. Coins or other prizes were tossed among the blindfolded players by the presiding noble, and the players used their hands and feet to find them. The game was written of with great disapproval as it provided plenty of opportunity for groping and other unseemly behavior!

To play this game you will need blindfolds for all players and a number of small prizes (gold-foil-wrapped chocolate coins work well for this). Select a fairly open, level area, either indoors or out, where players can stumble around without getting hurt. Players spread out across the playing area and blindfold one another. When everyone's eyes are covered, the presiding "noble" tosses the prizes into the air so that they rain down across the playing area. (A broadcast "seeding" motion is better than throwing the coins straight up.) On the signal "now," players scramble to collect as many prizes as they can find.

Shahma

Shama resembles some playground games of our own era. Two teams attempted to capture a child who was "it." The team which managed to surround "it" was the winner. Losers gave the winners a ride on their backs before challenging them to another game.

Snail

Snail was an Arabic form of hopscotch. Children traced a large spiral in the dirt: the snail. The object was to hop around the spiral on one foot, pushing a stone with the toes. The player to go first dropped a small stone in the "mouth" of the "snail" (the outside edge of the spiral). Holding the left foot in the left hand the child hopped on the right foot, nudging the stone along with her toes. When she reached the center of the spiral she was allowed to rest and, in some versions, to change feet. Then she had to push the stone back to the mouth of the snail. If at any time she pushed the stone across the sidelines of the track her turn ended.

Trigon

Trigon was played with small feather-stuffed balls the Romans had called folli. Three players stood in a triangle, each with a ball. The game was to keep all three balls in motion, tossing and catching them from one player to the other. The game could be played cooperatively, establishing a rhythm and making the effort to toss the balls so they would be easy to catch. It could also be played more competitively, throwing the ball hard in an effort to force another player to drop the ball. Spectators formed a circle around the game and entered the game to replace a player who dropped or missed the ball. (The rule was that if you threw the ball out of bounds you had to go after it and were replaced, which discouraged wild throws designed to be impossible to catch.)

SPORTS

Birjas

Birjas was a Byzantine competition designed to test and rank horsemen archers for the military. It was held in the hippodrome and the public display of honor or dishonor added to the tension of the game. The competitors rode in, one after the other, and had to shoot at the target (a small hoop mounted on a pole) in front of the judges. They were judged not only on the accuracy of their shot but also their form: remaining still in the saddle, keeping the horse's reins under control while shooting. Based on their performance the archers were designated as "excellent," "mediocre," or "inferior," and their pay for the year to come was adjusted accordingly.

You can play birjas on roller skates or skateboards. Make target rings from braided straw or cut them from cardboard or a plastic lid. If you make more than one size target you can have different levels of difficulty for each round. Tie or nail the ring to a stake or broomstick and stand it in a bucket of sand at the center of the playing area. Be sure that all the spectators and judges are behind the players! Players ride into the lane one at a time, shooting at the target as they pass. Judges score each player on their form: speed, balance and smoothness of the ride, as well as whether or not their arrow passes through the ring.

▦ Boat Racing

River travel was important in the commerce of the Middle East, and wherever traders moved goods up and down river by boat, sailors and boat owners competed to see which boat could complete the trip most quickly. The city of Baghdad was built over and around the Tigris River and four canals laced through its streets. On festival days the streets and bridges filled with cheering spectators as speedy little *dhows* with their triangular sails skimmed along the canals. Repeated warnings from the clergy against betting on races remain as evidence of the popularity of these races.

▦ Boxing

Boxing was one of the old Olympic sports that survived into the Middle Ages. The rules specified that blows were to be directed only at the head. Boxers wore leather helmets and ear protectors, and wrapped their fists and arms with leather for protection.

The *caestus*, a spiked leather strap over the fist, was a fearsome addition to the boxer's equipment. There were no rounds or breaks in the action, and boxers continued pounding each other until one surrendered by raising his index finger to acknowledge defeat. A referee watched for illegal hits and declared fouls, but did not interrupt the fight.

▦ Buskashki

This medieval game is still played by Pushtu nomads in Afghanistan. It is excellent training in the skills of hunting and fighting on horseback.

Teams can have as few as five or as many as a thousand players, and the size of the field depended on the number of players in the game.

A large circle is drawn in a field, and the carcass of a calf or goat is placed in the center of the circle. The players, on horseback, align themselves around the circle, with team members alternating. On the signal everyone rides into the circle to attempt to capture the carcass by hooking (or lassoing) it and dragging it out of the circle.

There is a prize for the player who succeeds in capturing the animal, as well as a point awarded to his or her team. Then the carcass is replaced in the circle and the game begins again. Play continues until one team reaches an agreed-upon winning score or until the carcass falls apart.

You can play buskashki on scooters. Stuff a sack with old clothes and sand (it should be fairly heavy and lumpy, not evenly distributed). Each player needs a stick with a hook on one end: the hooks made to hang clothes on the back of a door are good: about the right size and with rounded ends. Draw a chalk circle on the pavement and place the "carcass" in the center. Players line up around the outside of the circle, alternating teams. At the signal, everyone rides into the circle and tries to secure the "carcass" and drag it out of the circle. Once a player has hooked the "carcass" his teammates may try to keep the opponents away from it while he drags it out, but no deliberate crashing or bumping into other players is allowed.

▦ Chariot Races

Chariot races were introduced into the Middle East by the Romans during the years of the Roman Empire, and became one of the central features of life in Byzantium. Virtually everyone in the city was affiliated with one of the four teams (two, in later years) Blue and Green, Red and Yellow. Like modern Mets and Yankees fans, the divisions between these spectators extended far beyond the hippodrome to their politics and social interactions.

Several kinds of chariots were raced in Roman and Byzantine times. Those drawn by two or four horses were the most common, although as many as ten horses were sometimes driven together. The more horses on a team, the greater the challenge for the driver to keep all the horses together and coordinate their movements through a fistful of reins. Collisions and rollovers were not uncommon, and many a young man died in a tangled heap of reins, wheels, and horses.

Seven laps around a track of roughly 900 meters equaled one race. Tracks were straight up one side of the hippodrome and down the other with *spina* (posts) at each end of the track, which the driver had to turn around and come back. These sharp turns were the site of most of the serious accidents.

One uniquely Byzantine twist in chariot racing was the *diversium*. After a race had been won the winning and losing drivers exchanged their chariots and competed again, presumably to determine whether the victory was due to superior driving or superior equipment.

Chances are you don't have horses or chariots available, but even in medieval times children played at chariot racing with carts for chariots and playmates for horses. Today a teammate on a bicycle can substitute for a horse, with a wagon towed behind as the chariot. Lay out a track for the race, being sure there is plenty of room between the lanes so riders don't collide. A straight racetrack avoids the danger of the turn around the spina. One team should wear blue and the other green, and the fans wear and wave matching colors. The "emperor" stands on a platform or other high point and signals the start of the race by dropping a white cloth, and they're off!

▦ Episkuros

Episkuros was a popular ball game in the later years of the Roman Empire and the Middle Ages, and not unlike today's rugby. Two teams of equal size faced off against each other across a line marked with stone chips. Goal lines were similarly marked at each end of the field. To begin the game the ball was placed on the centerline, and on the signal both teams attempted to gain possession. Once in control of the ball, players attempted by throwing and catching (not kicking) the ball to carry or drive it over the opposing team's goal line, while the opposing players attempted to intercept or capture the ball and carry it the other way. The ball was probably a pig's bladder stuffed with hair, which would be about the size of a modern volleyball.

To play episkuros mark out a playing area on grass or dirt (traditionally sidelines were not marked). The more players you have, the larger the field should be; in reality people played in whatever space was available. Make a ball from leather or use an underinflated playground ball.

▦ Falconry

The sport of falconry, or hunting with birds of prey, is really two sports: the hunt, which is the supposed purpose, is sometimes almost secondary to the satisfaction of training the birds. The Abbasids were avid falconers, raising and training several different kinds of hawks for a variety of hunts.

To train a bird to hunt the falconer first had to tame it and train it to come to the falconer and sit on his arm. This training took time and patience, as well as techniques of depriving the bird of light, food, and sleep in order to make it compliant. Once the bird was accustomed to standing on the falconer's arm and being fed, it was hooded (to keep it from being distracted) and brought out among people and into noisy places so it wouldn't be startled. Finally field training began. Training began with tethered rabbits, pigeons, or gazelles, and it took months to bring a bird to a level where the falconer could comfortably turn it loose to seek and bring down prey and reliably return to the wrist.

▦ Gladiators

Roman gladiators were recruited from the many prisoners taken in Rome's battles and trained in government-operated schools. They competed in the circus in hand-to-hand combat, generally fighting with the weapons of their own people. Typically they battled to the death of one or the other. In the medieval Byzantine circuses, in contrast, the gladiators were professionals, hired by the emperor or other nobles to represent them in the ring. They battled for a victory declared by the official, although many died in the process just the same. The gladiator fights were among the first of the Roman circus events to die out, but the modified, professional form continued at least into the middle of the sixth century.

▦ Harpaston

Harpaston was a team game played with a small ball. From contemporary descriptions it appears to have been very much like volleyball except that instead of a net, a player called the interceptor roamed the middle line, attempting to steal the ball as it passed from one team to the other. The object of the game was both to keep the ball away from the interceptor and to keep it from touching the ground, as there are descriptions of players diving to save the ball before it touched the earth. Points were probably awarded if the ball touched the ground in the opposing team's side of the court. In some variations it appears that the interceptor was out if he was struck by the ball, and it's not clear how the scoring system treated balls caught by the interceptor.

Harpaston is easily adapted for play on grass or in a gym. A "dead" tennis ball will do, or you can make a ball from leather stuffed with dry grass. Mark the midlines of the court with lime if you're on grass. Divide the players into equal teams. Each team will take turns putting in the interceptor. If a team's interceptor captures the ball it is returned to that team. If the interceptor is hit by the ball he or she is eliminated. Teams will gradually shrink as the interceptors are eliminated. The game ends when one team has no players left.

⬛ Horse Racing

As chariot racing declined in the early centuries of the Middle Ages, equestrian events gained in popularity. While only a few women ever competed in chariot races, women and children jockeys had the advantage of lighter weight in horse racing. Riders not only competed for speed over fixed distances but also performed acrobatic tricks, leaping off the horse and back on again, or from one horse to another. Relay races on horseback were popular. Riders also threw javelins at targets and rode at each other with lances in mock battle. Riding in formation and performing complex patterns were other popular entertainments, very much like the shows marching bands perform during halftime at football games.

Not only can you race on bicycles but you can also ride in formation and throw "javelins" made from broomsticks at targets. For battles a "lance" padded with foam is best.

⬛ Lion Hunting

The caliphs and other nobility of the Islamic empires loved to hunt, and the ferocity of the lion made it a particular favorite. Lions were hunted on horseback, and the horses had to be specially trained in order to overcome their instinct to run at the sight of the lion. The trainer would feed the horse near a wooden lion for a few days, and then near a caged lion in order to accustom it to the sight, scent, and sound of the beast. Finally the horse would be repeatedly ridden up to the lion cage.

The lion hunt itself was designed to make use of the horse's speed. The hunters would provoke the lion, throwing stones at it, or teasing it with spears and clubs until it began to chase them. A horse can run longer than a lion, so when the lion began to tire the hunter would turn back and shoot arrows at the lion from short range. Finally when the lion was quite exhausted the hunter would finish it off with a knife or sword.

For hunting practice the Arabs used an ingenious dummy—a four-wheeled chariot with a stuffed skin attached to the front and another attached to the back. The front skin represented the prey, and the back one represented the hunter's dog or other hunting animal chasing the prey; so the idea was to strike the first one and not the second! This chariot target could be towed behind a rider on horseback or rolled down a hill to provide repeated practice.

You can construct a similar dummy on a wagon.

Musajalah

Footraces are a universal sport. No one needs to instruct youngsters in the details of "I can beat you to that tree" or "Last one home is a rotten egg." In the Middle East foot races of various lengths were a common event at local market festivals and church holidays. They were considered an appropriate competitive activity for women as well as men. Nobles set up races among their slaves for their own amusement (and for betting, although this was forbidden).

The stadium run of the Olympics was a single lap around the stadium: about 200 yards. Twice around was called a double-race and twenty-four laps, or stadia, was called the cross-country race. After the Olympics were banned in the fourth and fifth centuries these races became festival activities, with the distances marked in the street in communities without hippodromes. One early race involved the added challenge of carrying full jugs of water.

Musara'a

Musara'a (wrestling) was a favorite sport among the people of the Byzantine Empire. Both common people and professionals wrestled, and there are records about the different rules used in professional matches and how they could confuse spectators.

The wrestling pit was lined with clay and oil to make it smooth. Rain often made these pits slippery, and training gymnasia were equipped with both dry and wet pits for practicing so the wrestlers would be ready for either condition.

In professional matches, players began standing. When the referee gave the signal to begin, they leaned forward and wrapped their arms around each other's torsos. The referee watched for stepping out of the circle or for any illegal move. The object was to bring the opponent down flat (face down or up) on the ground (simply touching the knee to the ground was not a fall). Three throws were needed for victory.

Pankration

Pankration was a sort of combination of boxing, kickboxing, and wrestling. Although it some regarded it as combining "bad boxing with bad wrestling" it was still wildly popular as a spectator sport. Pankrators traveled the countryside with their managers, and matches between them were set up in the town squares or local gymnasia.

Pankrators wore no protective equipment, and were allowed to kick and to hit any part of the body with either the fist or the open hand. Gouging, biting, and other unsportsmanlike conduct were prohibited but frequent. Unlike wrestling, when a pankrator brought his opponent down the battle continued, with both players rolling in the dirt, grappling for a hold and using hands, feet, and knees to pummel their opponent. The match ended by knockout, or preferably, when one fighter conceded defeat by tapping the other on the shoulder. To this end professionals attempted to hold their opponents in a position that would not allow the other to move without dislocating a joint.

▦ Rami al-nushshab

Archery competitions were one of the forms of athletic activity specifically encouraged by the Prophet because they were training for battle. Because they were one of the few exceptions to the no-gambling laws, archery competitions were very popular events.

Persian bows were of medium length, about as long as the archer's span with arms outstretched. Bowstrings were made of twisted silk cords in the winter or rainy weather and leather in the warm weather (leather is difficult to stretch when cold). Some archers strung their bows with two strings, enabling them to use thicker or thinner strings without changing bows.

The Turks were considered the best archers in the Muslim world, especially on horseback. Their bows were small (about as long as a man's forearm) and light. They were well-suited to shooting from horseback, whether in war or when hunting. Built of layers of wood, they were strung to bend against the curve of the wood so that there was a great deal of spring in the bow. The bowstrings were made of wound silk and the nocks, or notches, on the ends of the bow were carved of horn.

This kind of bow took a long time to build and is difficult to recreate in a simplified way, but a bow made from a short piece of green wood will do (see Appendix).

Arab archers were trained to hold their arrows between their fingers and draw back the bowstring with the thumb, rather than the index finger and thumb hold the Europeans used. Many archers used a ring or leather guard to protect the thumb from the bowstring, and a small shield on the wrist of the bow hand which helped support the arrow. Both long (thirty inches) and short (fifteen to eighteen inches) arrows were used with these bows, depending on the task. Arabs used a variety of arrows, selecting different materials and styles for different purposes.

Bamboo and wood shafts with flint or metal points were all common. Archers practiced shooting at hoops, dummies, and game birds.

Archery competitions included a number of events. Flight shooting was purely a distance competition. Target shooting was divided into close range, distant, and moving targets. One target was a mock-up of a horseman stuffed with straw with a disk for a head and a shield at its side, each worth a different number of points when struck. Another was a gourd, mounted at the top of a tall pole. In another event four targets were set equidistant at the four compass points from the archer, who stood in the center. The archer began with four arrows in his hand and was required to shoot at all four targets without moving his feet. Trick shooting was a crowd-pleasing favorite, as archers took aim at a variety of targets, shot over their shoulders, behind their backs, under their legs, or fired more than one arrow at a time.

Sawlajan (Polo)

Polo, or sawlajan, probably developed in ancient times in the Mongolian steppe. During the Middle Ages polo was very popular throughout the Arab lands (Figure 6.4). Several versions of the game developed in different places. In Persia, polo became the national pastime and was played very much like modern polo.

The size of the field and the teams could vary, but the field was always very large: 150 to 200 yards wide and as much as 600 yards long. Teams were equal and fairly small: four to ten on a side. Goals were twenty-four feet wide with stone goal posts. The wooden balls were about the size of an apple. Polo sticks varied through time, beginning as a sort of "spoon" shape and gradually developing into a mallet.

By the medieval era the players' roles were distinct: there were goalkeepers who excelled in blocking shots and driving the ball away, and other players skilled in passing and shooting.

The game began with players aligned on the field: defenders back in front of their goals, attackers aligned on both sides of the centerline. The official rolled or tossed the ball into the middle of the field, and players raced for it, striking it so that it flew through the air toward the goal. (In India the ball was supposed to remain on the ground, but in the Persian game it could be airborne.) The game was divided into periods of specific lengths of time, each period ending with a bell. Both excellent stick-handling and excellent horsemanship were required for success in polo.

You can adapt polo for playground play on scooters using croquet sticks or field hockey sticks and a wooden ball from a craft store.

Figure 6.4. Sawlajan was a favorite game of Persian nobles. *Source*:
Dale (1905).

 Swimming

Swimming in Persia was done in an upright position, what we would call "treading water." Competitive swimming, therefore, was not a matter of how far or how fast one could swim but how long and how well. One noteworthy competition determined which swimmer could hold a tray full of drinks above the water for the longest time without spilling anything.

 Tyzhanion

Tyzhanion was a unique form of polo developed in Constantinople (Figure 6.5). Like ordinary polo it was played on horseback and the object was to control the ball and score goals. In this version, however, the ball was stitched of leather and stuffed: hard, but not nearly as hard as a wooden ball. The sticks had not wooden mallets, but woven racquet heads, like lacrosse sticks. This variation enabled the players to drive the ball along the ground or to scoop it up and toss it, either passing to a teammate or shooting at the goal.

With these innovations Tyzhanion became more a game of horsemanship and less one of strength. It also became a game for women as well as men.

Adapt tyzhanion by using scooters in place of horses, as with polo. Use lacrosse sticks or make a netted head by curling a slender branch into a "u" shape and lashing it to the shaft. Use netting from an onion bag or make a net from twine to cover one side of the head, leaving just enough slack for the ball to rest in the net (if it's too loose the ball will get caught in the net, too tight and it will be very difficult to carry the ball at all).

 Venationes

In the Roman circus one of the prime entertainments had been the wild animals. Huge numbers of lions, tigers, rhinos, elephants, bulls, and bears were kept beneath the coliseum and killed in the circus. Sometimes the animals were set up to fight and kill one another; sometimes they were used to kill prisoners; and sometimes they were fought by *bestiarii*, gladiators who specialized in fighting with animals. Training animals to fight, and then watching and betting on the fights remained an extremely popular sport in most of the medieval world.

In the Byzantine era these venationes, or animal battles, went through a gradual reform. While bloodletting was not unknown, the action was much more stylized, and the bestiarii were really acrobats, teasing and racing the animals before leaping to safety behind gates, upon platforms,

Figure 6.5. Tyzhanion was a form of polo played by women in Constantinople. *Source:* Dale (1905).

or into baskets that were hoisted above the reach of the beasts. The *canisterium*, a sort of mechanical egg, was particularly amusing to spectators, as the animal would push it around the arena the way a cat chases a catnip mouse. When the animal abandoned the canisterium, the acrobat inside could move it, sneaking up on the animal to startle it into further activity.

⊞ Weight Lifting

Weight lifting was not one of the Greek Olympic sports but was used in strength training, especially by wrestlers. The Abbasid caliphs encouraged and participated in weight-lifting contests. One caliph renowned for his strength was reported to have lifted nearly one thousand pounds over his head and taken several steps!

Accounts of weight lifting report the use of weights made from stones specifically for lifting (generally by the carving of handles on the stones). Other accounts tell of champions lifting ordinary objects such as wheelbarrows and iron doors.

To stage a weight-lifting contest, collect and weigh a variety of objects to use as weights. Have competitors take turns lifting first the lighter objects, and then the heavier ones. In each case the athlete must lift the object and carry it at least three steps, and put it down without dropping it.

⊞ Zijal

Zijal, or pigeon racing, was very popular during the time of the Abbasids. Although some clerics condemned it as a cause of gambling, it was ultimately approved as being useful for warfare, as trained pigeons served as message-couriers in battle.

Arab pigeon fanciers bred pigeons for speed and intelligence, keeping meticulous records of the lineage and performance of the birds. Trainers began teaching pigeons to return to their lofts as soon as the birds developed their flying feathers. Later the trainer began feeding the pigeons on a feeder at the roof of the house. This taught the birds both to return and to find their way around the city. Over time the trainer would carry the birds in baskets and release them a little further away each day, rewarding them when they returned home quickly. Because pigeons mate for life, the trainers would be sure to take only one of a pair flying on each day, keeping the mates in the dovecote as an added incentive for the birds to return.

Pigeon races sometimes covered distances of hundreds of miles, with the birds flying from one city to another or from the coast to an inland city. There are reports of birds flying from Cairo to Damascus in a single flight: a distance of more than six hundred miles. On the days of pigeon races spectators gathered on hillsides and rooftops to watch the birds arriving.

▦ NORTH AMERICA

Geologically the continent of North America stretches from above the Arctic Circle to the Isthmus of Panama, but for purposes of this book Central America and South America are combined under the heading of Latin America, and this chapter is focused on what is now the United States and Canada. While this decision reflects some significant cultural distinctions, the reader should keep in mind that the line between the Southwest of what is now the United States and the northern portion of what is now Mexico is only a river. It is safe to say that the desert Anasazi of what is now New Mexico and Arizona had more in common with the Mayan and Aztec people than with the Algonkian in the Northeast or the Inuit in Alaska.

The history of the people of North America before the arrival of the Europeans is sometimes difficult to document, as most of the Amerindians did not keep written records, and their oral histories often died with them in epidemics of diseases that arrived with the Europeans. Archaeologists believe that the people of the Americas arrived via a land bridge from Asia into Alaska before the last Ice Age, not all at once but in several different migrations. The Ice Age that ended eight thousand years ago drove the ancient peoples south into the narrow southern tip of the continent. Then as the glaciers receded and people spread out across North America, they developed distinct cultures that still had many common features derived from their shared history.

Archaeological evidence and the reports of the early settlers reveal a complex society. If we define a "nation" as a group of people sharing a common language, a number of different nations shared the continent. In the eastern woodlands, people lived in relatively small communities, mostly as hunters. In the Plains, the people were nomads, following herds of bison. In the Southwest there were larger, permanent communities with as many as ten thousand inhabitants, and agriculture was the predominant way of life. The Northwest was home to a society of forest fishermen, while far to the north, the Inuit and Aleut people had adapted to arctic and subarctic conditions. (Their nearest neighbors, the Algonkian, dubbed them "Eskimos," or "people who eat raw meat.")

Religiously, socially, and politically, these were very diverse cultures. Some groups were monotheists; others had many gods. Some lived in villages of tiny homes with just their immediate families, others built large communal dwellings, each housing twenty or thirty members of a band directed by a single head of household. A dozen or more such houses made up a town. The "apartment buildings" of the Pueblo Anasazi are well known. Some native groups had democratic forms of government; others were run by a small elite. The Iroquois League was a complex alliance that became the model for the American Republic. In the Northeast the Algonkian peoples had hereditary leadership positions.

Despite these differences, the sports and games of these varied peoples had much in common. Darts, arrows, and other target games developed skills necessary for hunting and for warfare. Games of chance provided entertainment and were sometimes used to seek guidance from the spirit world. There were dozens of ball games and hoop-and-pole games, hundreds of bowl and pit games, and perhaps thousands of stick games played in North America. Variations of the moccasin game were played from Newfoundland to New Mexico. All of these games shared basic structures and rules for play. Ring-and-pin games might be made from bone and antler, wood and leather, even bundled cedar needles, but the basic form of play was the same for all of them.

One North American sport that many people think of as ancient is sled-dog racing, but for the Inuit people of the far north, sled dogs were a form of transportation and especially of cargo transport. The first recorded sled-dog race wasn't held until 1908.

GAMES

▦ Agitci Kanahamogi

Many of the North American natives played stick games that rewarded a sharp eye and skilled hand. This version of the game, from the Sauk people of what is now Iowa, used 102 peeled willow twigs or straws, about one foot long, and a single, slightly longer stick with a point at one end, which was painted.

The willow sticks were held in a tight bundle, stood on end and then released, so that they fell into a tumbled heap. The object was to separate a predetermined number of sticks from the pile. Having examined the pile the player announced how many sticks he would separate (always an odd number) and pushed the dividing stick through the pile and into the ground. The sticks separated from the pile were counted. If the player succeeded in dividing the sticks as he predicted, he won one point and played again. If he had not, the turn passed to the next player. The game ended when one player had reached the predetermined number of points.

A variation of this game was played by the Huron. The complete bundle of sticks had to contain an odd number. The first player divided the pile and took the sticks as he or she separated them from the pile. The other player took the rest, and both counted their sticks. The player with the odd number won the hand.

To make a set of agitci kanahamogi sticks, cut willow twigs or use bamboo splints (see Appendix). You can also use broom straws, although they won't hold up as well. Purchased "pick-up" sticks work, but you will need several sets to make the game challenging.

⊞ Awithlaknakwe

This Zuni board game from the Southwest could be played by either two players or by four. If four played, partners sat opposite each other.

The awithlaknakwe board was a grid of twelve-by-twelve squares with six extra squares centered on each of the four sides (Figure 7.1). All the squares were divided on both diagonals. The pieces were one-inch disks of stone or, more often, clay. Half had a hole drilled through them to distinguish sides.

Each player began with six pieces placed in the six extra squares on their side of the board. Pieces moved one space at a time, only along the diagonals, or "trails." Moving horizontally or vertically was called "crossing the canyons," and only "priest" pieces had the power to cross canyons.

The object of the game was to move all ones pieces to the other side of the board, and to capture opposing pieces on the way. A piece was captured by being surrounded—that is, maneuvering one opposing piece to each side of it. Captured pieces were removed from the board. Partners had matching pieces, and could cooperate in capturing opposing pieces. An unusual feature of awithlaknakwe is that the first piece lost by each player or team was replaced with a "priest of the bow"—a larger piece which could "cross a canyon" (move one step forward horizontally or vertically) as well as moving along the trails (diagonally). No piece in this game could move backward.

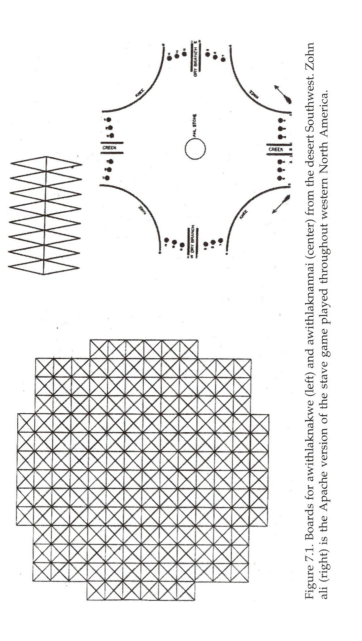

Figure 7.1. Boards for awithlaknakwe (left) and awithlaknannai (center) from the desert Southwest. Zohn ali (right) is the Apache version of the stave game played throughout western North America.

You can draw an awithlaknakwe board on paper or make a permanent game on a board. Buttons, checkers, or coins will work for playing pieces. Be sure to have two larger disks for the "priests of the bow."

▦ Awithlaknannai

Awithlaknannai was played by the Zuni. Because it is similar to ale-querque (see El qirkat in Middle East) some scholars have suggested it developed in Mexico after the Spanish introduced it there. Others believe it was pre-Colombian, pointing to archaeological evidence.

This game was played on a board of twenty-seven (see Figure 7.1) points, a line of nine in the center with lines of eight on either side, laid out so that the outside points fell between the inside ones. A line down the middle connected the nine inside points, and zigzag lines from each of the outside points to the two nearest inside points created eight tri-angles on each side of this center line. One player sat at each end of the board. Each player began with twelve pieces, eight on one outer line to his left and four on the center points closest to the player, so that the middle point on the board was empty. (The whole board could be dou-bled, in which case each player began with twenty-four pieces).

Players moved any piece one step in any direction along a line into a vacant space. Pieces captured one another by leaping over an opposing piece into a vacant space just beyond it, removing the captured piece from the game. Players were required to make a capture if one was possible.

This game board can be sketched on paper, painted on wood, or scratched on stone. Small stones or clay disks make authentic playing pieces, but checkers or coins work well.

▦ Bowl and Pit games

Variations of bowl and pit games were played all over North America. The playing pieces (dice) were sometimes flat seeds like plum stones, disks cut from antler, bone, or wood, or pebbles (Figure 7.2). The flat sides of the pieces were marked, sometimes simply painted or charred black and sometimes decorated with elaborate carved designs.

The tossing dish might be a basket, a wooden bowl, or even a blanket. In each case the pits were tossed and caught in the bowl, and the player earned points based on the combination of face-up and face-down pits. Most games included sticks for keeping score.

▦ Chun Wiyushnanpi

Chun wiyushnanpi was a Dakota stick game played with a large bun-dle of green sumac sticks. One of the sticks was marked. One player

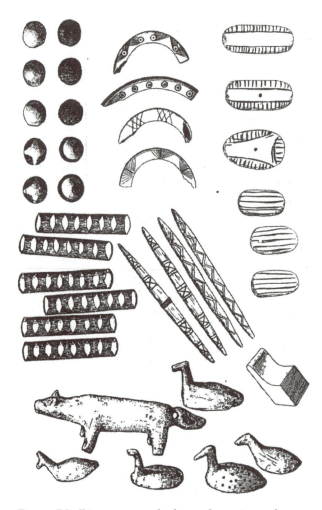

Figure 7.2. Dice were made from plum stones, beaver teeth, bone (left to right, top), split sticks, carved sticks, bone (center), and ivory (bottom). *Source*: Adapted from Culin (1975).

divided the bundle into two portions and the other would choose one portion. The player with the marked stick would win the hand.

▦ Congaree Estimating

This simple game was played by Congaree women in what is now the Carolinas with a bundle of fifty-one split reeds, about seven inches long. The first player mixed the reeds in her hand and then tossed part of the bundle to her opponent, who had to catch them and guess how many there were in her hand.

⊞ Crows' Feet

The Cherokee lived in the southeastern part of North America. They made string and fabric from plant fibers, especially wild hemp and the inner bark of the roots of the mulberry tree. The Cherokee also spun string from the hair of possums, bears, and bison.

For this Cherokee string game you need a string from four to six feet long. If your "string" is a piece of hide you can stitch the ends together. Otherwise bind or tie the ends together to make as small a lump as possible.

Lay the loop open across your lap. With hands face down about six inches apart, slide your little fingers under the near string. Hook your index fingers over the far string, draw toward body over the near string and then slide the index fingers under the near string. Then turn your hands over and hook index fingers under the far string of the loop as it extends beyond your hands. Draw it toward you and bring it up between the index strings and little finger strings, dropping the far string off the index fingers as you bring the new strings up.

Finally, drop the cross string from the middle and fourth fingers (or use your thumbs to lift the palmer string over the middle and fourth fingers). Turn your hands toward you as you spread them apart, and crows' feet will appear at each end.

⊞ Ga-hi-ki (Butterfly)

The Navaho and Pueblo were accomplished weavers who spun cotton string for making household items from rugs to clothing to net bags. This string was also useful for games and figures. Later, after the Spanish introduced sheep to the area, the Navaho adapted their skills and began to make the woolen blankets for which they are known today.

This Navaho string figure works well with a string about sixty to seventy inches long. Try to make the knot as small as possible or bind the ends together.

Begin with the loop between your thumbs and index fingers (Figure 7.3). Cross the right hand in front of the left to make a small loop. Bring your index fingers through the small loop toward you, then put your thumbs away from you through the large loop. Straighten your index fingers and spread your hands apart, palms out.

Hang onto the thumb string by bending your thumbs, and twist the index finger loops five times by bending the index fingers down toward you and straightening them up again. Insert both thumbs from the bottom through the index finger loops, and separate the thumbs and fingers as you turn your hands

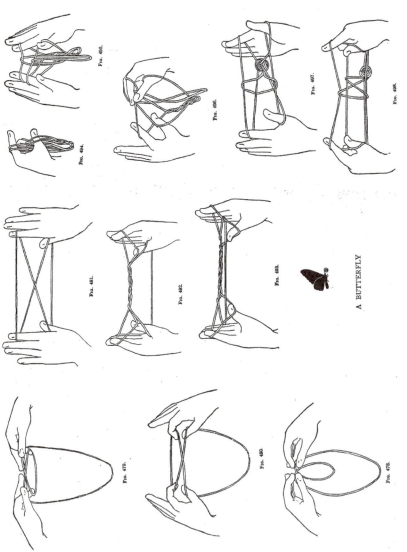

Figure 7.3. Ga-hi-ki is a Navaho string game. *Source:* Adapted from Jayne (1906).

*toward each other. Use your teeth to lift the lower thumb loop up over the thumb
(and over the upper thumb loop) on both hands.*

*You now have, on each hand, a triangular loop around the thumb and one
around the index finger, with a double strand stretched across the middle
through several twists. The next step involves switching the direction of the
loops, not as complicated to do as it sounds.*

*First, bring your hands together and hang the right thumb loop on the left
thumb and the right index loop on the left index finger. Turn your left hand so
your fingers point away from you. Put your right thumb and index finger
together and place them beneath your left thumb between the two loops. Separate
your right thumb and finger, transferring those loops. Do not pull yet. You
now have the left-hand loops both hanging on the left index finger. Pinch both
strings between your right index finger and thumb and slide your left index
finger out. Now copy the transfer, placing your left index finger and thumb
between the left-hand loops and separating them to pick up those loops.*

*Pull your hands gently apart. The twisted strings coil into the butterfly's
proboscis. Use your middle, ring, and little fingers to pull the furthest-out index
string and the closest thumb string down and together to form the butterfly's
body. By moving your thumbs and index fingers you can flutter the butterfly's
wings!*

⊞ Gla'atagan

This game from the Haida people of the Northwest Pacific was played
with a piece of wood, bone, or ivory carved so that it had a block-shaped
base with or top that curved up on one side; sometimes described as a
"chair" shape (Figure 7.2, lower right). The block was held by the long
thin end and tossed into the air so that it would spin over and over.
Points were scored by the position of the block when it fell. Curved-side
down, so that it rested on the back and base of the block, or flat on its
longest side, earned one point. Standing on its base was worth two
points, and lying on its front or shortest side without tipping forward
was worth three points. If the block landed on one side or the other no
point was scored and play passed to the opponent.

*You can make a gla'atagan block from modeling dough (see Appendix) or
carve one from softwood.*

⊞ Hotchi-kin

Variations of stick games were played across the land using wooden
splints, willow twigs, fine bones, or porcupine quills. In this Hupa version a large number (fifty to one hundred) of sticks of equal length and
size were prepared, and one was marked with a line or notch around

its middle. The first player mixes all the sticks between his or her hands and then quickly divides them, holding out two bunches. The second player had to guess which bundle included the marked stick. This game was also a convenient way of determining which player or team should go first.

▦ Ja Chawa

This Omaha variation of a stick game began with the sticks piled in the center of a circle. Each player took a bundle, without counting how many he or she took. Once all the sticks were picked up, the player holding the smallest odd number was the winner. The trick here would be to pick up as few as possible, but since the picking up continued around the circle until all the sticks were taken, a player couldn't simply take one and be done.

▦ Moncimon

Bowl and pit games were the Native American equivalent of the modern poker game. Moncimon, a Cheyenne version, even looked rather like poker. The game was played by pairs of players sitting opposite one another. The playing pieces were five flat seeds or stones marked on one side, three with crosses representing human faces, two with bear paws. All were blank on the back. The game also required a basket woven of grass, about 8 inches across and 4 inches deep. Each person had eight counting sticks for scoring.

Scoring was based on the way the pits fell. Three crosses and two bears was worth eight points, an instant win. Two blanks and three crosses was worth three points. Two bears and two crosses was worth one point, as was two bears and three blanks or five blanks. Other combinations earned no points and ended the player's turn.

The first player tossed the stones up, smacked the basket against the ground, and then caught the falling stones in the basket. She calculated her score and collected scoring sticks from her opponent. She then continued until she lost her turn, when she passed the basket to the next person. The first player to accumulate eight points was the winner.

▦ Mukesinnah Dahdewog

Moccasin games were very popular in North America. The moccasins could be real moccasins but were often specially made for the game and sometimes were more cup-like than shoe-like. For this Chippewa version small moccasins were usually used. Four small shells, stones, wooden "pearls," or even pieces of stick were used for hiding. One of the four would be marked. Beans were the usual counters, though sticks could be used. One hundred two counters was a common number. The pointing stick was often decorated.

Mukesinnah dahdewog was often played between people of different villages or even different tribal groups. Players divided into two teams. While a single player was the hider or pointer in each round, his teammates assisted by chanting or drumming (if he was the hider) or by watching and giving suggestions to the pointer.

Four moccasins were turned upside down on a blanket, or partially buried in the dirt. The hider, holding the four shells in his hand, rapidly slid his hand under one moccasin after another, all the while waving the other hand, moving his body and chanting in an effort to distract the guessing team. Eventually he deposited one shell under each moccasin. Using the pointing stick, the guesser lifted first one and then another moccasin to reveal the hidden balls.

In some versions of the game the best score was given for locating the marked ball on the first try (ten points for finding it on the first try, five for the second, and one for the third). More often the guesser attempted to locate the unmarked balls first, and each unmarked ball uncovered before the marked ball was revealed added to the point total: if one unmarked ball was uncovered before the marked ball, the guesser won 10 points, if two, the guesser won 20, and if all three unmarked balls were uncovered the guesser won 50 points.

▦ Pissinneganash

To play this Narragansett variation of the stick game the dealer shuffled the straws and separated them into as many bundles as there were players. The bundles were then rearranged. Each player selected a bundle, and the one who chose the bundle with the odd number of straws was the winner.

▦ Reed or Stick Games

Many of the earliest European explorers in the Northeast commented that Native Americans shuffled and dealt rushes or straws in the same way Europeans used playing cards. As games that combined an element of chance with some learned skills, stick games could be considered the North American equivalent of card games in Europe and dominos in Asia. Sets of sticks consisted of from thirty to one hundred or more thin sticks, reeds or quills. The sticks were from four to seven inches long and very thin, so that a large number could easily be held in one hand.

The sticks were painted or carved in distinctive patterns: sometimes with lines and spaces, others with designs representing animals, birds, or fish. One stick, the *dijl*, was left unmarked.

Unfortunately most of the games played with these sets were never written down. We have details of only a few simple variations. It seems certain that since the sticks were marked differently, they must have had different point values or ranks, but the notes by European explorers nearly always admit to being unable to figure out the games. We can perhaps sympathize if we imagine trying to figure out the rules for poker, rummy, or bridge by watching the game being played in an unfamiliar language.

Sometimes the stick game was played in a fashion similar to the moccasin game (see Mukesinnah Dahdewog), with the dealer hiding the bundles of sticks under shavings or cloth, shuffling them back and forth and then challenging the opposing player to choose the bundle including the dijl (see Chun Wiyushnanpi, Congaree Estimating, Hotchi-kin, Ja Chawa, and Pissinneganash).

Slahal

Variations of this percussive guessing game were common in the Pacific Northwest. Slahal could be played by two to six players, or a larger group would be divided into teams, with a leader on each side who delegated the mixing and guessing responsibilities among his teammates.

The game required two pairs of bones, typically about two inches long. In each pair one of the bones had a thong tied around its middle or a line painted or etched around it. (For team play two pairs of bones might be used simultaneously). There were eleven counting sticks—ten matching and one "king" or "bull" stick, which was larger than the rest. The players knelt on opposite sides of a flat board or paddle, on which they drummed while the bones were being mixed. When the game began each side had five counting sticks, which they stuck into the ground on their side of the paddle (some versions of the game included a carved stand for the counting sticks). The king stick was laid beside the paddle. It would go to the side that won the opening play.

The referee handed each team a pair of bones, which they mixed, rolling them between the hands, on the thighs, or on the ground while teammates drummed on the paddle. When the referee shouted "now!" the mixers held out their fists, with one bone concealed in each. As the teammates offered suggestions, each mixer indicated where he thought the other had concealed the marked bone. The one who chose correctly received the first play, and the king counter was moved to that side, giving that side an advantage.

Play proceeded in the same way, mixing the bones and holding out the fists for the opponent to guess which hand held the marked bone. A correct guess won the guesser one of the mixer's counters and the next play. An incorrect guess forfeited two of the guesser's counters to the mixer, and the mixer played again. When one side had all the counters, the game was over.

A variation of this game involved tossing the bones, rather than hiding them in the hands. In this version points were scored (and counters claimed) by the way the bones fell: both round side up, both round side down, marked round side up and plain round side down, or plain round side up and marked round side down.

You can save bones for slahal from the dinner table and paint them, or make pieces about two inches long and rounded on one side from modeling dough (see Appendix). Each pair should have similar markings, but one should be noticeably plain in the middle while the other is marked there. Counting sticks can be left plain or painted and polished.

▦ Smetale

Most of the people of the Pacific Northwest played games with dice made of beaver teeth, which are semicircular, curved on one side, and about one and one-half inches long. Carved semicircles of wood were used for the same game. Some communities considered this a women's game; others strictly forbade women even to watch it!

The dice were paired: Markings on the dice designated two as male and two as female, and linked them in couples (so one pair might have three marks and the other four or five, the female marked with circles and the males with lines, or chevrons). One of the dice had a string tied around its middle. Most sets also included some kind of counters: small bird's bones, painted sticks, or seeds were common counters.

Two people could play the game or the group could be divided into teams. One player tossed the dice. Each combination had a different value: If all the blank sides or all the marked sides came up, the player earned two points. Any of the three possible pairs—two men, two women, or one "couple" face up and the other pair face down—earned the player one point. If the dice with the string landed face up and all the others were face down, that was worth four points. Any other throw earned no points and ended the turn. For each throw the player collected counters to record points scored. The game either ended when all the counters had been claimed or it could go on, with players capturing and recapturing counters, until one player had collected them all.

You can make smetale dice from modeling dough.

⊞ String Games

Amerindians made string from animal hide or sinew, plant fibers, and animal and human hair. String figures often illustrated stories or jokes. Grandparents taught complex figures to grandchildren, who practiced them and passed them down through the generations (see Crows' Feet, Ga-hi-ki).

⊞ Tingmiujang

The people of the arctic region are still well known for their beautiful animal carvings. This Inuit animal dice game was played with a set of fifteen small figures of people, birds, and animals, carved in bone, ivory, or wood (Figure 7.2).

Players sat on the ground around a board or piece of hide. The first player shook the pieces (sometimes in a bowl) and tossed them into the air. In the first variation of the game, the player got to keep any figures that remained standing. The next player tossed the remaining figures and so on around the circle. The player who collected the most figures won. A second variation of this game assigned points to each figure, and depending on the shape of the figure, different values if an animal landed upright or on its side. In this version each player tossed all the figures on each play, and the player who accumulated the most points won.

A third, faster variation gave each figure (and its points) to whichever player it was facing when it fell.

⊞ Totolospi

The Hopi game totolospi looks like Hawaiian konane (see Oceania) or French fierges (see Europe) but was played very differently. The board was a large grid with a diagonal line marked across its center from northwest to southeast. Playing pieces were clay disks, different kinds of seeds, or colored stones, and when the game began all the intersections on the board were covered except those on the diagonal line, with the dark pieces to the north of the line and the light pieces to the south of it. (So each side began with as many pieces as there are squares on one half of the board: if the board was a ten-by-ten-square grid, each side would begin with forty-five pieces and the ten spaces on the diagonal would be empty. The actual number of pieces in the game depended on the size of the board.) Players sat at the ends of the diagonal line (by the corners of the board). A stick charred on one side was tossed up to determine which side (light or dark) would go first.

Pieces moved horizontally or vertically, dark moving toward the southeast corner and light toward the northeast. Both players could move on the diagonal line but never across it. The pieces moved up and down the diagonal line, where all the contact between the pieces took place. A piece on the diagonal line with an empty spot behind could be captured by an opposing piece, so players kept all their pieces moving toward the line. The player with the largest number of pieces left when no more moves were possible was the winner.

You can draw a totolospi board on paper and play with coins, or paint it on a board, or etch it on stone and play with colored stones for an authentic game.

⊞ Vaputi

This hidden ball game sometimes had ceremonial significance for the people of the Southwest, although it was most often just played for entertainment. The four hiding tubes, made from wood or cane, were often decorated and named. Sometimes they represented gods, sometimes the directions North, South, East, or West. The game could be played as a divination ritual, to determine whether the growing season would be wet or dry, or what the outcome of a planned battle might be. Game tubes are often found in the dress of *kacina* dolls and were sacrificed to the war gods by the Hopi and Zuni people.

To determine which player would go first, the Zuni would flip a stone disk; dark on one side, and call "light" or "dark" the way modern Americans flip a coin. The Papago method of selection was virtually a game in itself: they began by giving a pair of tubes to each player. Each hid a bean in one of the tubes (waving hands and chanting to try and distract the other's eye) while at the same time trying to spy which tube his opponent was hiding his or her bean in. Each then filled the tubes with sand and tossed them in front of the opposing player. Simultaneously they pointed to show which of the other's tubes they thought hid the bean. They repeated this until one correctly located the bean and the other did not. The winner took all four tubes and the true game began.

To play, the hider placed the ball inside one of the tubes, re-arranged the tubes on the ground and filled them with sand. In some games the four tubes might be covered with a blanket, or the hiding team could hold a blanket in place as a screen. In others the skill of the hider in disguising his or her moves was part of the game.

The guesser took the tubes and divided them into pairs. Having decided which tube hid the bean, the guesser crossed the other pair of tubes and then poured out the selected tube. If the bean was there, the guesser won the round and took the next turn. If it was the wrong tube, the hider revealed the location of the bean. The hider was awarded points and drew corn kernels from the pile as counters: 4 if the bean was in the single remaining tube, 6 if it was in the bottom tube of the crossed pair, and 10 if it was in the top tube. The hider continued to hide until the guesser successfully located the bean.

You can make tubes for vaputi from paper-towel tubes, but pieces of bamboo or sugarcane are more authentic. Plug one end with modeling dough, and decorate the tubes with paint. Use beans for hiding and corn seed for keeping score.

⊞ Wa'lade Hama'gan

This is complex bowl and pits game of the Penobscot people of the Northeast. It was played in three stages. In place of simple counting sticks, more frequently used in bowl and pits games (such as in waltes), wa'lade hama'gan required three kinds of counters: fifty-six narrow "1-point" sticks, four flat "16-point" sticks, and a crooked stick, which was the last to be won.

In the first round of the game players rapped the bowl on the ground to shake the dice and score. No points were won if four or fewer pits came up matched. Five alike (either face up or down) won three narrow sticks and another roll. If the second roll also resulted in a five, the player won nine narrow sticks and another roll. A third five won a flat stick.

A six-alike roll was worth a flat stick and a roll-again. A second six alike won two flat sticks and a third consecutive roll of six alike earned three flat sticks.

The last stick awarded was the crooked stick, and the player who won the crooked stick was also awarded two narrow sticks from her opponent's pile.

In the second stage of the game, the counters were moved into new piles. It became important to keep track of the points as the value of the sticks changed from one pile to the next! A roll of five allowed the player to move a narrow stick into a second, or "treasure," pile. A second roll of five moved three narrow sticks into her treasure pile. Three consecutive fives moved a flat stick into the treasure pile. Each stick in the treasure pile was potentially worth four sticks from the opponent's collection pile. If the player rolled a six she moved a narrow stick into the third, or chief, pile. Two sixes were worth two flat sticks and three sixes worth three flat sticks in the chief pile. Sticks in the chief pile were worth four sticks from the opponents' treasure pile plus one flat stick or sixteen narrow sticks from the collection pile.

When one player believed she had enough sticks in her treasure and chief piles to bankrupt her opponent, she called for the final phase of the game—paying up. For each stick in the treasure pile, she received four sticks from her opponent's collection pile. For each stick in the chief pile, she received four sticks from her opponent's treasure pile and sixteen (or one flat stick) from her opponent's collection pile.

If she was right in her estimate, she won the game unless her opponent held the crooked stick. If the bankrupted player was holding the crooked stick she was entitled to three final rolls of the dice. If she rolled three consecutive fives or sixes she won the game anyway. If the player who called for the end game was wrong, she had to pay her opponent according to the sticks in her opponent's treasure and chief's piles and stage two of the game continued.

⊞ Waltes

In this Micmac bowl and pit game the playing pieces were made of polished caribou shinbone and engraved with a six-pointed star. The waltes, or dish, was a made from a slice of hard rock maple, almost a foot across.

Waltes could be used for divination; that is, a question might be asked and the results of the toss interpreted as the answer. More often, the game was just a game, played sometimes for counting sticks and sometimes for valuable stakes. Most waltes games included fifty-one counting sticks. Some versions included 5-point sticks as well.

Six playing pieces were placed in a large shallow bowl or pan. The first player held the dish in both hands and rapped it hard against the ground, causing the disks to bounce into the air and drop back into the pan. Each disk that fell decorated side up was worth one point, except that if all six fall decorated side up, the player scored 50 points.

The first player collected the appropriate number of counting sticks and passed the waltes to the next player. The first player to reach a predetermined number of points (often 51) won the game.

⊞ Witcli

This Pomo stick counting game required a large bundle (at least three hundred) small sticks for the game and eight larger counting sticks to keep score. The first player took a handful of forty or fifty sticks from the pile and held them out for the other player to observe. The second player had to guess how many would be left over (1, 2, or 3) when the handful was divided by four. Then the first player counted the sticks off by fours (like dealing cards). For each correct remainder guessed, a player was awarded one of the counting sticks. Once the eight scoring sticks have been won the game continues with players taking scoring sticks back from each other until one has accumulated all eight and is the winner.

You can use toothpicks for counting sticks and pencils for scoring sticks for witcli.

⊞ Zohn Ali

Zohn ali, also called patol, was a game generally played by the Kiowa people. They were a nomadic people who were bison hunters. This game is similar to the game of sholiwe and wash'kasi, (see Latin America), and the Kiowa were probably related to the Anasazi. It is also very like the Apache zsetilth (see next entry). The zohn ali board was drawn or stitched on a blanket or hide (Figure 7.1), with four "paths" marked to align with the four compass points and four semicircular corners (called knees, which probably explains how the board was held flat on the ground) equidistant between them. A path of spots was marked around the board, with three between each "knee" and its adjacent path. The north and south paths were called creeks or rivers, and the east and west were called dry branches or gullies. There were four stick dice, each about ten inches long and five-eighths of an inch wide, rounded on one side and flat on the other. All the dice had a long groove down the flat side. On three dice the groove was painted red and on the fourth it was green. Each team also had four counters—pebbles, beans or counting sticks.

The game could be played by any number of players divided into two teams. Each side stuck an awl into the cloth at one edge of the south river. The first player held the dice bundled in his or her hand and threw the bundle down on the stone so that the ends hit the stone together and the dice bounced out onto the cloth. Each flat (lined) side that fell facing up dice was worth one step, but if all four fell flat side up that play was worth 6, and if all four fell flat side down that was worth 10. If the green line fell face up, the team got another turn.

The teams moved their awls in opposite directions. Rivers and gullies had to be "jumped" over, so if a throw landed an awl in the river, that team had to give the other team a counter and return to the start. If a turn ended in a gully, that team lost its next turn. If one team "caught" the other by landing in the same space, the awl that was caught had to start over, and that team forfeited a counter.

By completing a lap a team won a counter from the other team. If there were any steps left in their final throw, they could begin another lap. (They didn't leave the board; they just went around again.)

The game ended when one team had lost all of its counters.

⊞ Zsetilth

Zsetilth was popular among Apache women, although men sometimes joined in. The journey motif is in keeping with the nomadic lifestyle of these Plains Indians.

A circle of stones is laid out on the ground, four groups of ten stones each with four gaps, or "rivers," dividing the groups. The gaps were aligned with the four points of the compass. A large flat stone was placed in the center of the circle. Each player had a distinct piece to move around the circle. A set of three staves or sticks, each painted white or yellow on the rounded side and black or red on the flat side served to determine play. Two or more players could play the game, or a large group may choose to play in teams.

Players were allowed to begin at any point on the circle, and the object of the game was to complete the circle and return safely home.

The first player held the staves in a bundle in her hand and tapped the end of bundle against the center stone, releasing the staves as they hit the stone. If they fell with all three flat sides down, the player moved ten spaces and had another turn. Three flat sides up was worth five spaces. Two flat sides earned three spaces and a single flat side was worth one. If the game was played by two people, they moved in opposite directions. If more than two played, everyone moved in the same direction, North to East to South to West.

If a player's piece landed in a river, that player was required to begin again from the spot where she began. If a player landed on an occupied stone, the player already there was "bumped" and had to start over. (If the game was being played in teams, two teammates could occupy the same stone.)

The first player to return to her home stone was the winner.

PLAY

⊞ Ajaqaq

The Inuit people of the Arctic had a variety of ring-and-pin games (Figure 7.4). Sometimes they used the skull of a small rodent, with its various sized openings, as the "ring." More often ajaqaq were carved of ivory in the shapes of foxes, polar bears, and even fish, with a number of holes drilled into the shape. Each hole was worth a different number of points, and the object of the game was to accumulate the most points. Ajaqaq could be played as solitaire, or players could take turns and compete for the higher score or to a predetermined number.

⊞ Ak Sa Lak

Tugging and pulling games are very common. Children do not need to be taught these games, they invent them spontaneously. Among the Inuit people of the North American Arctic, however, these games were more developed and were often played by adults.

The Inuit made a sort of handle, called an *aksalak*, for tugging. Two pieces of bone, antler, or wood were tied together with a leather thong. The handles were small: the bones just long enough to fit into the palm of the hand, and the thong only a few inches long. Players sat opposite one another, legs stretched in front of them and feet touching. Each held one end of the aksalak in one hand. At the signal, both began to pull. The object of the game was to pull the other player to a standing position.

A variation of this game was a young person's courting game. A young man and woman stood on one foot, face to face, hands behind their backs. Each held the ends of a very small aksalak between the teeth. At the signal, each tried to pull the other over.

You can make aksalak in different sizes from pieces of wood or plastic. Use a bootlace to tie the two pieces together. Wrap it securely around each piece several times, crossing back and forth, and then wrap the lace around itself in the middle to form a solid cord.

⊞ Aratsiaq

The Inuit people who lived on the islands in the strait between what is now Alaska and British Columbia played this high-jumping game. A pole was set in the ground with another lashed to it at an angle. A piece of fur or other target was hung on the end of the brace. Each player began from about ten feet away, ran and jumped into the air, trying to kick the target. In order for the kick to count, the player had to land on the kicking foot and remain standing! A variation of the game required the players to hit the target with both feet.

To play aratsiaq, suspend a target in an open area, preferably with a soft landing spot: snow or sand or gymnastic pads. Begin with the target fairly close to the ground, to begin to develop the kicking-and-landing skills. As your skills improve you can raise the target higher, and the player who kicks the highest wins the game.

⊞ Arrow Games

Since skill with bow and arrow was essential for both hunting and fighting, young people across North America competed in many different archery games. One common game was a test of speed. Players would shoot arrows into the air, one after the other as fast as they could. The winner was the person who could get the largest number of arrows into the air at once. To do this it was necessary for the first arrow to be shot very high indeed, and for the players to be able to reload their bows quickly from the supply of arrows clutched in the bow hand.

Target games included shooting at fixed and moving targets. For a fixed target, one player would paint an arrow black or wrap it in buckskin, then shoot it 50 to 75 feet away so that it stuck into the ground. All the players took turns shooting at it, and the one whose arrow came closest was the winner. A variation of this game had two arrows stuck into the ground on either side of a hill. Players divided into teams, and standing beside one arrow, shot at the other.

For a moving target, players made balls of grass. One would toss a ball into the air and everyone would shoot at it, with the winner being the one to pierce it. Another, more dangerous moving target game had one player run while carrying a cactus root on a handle over his head, while the others attempted to hit the root with their arrows.

You need a wide-open area to shoot arrows into the air. For suggestions on making bows and arrows see Appendix on North American sports.

⊞　Buhtse (Foot Juggling)

Many of the North American peoples enjoyed bouncing a ball off the foot and knee, with the object being to keep it from dropping. This was particularly popular among girls and women. Sometimes the players would compete to see who could bounce the ball the greatest number of times, or the first to reach one hundred hits was the winner. Balls for this game ranged in size from two to ten inches in diameter, with six or seven inches being most common. They were made of leather and stuffed with hair, so that they were quite light. In the Southwest small wooden cylinders were also juggled with the feet.

This game is almost exactly the same as the soccer drill of bouncing the ball off the feet and knees, except that the ball was not rubber or inflated, so more upward force was needed to keep the sequence going. Make a buhtse ball from fabric and stuff it with dry grass or crumbled newspaper.

⊞　Dart and Ring Games

These games, a variation on the hoop-and-pole game (Figure 7.7), were played all over western North America. In some places the rings were made of grass or cornhusks, in others of twigs covered with buckskin or bark. Some games were played with rings as large as six inches across, some with rings as small as an inch. The darts, too, were made from different materials by different tribes. Some used simple sticks, sharpened on one end and with the bark peeled. Others constructed more elaborate darts from wood or corncobs, with feathers on one end to improve their flight. Children marked their darts so they could tell them apart.

Players sat in two lines, facing one another across an open space. The bowler rolled the ring from one end so that it passed between the lines, and the players threw their darts in order to hit the ring. No points were scored by tossing the dart through the ring—it was necessary to bring the ring down to score.

Try making a variety of rings. Curl small branches into circles and lash the ends together with twine or vines. Continue wrapping the vine around the whole ring so it will roll smoothly. Braiding cornhusks or bundles of straw together and binding the ends makes a different sort of ring. Make darts as described.

▦ Dart and Target Games

Most of the North American peoples played games with darts and targets. Unlike European dart games, however, these targets were generally placed on the ground. The object was to toss the dart upward so that it would fall down into the center of the target. Counters were used to keep score and the first person to reach an agreed-upon amount was the winner.

You can use the same darts and rings for the target game as for dart-and-ring games.

▦ Gaqutit

This game was a popular pastime during the long winters on the Plains. Men would gather in one tipi, women in another to play late into the night.

Players divided into two teams, and each team had a *gaquaä*, a small piece of wood painted red or black or marked with a string tied around it. A large number of tally sticks, corn kernels, or some other sort of counter was the only other equipment necessary.

One team hid the gaquaä, passing it from person to person, while the other team guessed where it was. All the members of the hiding team chanted or sang and moved their hands and arms, each appearing to receive or pass on the gaquaä simultaneously. The guessing team watched closely, and when one thought she knew who had the gaquaä, she pointed and shouted "there!" If she was correct, her team collected a tally stick and became the hiding team. If she was incorrect, her team had to pay a tally stick to the hiding team, which continued to shuffle the gaquaä.

⚏ Gawasa (Snowsnakes)

Snowsnakes was a very popular pastime for all the peoples of the northern parts of North America. From the great Northwest to the shores of the Atlantic, boys and men alike spent many hours carving, painting, and polishing their wooden "snakes." Some were designed to look like a snake, a fish, or a duck. Others were sleek and smooth with little curve, built for speed. Some were heavy at one end, designed to push their way through if they were caught in the snow. Most snowsnakes were six to eight feet long, although they could be as short as two feet or as long as ten feet.

Snowsnakes could be played in an open field, on the surface of a frozen pond, or even in tracks made especially for the purpose by dragging a log through the snow to pack down a trench. The tracks could be made even more slippery by sprinkling them with water and letting them freeze.

The snakes were thrown by holding the snake's "tail" in one hand, with the index finger against the end, and the other hand supporting the weight of the snake. Reports are that snakes on iced trails may have achieved speeds of one hundred miles an hour and traveled as much as a mile.

Players took turns tossing their snakes, with a quick snap of the wrist so that they skimmed along the surface. The snake's stopping point would be noted, and then the next player would try. Generally the snake that went the furthest was the winner. Sometimes points were awarded to the snake that went the furthest and then to the second-, third-, and fourth-place snakes, and the game was played to a predetermined total score.

On a wide icy surface, such as a pond, players could build multiple tracks side by side (ridges of snow keep the snakes headed in one direction) and toss their snakes simultaneously, racing them for both speed and distance.

Make snowsnakes from straight saplings or garden stakes. Sand the wood smooth, and shape the head into a point. Decorate your snowsnake with paint or carve designs in the back (keep the bottom smooth for speed).

⚏ Hoop and Ball

This Osage game required a prepared playing area and some sharp-eyed judges. The field was divided by three parallel lines, about fifteen yards apart. Teams lined up along each of the two outside lines, with each player opposite a space between two opposing players. Each team had a roller, and these two stood at opposite ends of the center line.

The roller rolled the hoop, which was about two feet in diameter, as fast as possible along the center line. The opposing roller won a point for his or her team by catching the hoop, then rolled it back as quickly as possible. The side players attempted to throw balls through the hoop as it rolled past. Judges on each end (or the rollers) watched the balls and awarded points for each ball that went through the hoop.

To play make hoops from slender branches curled into a circle and lash the ends together with vines or twine. Continue the wrapping around the hoop to make it roll smoothly.

▦ Illupik

Inuit hunters tied an *avatuk*, a sealskin bag inflated with air, to their harpoons so that when they had killed a seal the weapons would float. Inuit children used the avatuk for a jumping game: two players would swing the rope so the avatuk skimmed back and forth across the ice or ground, and the third player would try to jump over it when it came near.

▦ Kinxe

This game was played among the Kwaiutl people in what is now British Columbia. Each player had a stick, four to eight feet long, and a ring, eight or nine inches across made of sticks and wrapped in cedar bark. The players divided into equal teams, and decided in advance whether to take turns tossing the rings, or to have everyone toss their rings at once. Once the rings had been tossed, each player tried to capture as many rings as possible, either by catching them in the air or scooping them off the ground. The game was won if one team managed to catch all the rings, otherwise, the rings were given back to their owners and another round is played.

▦ Lukia

This game of the Kwaiutl people was a favorite of young boys. Players divided into two equal teams with from two to twelve on a side. Each team had a goal stick, which was placed in the center of the playing area. Each player had a throwing stone, a piece of polished lava about as long as the palm of his hand and half as big around as his fist. The teams alternated turns, each player throwing the stone to come as close to the goal as possible. The next player might try to get closer, or might attempt to knock his opponent's stone away. The last player for each team had two stones, and the team would save their best players for last, as he might be able to knock the opponent away and then land his final stone close to the mark. The first team to win ten rounds won the game.

⊞ Nalugatuk (Blanket Toss)

"Blanket tossing" is probably the game most people think of when they think about the "Eskimos," or people of the Arctic. Its surprising origin was as a hunting tool: a hunting party would bounce one member high into the air from a blanket to look for distant caribou. It soon became a test of courage for young men and eventually just a source of amusement for anyone. There were several variations of the game. Ten or more people held a skin tightly between them, and either cooperated with the jumper to try and get him as high as possible, or competed with him by trying to make him lose his balance and fall over. For a competitive game, players divided into two teams. If the object was to knock the opponent over, the members of one team held the blanket while representatives of the opposing team jumped. When the object was to see who could leap the highest, the jumper's own team held the blanket, and the opponents judged the height of the jumps.

⊞ Nauktak

In this Inuit jumping game the player first measured his height by lying on the ground with his feet against a wall. Another player marked the ground at the top of his head. Then the player crouched by the wall and leapt up and out, attempting to jump as far as he was tall.

⊞ Nullugaut

This Inuit spinning target game can be hazardous to the hands, but the Inuit people wore heavy mitts for protection while playing it. The mitts also made the game more challenging.

A piece of wood or bone—the target—was drilled with holes on both ends and another through the middle. Pieces of sinew were passed through the end holes and the target, and the target was hung from a pole or from the roof of a house (inside) so that it was at the player's head level. A weight on the string below the target helped keep it steady. Each player had a short spear, about three feet long, tipped with a piece of bone thin enough to pass through the center hole of the target.

The players stood around the target, which was set spinning. Then each player tried to stab the target through the center hole as it spun.

Make a nullugaut set with a piece of wood or cardboard for the target and pencils or long slender branches for spears. Stand back far enough to avoid being hit by the player on the other side, or wear eye protection as well as mittens!

▦ Oijumik Akimitaijuk Itigaminak

Intuit children playing this jumping game in the Arctic developed balance and strength in their legs that were valuable in hunting at sea, although no doubt they only thought it was fun. Each player crouched down and grabbed his or her toes, then tried to jump as far as possible without letting go.

Try it—it's harder than it sounds!

▦ Pokean

This Zuni shuttlecock game was very similar to the Maori bowgitee or the Japanese game hago abosi. The Zuni would weave green corn husks into a flat box about two inches square, and fasten feathers to one side of it. This was called a *pokinanane*. Using the flat of their open hands players batted the pokinanane up into the air, and tried to see who could keep theirs aloft the longest.

You can make a pokinanane from cornhusks. Tear them into strips about an inch wide and weave four of them together at their centers, then fold two up on opposite sides and weave the other strips through them. Fold over again and once more to complete the box. Fasten two feathers to the box by inserting their quills through the husks far enough for the barbs of the feathers to hold them in place.

Players can compete as individuals or as teams.

▦ Ring and Pin

Ring-and-pin games, often called by the French term *bilboquet*, were popular throughout the North American continent. The basic game is simple to describe and difficult to do: holding the pin in one hand the player swings the target up and out, and as it falls attempts to pass the pin through the target.

Ring-and-pin games were made from all sorts of material, from ivory in the Arctic to gourd shells in the Southwest to bundled pine needles in the Northeast (Figure 7.4). Skulls of small rodents, with their multiple holes, were common targets. Ivory or bone targets were sometimes carved to resemble an animal, with multiple holes drilled into their sides for catching. Sometimes a piece of hide with a number of holes in it was attached at one end of the string. Then from four to nine rings were strung on the string. Bone or wooden rings often had holes drilled through them, and in some games the rings were of differing sizes or

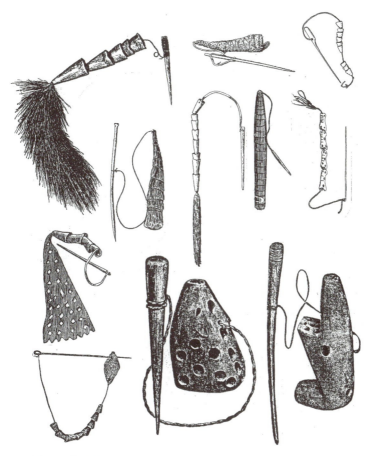

Figure 7.4. Ring-and-pin games of dexterity were made of materials as diverse as wood, ivory, hide, bundled pine needles, moose hair, and the phalangeal bones of deer and seals. *Source*: Adapted from Culin (1975).

had different sized openings so that some were more difficult to catch than others. Finally the string was tied to the pin; a stick or bone that usually tapered at one end.

The simplest form of the game was the equivalent of the ball-and-cup games of Europe: catch the target on the pin. Multiple targets allowed for more complex games: catch the rings in a particular order, or win different points depending on which hole in the ring or the hide the pin passed through.

You can make ring-and-pin games from many different materials, just as Native Americans did. Use the modeling dough (see Appendix) to fashion disks or animal shapes with a variety of holes. The decorative gourds sold in grocery stores in the fall can be cut into rings for ring-and-pin games, or you can cut disks from pumpkin rind and let them dry. Bundles of pine needles bound with vine string are completely authentic. A butcher shop or slaughterhouse may be able to provide phalangeal bones (the long bones of the foot), the bones most commonly used for ring and pin. A piece of heavy cloth or leather with several holes in it is the last target, and keeps the rings from sliding off the string. The sticks or pins for the games ranged from three or four inches long to nearly a foot: the shorter the pin, the better control you will have.

▦ Sakumship

This two-person ball and racket game was played by Topinagugim girls and women in what is now California. Players stood about fifty feet apart, with a basket-shaped racket in each hand. The ball was about four inches in diameter, made of buckskin and stuffed with hair so it was quite light. Players used the baskets to toss and catch the ball, and used tally sticks to keep track of forfeits. A forfeit was charged either for failing to catch the ball or for tossing it in such a way that the other player couldn't catch it: over her head or too short or wide. Players often put up stakes before the game and divided them after according to the number of forfeits each had accumulated.

Sakumship baskets were described as being very similar to amatah baskets (see amatah for suggestions for constructing these).

▦ Swimming

Almost all of the peoples of North America were accomplished swimmers. Swimming was, of course, an essential life skill for those who lived and traveled along the lakes and rivers. It was also a great source of fun. Boys and girls did not swim together, but both sexes enjoyed playing in the water, diving from the banks, leaping from overhanging branches, or swinging out over the water on a vine. Riding a log down a river was a challenging game for an adventurous group of boys.

▦ Tobogganing

Toboggans were sleds used by the peoples of the Northwoods to transport bundles from place to place. The Coughnawaga of Canada are credited with beginning to use the sleds just for fun, speeding down snowy hillsides and racing to see who would go the furthest or reach the finish line first.

▦ Tug-of-War

Tug-of-war was a game common to many of the native people of North America. Inuit players used ropes made of leather. Further south, ropes of braided hemp were used. The game was simple: players lined up on each end of the rope, and at the signal each team tried to pull the other across the center point.

⊞ Uiwak

Tops are virtually universal, but the Aleut people of the far north had a particular fondness for tops. Many, many examples of spindle tops have been found in these areas. This favorite top game for both boys and girls required a player to get the top spinning well, then run out of the shelter and around the building, trying to get back inside before the top stopped spinning.

⊞ Unkalugit

This football game from what is now Canada was primarily a woman's amusement, although men and boys played it in some places. Two pairs competed against each other. Players stood opposite their partners, and each pair had a large ball. The first player bounced the ball against the ground midway between herself and her partner so that it would bounce toward her partner. Then her partner hit the ball back, using her open hand or foot. It was also permissible to kick the ball up into the air and then hit it toward the partner. The goal was to keep the ball moving; the pair with the fewest misses and dead balls won the game.

SPORTS

⊞ Akraurak

This football game was a favorite sport among the Inuit people of far north, where everyone from toddlers to the elderly joined in the game. Two players were designated as captains and chose sides so that the teams were evenly divided and matched. The goals were marked on the hard-packed snow and players lined up in front of their goals. The game began with the players kicking the ball back and forth between the lines of players, until one side managed to drive it through the other's line. Then the players chased the ball and tried to kick it through the other's goal. There were not specific positions but players would choose to chase and shoot the ball or to hang back and defend the goal based on their own abilities.

Akraurak balls varied in size, from three to eight inches in diameter. Typically they were stitched of hide and stuffed with a mixture of hair and feathers, grass and moss, and some wood shavings or even bone for weight.

Play akraurak on a packed, snow-covered surface if you can. The ball moves differently on the snow, and so do your feet! (In the Northeast the Algonkian people who migrated to the seashore for fishing each spring played a similar game on the beach, so if you don't have snow you can play on sand instead.)

▦ Amatah

This variation on the ball-and-racket game was played by Miwok people in what is now California. Among some groups it was strictly a women's game, while in other tribes men and women played amatah together.

The rackets, called amatah, were baskets woven of willow splints, about eighteen inches long including their short handles. Each player had two baskets, one larger and deeper than the other. The ball was about three inches in diameter, made of buckskin and stuffed with grass or hair.

Play took place on a large field with goals marked at each end. The ball was tossed into the air at the center of the field, and players used the deep basket to catch and toss the ball, or carried it in the deeper basket using the shallower basket as a cover while running with the ball. The object was to carry the ball through the other team's goal.

You can make amatah from willow branches just as the Miwok did, curving the branches into loops and binding their ends to make handles, then weaving smaller branches across the loops to form the baskets. Jai alai rackets will also work, as will the plastic scoops children sometimes take to the beach. Make the ball as described above or use a foam play ball or juggling ball.

▦ Archery Contests

Skill with bow and arrow was essential for hunting, so it is not surprising that archery was also the subject of friendly competitions. Different types of targets made for different kinds of games.

The people of the eastern woodlands set up targets of deerskin stretched over large frames made of branches, which they hung in trees or on poles about eight feet off the ground and about fifty yards apart. Teams representing different villages or families stood by their targets and shot at their opponent's targets. Each team would shoot twenty-one arrows, and the team with the largest number of hits won the contest.

In the Plains, archery contests involved very small targets at much longer distances. These distinctions undoubtedly reflect the difference in hunting conditions in those regions: Eastern hunters stalked and tracked their prey through the woods and had to get quite close to them to see them. In the grasslands, tracking and locating the animal were less important than being able to strike from a distance.

A different contest was held in the desert southwest, where the target was a ball wound of the fibers of the yucca plant. A string of buckskin was wound into the ball and a small stick attached to the string, so that when the ball was thrown into the air, the stick acted like the tail on a kite, to keep the ball's descent steady. In the contest, the ball would be tossed high into the air, and as it fell players would shoot at it, scoring points for each hit.

Using commercially available bows and arrows will yield the most precise shooting, but making your own bows will feel more authentic.

You can make eastern-style targets from hulu hoops covered with fabric. For a more authentic target make your hoop from a slender sapling, curled and lashed into a circle. Hang targets from climbing apparatus, basketball hoops, or trees. For Plains-style targets make hoops about a foot across from small branches. The southwestern moving target can be made exactly as the Native Americans made them if you dry yucca leaves. For a simple modern version, place a tennis ball into an onion bag, tie it shut and tie a stick as a tail to the string.

▦ Canoe Races

Canoes were the primary method of transportation for the people of the wooded areas of North America. In the eastern woodlands canoes were made of bark, stitched and stretched over a frame. Other boats were made of hides stretched over wood frames. Heavier canoes could be made by hollowing out a treetrunk. In the Pacific Northwest dugout canoes made from giant Sequoias could hold up to fifty people for a foray into the ocean. Sometimes they lashed two of these together to form a very stable catamaran-like vessel.

For racing the lightweight canoe was best. Canoe regattas brought racers from many villages together, each bringing the best canoes they could make. The games included races for speed over distance and around obstacles. Paddlers raced standing in their canoes for top speed! Another race involved paddling out to a predetermined distance, swamping the canoe and swimming back, towing the canoe behind. There would also be tug-of-war matches, where two canoes were tied end to end and the players would paddle in opposite directions, with the winner being the one who dragged the opponent's canoe past a marker.

Any of these events can be practiced today without modification.

▦ Chungke

People played chungke across southeastern North America, and the *chunk yard* or playing area was located in the center of most Chocktaw and Muskogee villages. The explorers Lewis and Clark reported seeing a chungke court built of logs as far north as the Dakotas. The chungke playing area was as much as two hundred feet long. The soil in the area would be dug out to a depth of one to two feet and often used to build seating along the sides of the field. The field itself was packed flat and smoothed with clay. Often sand was sprinkled on the surface before playing.

Two players at a time could play. When villages competed, each would put together a team. At the match, each player would compete alone against a player from the opposite team, with the scores accumulating.

The game was played with a round polished stone as a target. The size of the target stone varied from one tribe to another. Some stones were about a foot across and two inches thick. Others were much smaller, two to three inches in diameter. Each player had a lance or pole, about eight feet long and sharpened at one end.

One player would throw or roll the stone down the field. Both players would chase the stone. The object of the game was to throw the lance so that it stopped just ahead of the spot where the stone stopped. The closer to the stone, the better the throw. In one version of the game, two points were awarded to the player whose lance was closer to the stone. If the lances were equally distant, then each would receive one point. In another version, the lances had four strips of leather attached along their lengths, and the player would receive one, two, three, or four points if one of the leather strips was touching the stone when it stopped. In yet another version of the game, only the player who had not rolled the stone could score. The player who rolled the stone would try to prevent the other player from scoring, throwing his lance in order to knock the other's off its flight or to come to earth between the opponent's lance and the stone.

You can play chungke with a target made of wood, or for a more authentic target, you can buy round concrete landscape "stones." Lances made from saplings or broomsticks are easy to make. Tie and glue strips of fabric about every foot along the lances for that version of the game. Loose sand will make the disk hard to roll, so unless you have hard-packed dirt a paved area or a wooden floor will make a better chungke playing area.

▦ Double-ball

Double-ball was almost exclusively a women's game. It was played mostly west of the Mississippi.

Like lacrosse and shinny, double-ball was a game of scoring by passing a ball through a goal. In double-ball the "ball" was actually a pair of balls or pieces of wood, one on each end of a piece of leather string. The balls were generally stuffed with hair or bark and often weighted with sand. The string could be quite short but more often was a foot long. The double-ball stick was a thin, flexible piece of willow, curved slightly at the end. (Beginners' sticks sometimes had a notch toward the end to help hold the ball.) The ball was controlled and tossed by the string around the end of the stick.

The double-ball field was generally three or four hundred yards long and nearly as wide, although some were as long as a mile. Players had positions, or zones, to defend, but there was a tremendous amount of running in this game just the same. The goals might be conveniently located between trees twelve to fifteen feet apart at the end of the field, or poles or piles of dirt would be used. Play was very much like lacrosse—the referee tossed the ball up to begin play, and the players scrambled to control, pass, and throw it toward their opponent's goal. Play continued until one team reached an agreed-upon score.

Make double-balls from fabric and stuff them with grass. Add sand and let it sift around the grass for weight and stability before stitching the balls shut. Twine is slippery so a leather thong is better for holding the balls together. A pair of leather bootlaces will yield string for six double-balls.

The sticks for double-ball need to be flexible, so you should cut them fresh if you can. Peel the bark away to leave the smooth wood (you can leave the bark on the hand end of the stick to make it less slippery).

Practice tossing the balls back and forth over a short distance first, then gradually spread the players apart. Once everyone learns tossing and catching, mark out a playing area, set up goals, and divide into two even teams. The more players you have the bigger the field should be.

▦ Foot Racing

The running ability of the native people of the Americas quickly became legendary among the European explorers. Never had they encountered such strength and endurance. In the southwest of North America and in Central America, long-distance running was the primary competitive sport among the people. Races of one and two hundred miles were common, and there are so many reports from so many sources of runners covering 25 miles in two hours that they seem likely to be accurate, although that easily outstrips the records of most modern marathoners.

Running barefoot and wearing very little clothing that might restrict their movement, Native American runners picked their way through the mountains, over rocks, and along streams. They kept their arms close to their bodies and their steps steady, not sprinting but still making amazing speed. Runners carried messages throughout the territories and were important to the tribal economy and military preparedness. But running was not just a job, it was a sport.

Runners trained for big races by wearing bags filled with sand around their ankles for weeks in advance. This strengthened the leg muscles, and when they were removed for the race the runner's feet felt "lighter than air." They painted their legs with designs representing speed and agility, and painted symbols of their clans and families on their chests and backs.

In the West and Southwest, races were held on tracks built for that purpose, and spectators lined them as they do today. Other races were between villages or pre-arranged points, with judges at both the starting and the finish line. One anthropologist reported running tracks in the prairie designed in an arc, so that although they were three miles long, the starting and finishing lines were both within sight of the judges. On tracks races could be run in groups, with each group's winner going on to race against the other.

Organized races were announced by messengers, and the runners gathered at the appointed time and place bringing blankets, baskets, or other stakes which they contributed to the prize. Some races featured teams representing different villages, others were individual events. Runners were divided according to gender and age group, and if there were many runners a race would have heats, with runners competing in groups, and the winners of each group going on to run against each other. There were short races of about 100, 300, and 400 yards as well as longer runs of a quarter- and half-mile, in addition to the long-distance racing described above.

⚏ Harpoon Throwing

Harpooning a whale from a small boat in an icy sea required balance, strength, and accuracy. The Eskimo men of Baffinland practiced these skills with this competition. A line was hung from an inclined pole, and part way down the line a ring carved from ivory was tied. Fringes of skin tied on the ring and the line made the target harder to see, and since it was tied to the line, it was somewhat mobile. The competitors stood at a predetermined distance and threw the harpoon, attempting to get the harpoon through the ring. As many as succeeded would then try again from a greater distance, until finally one was the acknowledged champion.

For a harpoon contest you can make rings of different sizes by curling and lashing thin branches, or cut them from heavy cardboard. The larger the ring, the easier it will be to hit. Tie the rings into long lengths of string, and tie one end of the string to a basketball hoop. To make the target more stable, tie or weight the other end of the string down. Your harpoon can be a three- to four-

foot stick cut from a sapling or a broomstick, or a javelin if you have access to track and field equipment. Begin tossing the harpoons from about ten feet back, and move the line back two or three feet each round. Station judges on a line with the targets so they can see whether the harpoons actually pass through the rings.

Juggling Race

Juggling was a popular pastime among many of the Native Americans. People juggled stones, balls, bones, and chips just to amuse themselves or while walking from place to place. The juggling race, a woman's competitive sport, was a natural outgrowth of this. Once the course had been described, the players began on a signal, ran down the course, around a marker at the other end, and returned—all the while keeping three or four balls in the air. If a ball dropped, the player started over or was disqualified.

Unless you're an accomplished juggler, it's challenging to run and keep just one or two stones in the air! Use small stones or make juggling balls of leather or fabric. Fill the balls with birdseed and a little sand for stability. Mark out the race course. You may choose to have three or four parallel tracks so that racers don't need to worry about running into each other.

Müla

Müla was a relay game for two teams played by the Wasama people in California. It was played with wooden balls and sticks such as those used for shinny, but required fewer players. A course was marked out between the starting line and the goal, one-quarter- to one-half-mile long. Stations were marked every five hundred feet or so along the way. A player from each team stood at each station. The first players hit the ball from the starting point toward the first station. Once a team's ball reached the first station the team member at that point took over and hit the ball toward the next station. The last player had to get the ball across the goal line. The team with the smallest number of strokes won the game.

For müla you will need a stick for each player, about three feet long with a slight bend at one end, and a wooden ball for each team. A wooden ball about three inches in diameter from a craft store will work. Mark out a course with a starting and finishing line, and place a stake in the ground at each station.

Ndashdilka'l (Shinny)

Ndashdilka'l, as the Navaho called it, was another sport widespread across the North American continent. In many places it was a woman's

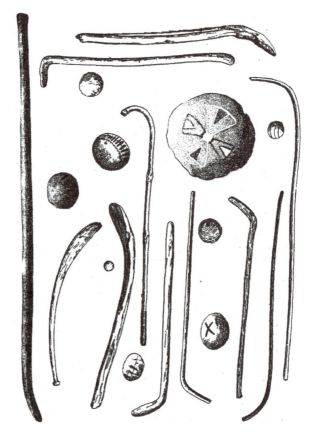

Figure 7.5. Sticks for shinny games could be deliberately curved, or a naturally crooked stick might be
used. *Source*: Adapted from Culin (1975).

game, although young boys played as well. In a few places this game,
called "shinny" by the Europeans, was played by mixed teams of men
and women as palitún was in South America.

Shinny was very similar to modern field hockey. Shinny sticks were
typically about three feet long, with a curved end (Figure 7.5). Shinny
balls were anywhere from golf-ball to baseball-sized. In the West, shinny
balls were often made of bone or wood, while in the East people more
often made shinny balls from buckskin, stitched, and stuffed. The decoration of both balls and sticks was elaborate and a matter of some pride
for the players.

Shinny was played both on grass and on the ice. The playing area was
similar to a lacrosse field although not generally so long: two to three
hundred yards was typical for shinny. A team could have anywhere

from ten to one hundred players, and a larger team needed a larger field. Goals could be ten to twenty feet wide, marked with sticks in the ground or even piles of blankets, but more often the goal was a single pole or tree at each end of the field, which the players had to strike with the ball to score. Players were often divided into defenders of the goal and offensive, scoring players.

To begin the game the teams lined up facing each other across the centerline of the field. The referee placed the ball into a shallow hole at the center of the field or, in some areas, tossed it into the air. Both teams immediately began to try and gain control of the ball. As with lacrosse, the ball could not be touched with the hand—all passing and shooting was done with the shinny stick. Unlike modern field hockey, however, the passing tended to be over the heads of the players, and a skillful player could strike the ball on the ground in such a way as to loft it several hundred feet toward the opposing goal.

Shinny sticks were made by curving the end of a three-foot stick and tying it in position when it was green so that it would dry curved. You can make shinny sticks the same way, or use field-hockey sticks for a quick substitute, though the end of a shinny stick would be not be flat on one side the way a field hockey stick is.

⊞ Pagadanowak (Lacrosse)

Pagadanowak, or bagataway, was the premier sport of the North American people. Variations were played in every part of the continent except the southwestern deserts (Figure 7.6). To the players, it was simply "the ball game," but French explorers called it "la crosse" because it reminded them of the European stick-and-ball game (see Bandy).

Lacrosse fields varied in size according to the number of players and the space available. On average they seem to have been about 200 yards wide (twice as wide as an American football field is long) and between one-fourth- and one-half-mile long. In most variations the goals were tall and narrow, about six feet wide and as much as twenty feet tall, with a crossbar at about ten feet.

Many different styles of rackets, or sticks, were used in the ball game. In general the people of the Southeast used a stick with a round net or basket attached at the end. Northern players used sticks curved at the end with netting across the curve. Northern peoples used longer sticks, often as tall as the players themselves. Southern sticks were traditionally shorter. Above the Arctic Circle players used nets with handles so short they were really not "sticks" at all. Southeast peoples played lacrosse with two sticks (see Toli), while in the North the single, longer stick was controlled with both hands.

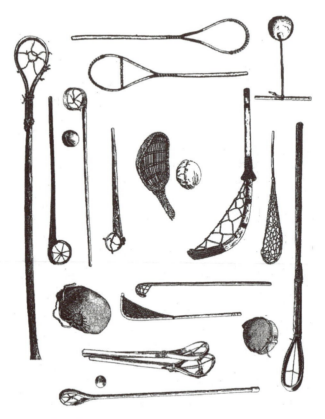

Figure 7.6. There were many variations of the ball-and-racket game, now called lacrosse. *Source*: Adapted from Culin (1975).

Lacrosse balls were often wooden, generally made from a knot, that particularly hard, twisted wood that forms in the trunk where a branch grows from a tree. These slightly egg-shaped knots were carved, polished, and painted for the lacrosse game. Some people used a buckskin ball stuffed hard with hair for lacrosse.

It was important that the teams were of equal number, and since the total number on the field was so large, opponents would line up and pair off before the game to count off. In intervillage contests anywhere from fifty to several hundred people would play for each team. Four or five referees typically watched a match, but for the most part the players were responsible for maintaining fair play.

The game began at the center of the field. In some games a referee tossed the ball into the air to begin play. Others began with a player from each team facing each other with their rackets pressed together.

The referee placed the ball between the rackets and gave a signal, at which the two players lifted the ball into the air. Once the ball was in play, all players attempted to catch, pass and throw it through their opponent's goal. A single point was scored for each goal, and the game would be to a pre-arranged total, generally between twelve and twenty. It could easily take more than half a day to achieve this score, and play became increasingly energetic as the score approached the final goal.

The ball could not be caught or thrown with the hand—only the sticks could be used. Running, jumping, and leaping over one another, scuffling with sticks for a ball on the ground, racing to carry the ball toward the goal, or flailing to knock the ball out of another's racket were all part of the sport. With no protective clothing or equipment it is not surprising that players were frequently injured. At times two players would begin to fight on the field, but the game would go on around them. The referees sometimes broke up the fights with sticks or whips, but most often the players resolved their differences and returned to the game.

Lacrosse is very popular today, so equipment is readily available. "Fiddle sticks" designed for learning to pass and catch the ball are a good introduction to the game. Play with a soft practice ball, or make a ball from leather stuffed with seeds, or use a wooden ball from a craft shop. (A modern lacrosse ball is made of rubber and bounces.) Eye protection is not authentic but highly recommended!

Practice tossing, catching, and carrying the lacrosse ball before attempting to play a game. Divide the group into equal teams and mark goals at the ends of the playing area. Modern lacrosse goals are like soccer goals but smaller. Traditional goals were high: uprights might be as much as twenty feet tall, and the ball had to clear crossbar, ten feet off the ground, to score.

▦ Sawa Puchuma

The peoples of the West Coast competed at casting stone balls with their feet. The ball, about four inches across, was picked up with the toes and rolled onto the top of the right foot. The player had to keep the left foot planted while lifting and throwing the stone as far as possible with the right.

You can use a baseball to practice sawa puchuma.

▦ Tahuka or Haka (Netted Hoop)

In the more common hoop-and-pole games (see tutava) the object was to get the hoop to fall onto the pole, and no points were scored by passing the pole through the hoop. In the netted hoop games of the northern Plains, vines, plant fibers, or leather strips were woven through a ring, creating many small spaces. The object of this game was to pass a dart through the net, preferably through the center of the net, called the "heart." The netted hoop games also involved an element of defending a goal.

Among the Oglala Dakota, the hoop for the netted game was about a foot across, and the rawhide net was tightly woven, so that the spaces were not very large. At each end of a field, about one hundred feet long, a "man" was set up: a stick split at one end so that it had four "feet" on which to stand. (Some scholars have asserted that this game was once played with the corpses of fallen enemies as goals, but there is no hard evidence of this.) The darts were long, nearly four feet, and split on one end so that they could be propelled with a finger. The teams lined up in front of their "men." Each in turn threw a hoop to try to knock the other team's "man" over. The defenders tried to spear the hoop as it rolled by. If one of the defenders managed to spear the hoop through the "heart," he grabbed the hoop and chased the other team, trying to hit the person who threw the hoop with it.

An interesting twist in this game is that it recognized both a winning team and a winning player. The team that knocked over the opponent's "man" most often won the game; the player who pierced the "heart" of the net most often was the winner player. The winning player did not need to be on the winning team.

To play tahuka, make a ring from a thin piece of branch, curled into a circle and lashed together. Cover the hoop with a piece of net from a bag, or for a more authentic target, use a sheet of woven cane made for chair seats or baskets. Mark the "heart" by coloring the center of the net or by weaving red ribbon through the net around the center point. Make darts from light sticks or bamboo splints. Cut notches in the butt ends. The tips do not need to be sharpened but they should be smooth and tapered. To propel the dart, hold it on top of the middle finger with the thumb, and place the index finger against the notch. The forward motion of the arm and the flicking of the finger combine to give speed and direction to the dart. To make the "man," you can split one end of a one-inch-diameter branch into four pieces by making two slices at right angles across the end with a light saw. You may find it easier to make the target by bending two green branches, three or four feet long, in half and binding the bent ends together so that the "feet" splay out.

Create the playing area on a playground or in the gym by setting up the "men" at opposite ends of the space. Players on the "serving" team stand in front of their "man" and bowl at the opposing target. The defenders can move back and forth as they try to spear the target as it approaches, but they cannot run past the centerline toward the opposing goal.

Toli

In the southeastern part of North America the ball game (see paga-danowak) was played with two sticks, called *kapocha* in the Chocktaw language. Players carried the ball by holding it between the netted ends of the kapocha. Sometimes the goal was a single post, which had to be hit with the ball in order to score. Another variation had two posts quite close together. The ball had to be thrown between the poles to score a point.

Tutava (Hoop and Pole)

Hoop-and-pole games were very common among the people of the Plains and the West. Tutava, the Walapai name, comes from the South-west. Two basic forms of hoop and pole were distinguished by different types of scoring. In both types, the game itself consisted of trying to spear the rolling hoop, and the game developed and rewarded skills essential for the hunt.

The hoops for hoop-and-pole games were often made from reeds or supple twigs, curled into a circle and bound tightly with grasses, hide, or bark. In the Northwest, hoops were made by bending a small branch into a circle, covering it with hide, and then filling the cover with sand. Packed tightly this made a very solid, well-balanced hoop for rolling.

The lances or poles for hoop-and-pole games were commonly six to eight feet long, light, and strong. They were generally pointed at one end and often bound with hide at the other to provide for a good grip.

The field for hoop and pole was generally quite large. Teams lined up on either side of the field or, in some versions, in a V-shape. The player chosen to begin the game (generally by lot) rolled the hoop between the lines of players, who chased it as it rolled down the field. The object of the game was to throw the lance so that it would just catch the hoop as it fell over.

In the simpler version of the game, if the hoop fell over onto the lance, the team whose player's lance it was scored one point. Four points won the game. If the tip of the lance was within the hoop, the team won four points and the game immediately—but if the lance was through the hoop, no points were scored.

In the more complex version of the game the hoops were marked with porcupine quills or beads (on the inside of the ring, so they didn't in-terfere with the rolling). Each marking represented a different point value, and whichever marking touched the lance was the score for that throw (Figure 7.7).

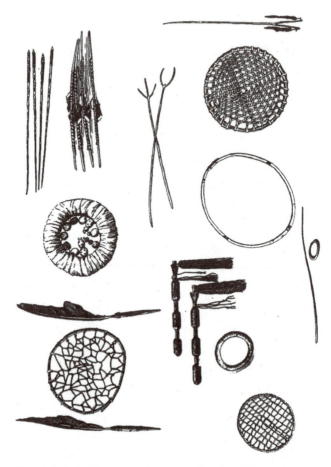

Figure 7.7. Markings on hoops and poles represented the scores for different positions. *Source*: Adapted from Culin (1975).

⊞ OCEANIA

More than 25,000 islands make up the part of the world known as Oceania. Ranging in size from the continent of Australia to some volcanic atolls barely large enough for a tree to take root, these islands are spread across ten million square miles of the South Pacific. Some have had human populations for at least fifty thousand years. Others were settled less than one thousand years ago.

The fact that so many animal species in this region are unique demonstrates that there cannot have been overland accesses between Australia and the mainland of Asia. The peoples of Oceania have always been seafarers. The first human beings who settled in Australia, New Zealand, and the rest of the Pacific islands came by boat, traveling from Southeast Asia across the South China Sea to the islands now part of Indonesia and Papua New Guinea. From there they journeyed east, north to the Philippines, south to Australia, and ever eastward across the Pacific, settling Micronesia, Polynesia, and a host of smaller islands, developing into disparate cultures as Asia became a distant memory. Eventually these rocky paradises would be explored and claimed by competing nations of Europe.

The legends of the South Seas were filled with stories of people who sailed off in the night in search of new lands or missing loved ones. Wayfarers traveled by "star maps," navigating by noting the points where the stars appeared over the horizon and the track of the sun across the waves as it rose and set. Experienced navigators mapped the routes between islands with sticks laid on the sand, which younger sailors memorized, and each generation explored and settled islands further from the mainlands.

Figure 8.1. Wayfarers traversed the open ocean in outrigger canoes. *Source*: La Trobe Rare Books Collection, State Library of Victoria, Australia.

Seventeenth-century European navigators, struggling to circumnavigate the globe with the most advanced navigation technology available, were astounded to hear these tales of local wayfarers traversing the open sea. They were amazed by outrigger canoes stable enough to carry as many as fifty travelers, and primitive sailing vessels that outmaneuvered and outraced their own. Not until the twentieth century did modern scientists begin to believe in the techniques of the ancient sailors.

Wayfaring canoes were built from dugout logs, fitted with "outriggers"—poles with floats on the ends to stabilize the boat (Figure 8.1). Sometimes two canoes were attached with planks between them, providing space for passengers and cargo. These boats were paddled like canoes, but also had huge sails made of woven palm leaves that sailors could tack but could not strike, so that even in a storm the boat would have to ride the wind. The wayfarers not only navigated by the stars, they were astute forecasters of the weather.

Although civilization dates back thousands of years in Australia, New Zealand, and Micronesia, Europeans didn't "discover" these lands until the 1700s, and the local people had kept no written records. Nowhere else in the world does the term "prehistoric" mean "before 1788," as it does in Australia.

Fortunately for our purposes those early Europeans were fascinated by the lives of those local people, although they considered them "savages." They took extensive notes on all manner of activities, including sports still mostly unchanged by contact with outsiders. A number of these games are described here.

Everywhere the Europeans sailed they found people whose lives appeared unspeakably exotic. They marveled to see adults spinning and tossing giant tops, swinging on ropes suspended over the edges of cliffs, completing elaborate string figures, and playing tournaments of board games with hundreds of pieces. Then there were activities the Europeans had never dreamed of: tossing boomerangs; surfing; cliff-jumping; and "sling-shotting" people out of trees. They were even land diving from high towers, with vines tied to the ankles just long enough to keep the diver's neck from being broken. Remarkably, the rate of injuries associated with these activities seems to have been no higher than it is for, say, bungee jumping today.

The people of the South Seas played games that developed hunting and fighting skills, but they also valued recreation for its own sake. Men and women continued to play throughout adulthood. Many of their games were cooperative rather than competitive, and gambling did not seem to have been the scourge here that it was in other parts of the world.

Throughout Oceania games with similar names and rules were played by people in different cultures, probably a legacy of their common ancestry. At the same time a few games were played in the Pacific that recall the hidden-ball and moccasin games of North America, a tantalizing hint of possible contact in that direction as well.

The story of the Western contact with Oceania is not without controversy. Having found people they considered uncivilized, the European response was either to civilize them or deny their humanity. England turned Australia into a penal colony. The Dutch East India Company, finding the spice trade less profitable than they had hoped, turned to shipping opium and slaves. The United States tested atomic bombs on the Bikini islands. These issues are certainly outside the scope of this book. But perhaps we in the modern era can learn something about civilization from those playful people.

GAMES

⠿ Konane

Konane was a game played on Hawaii long before the Europeans "discovered" the islands in the 1770s. Great stone boards, once carved into lava flats (Figure 8.2), have been found on the island, some lined up for "tournament" play, another in the center of a great arena. Apparently konane, like modern chess, could be a spectator sport. Because of the

Figure 8.2. Konane boards like this one were carved into lava flats on Hawaii. *Source:* University of Hawaii Committee for the Preservation of Hawaiian Culture and Language, Bishop Museum.

heavy betting (sometimes to the point of loss of life) associated with konane, early missionaries condemned it. European checkers quickly overtook the local game, and in the early twentieth century it was feared that there would soon be no one left who could play konane. Since then a movement to recall and revitalize indigenous traditions throughout the world has led to a renewal of the old cultures, and a version of konane is now taught to Hawaiian children and tourists as a part of Hawaiian heritage.

The board, *papamu*, is a grid of small depressions or holes. Ancient boards had from as few as sixty-four to more than two hundred holes on a board. A ten-by-ten-square grid makes for a manageable game. Black lava pebbles and white coral fragments were the traditional papa, or pieces. A ten-by-ten papamu requires fifty pieces of each color.

To begin the game, the pieces are placed on the board, filling every hole with colors alternating in diagonal lines. Each player sits so his color is in the right-hand corner hole of his home row.

One player picks up two papa from the board, one of each color, and mixes them behind his back. He holds his closed hands out in front of the other player. Whatever color is in the hand the other player chooses is the color she will play. The papa are then returned to the board. The black player goes first and removes a black papa either from the center of the board or the corner and places it in front of the white player. Now the white player chooses one of the white papa adjacent to the empty space, and presents it to the black player.

For the rest of the game, players capture (and remove) their opponent's papa by jumping over them. Papa can move frontward, backward or sideways but not diagonally. One papa can make multiple jumps in the same direction on the same turn, but may not change directions during a turn. Multiple jumps and captures are not mandatory.

Since the only way to move is to jump, once a player cannot jump over any of her opponent's pieces, she has lost the game. Since black has the advantage of deciding where to begin the game, players alternate colors for the next game.

You can play this game on paper with checkers or coins. Scoop out depressions in the sand or scratch lines on a flat pavement stone and play with light and dark pebbles for a more authentic game.

▦ Lulu

Hawaiian dice were round discs of lava, smoothed and painted. Lulu was played with four discs. Each was painted on one side with two lines dividing it into quarters, and then red dots were added to one, two, three, or all four sections.

The object of lulu was to be the first to accumulate one hundred points.

Players shook the dice in both hands and rolled them on the ground. If all four came face up, the player received ten points and rolled again. Any dice that fell face down were picked up by the next player and rolled, adding points to that player's total.

Make lulu discs from salt-and-flour dough or search for four smooth stones of similar size and weight in a riverbed.

⊞   Manu

Manu was a game played on Hawaii that was very similar to the fox-and-geese games of Europe and the Leopard games of Southeast Asia. The word *manu* can mean "bird" and may have referred to the hopping movement of the stick.

The manu board could be scratched on a flat rock with a stone or traced in the dirt. It was a central square with four rectangular arms, each arm and the square divided on both diagonals, so that the board had seventeen intersections, or points. One player had thirteen *pa-ka*, or small stones. The other player had a single stick, called the *la-au*. The pa-ka could move one point at a time, and the goal for that player was to surround the la-au. The la-au could move one point at a time but could also capture by jumping over a pa-ka into a vacant point beyond, and the object for the player of the la-au was to capture so many pa-ka that the rest could not surround it.

You can draw a manu board on paper or scratch it on a flat stone with another stone. Pebbles and a stick should be easy to find.

⊞   Mu Torere

Mu, or Mu Torere, is a deceptively simple-looking game still played in Australia which is quite challenging to play. Many early anthropologists, perhaps not giving the native people credit for developing such a game, believed it must have been developed from the draughts or checkers introduced by the Europeans. Local people insisted it was an ancient game. It is likely that the local people used the Maori word *mu* to describe the European game as well as their traditional game, thus leading to an erroneous conclusion. The games are not really very similar!

A mu board is an eight-pointed star, which can be easily scratched in the sand as four crossed lines (like an asterisk). The points or spaces are the eight points of the star and the center, or *putahi*. Each player has four pieces: black (lava) or white (coral). The game begins with all the black pieces on one side of the circle and the white pieces on the other. Black always goes first, and players alternate colors for succeeding games.

There are only three moves: into the center, out of the center, and from one point to an adjacent, vacant point. Any piece can move into an empty adjacent point, but a piece can only move to the center if it is adjacent to one or two opposing pieces. (Thus on the first move black can only move one or the other of the two end pieces to the center.) The object of the game is to make it impossible for your opponent to move.

You can draw a mu board on a piece of paper and play the game with coins or checkers, or scratch the board on a rock or draw it with charcoal on bark and play with pebbles for a more authentic version. It's harder than it looks!

▦ Naun (The House)

This two-person *whai* (string game) was played by the Maori in New Zealand and the Yap of the Caroline Islands.

Each person begins with a loop, a piece of string about six feet long (Figure 8.3). The Maori used a length of sinew or hide; the Yap used twine made of plant fibers.

Both players do the first steps: Stretch the loop around the little fingers; turn hands palm away from you, and slide thumbs up under the near (top) string. Turn hands to face each other. Slide the right index finger under the left palm string and draw back. Slide the left index finger under the right palm string and draw back.

Now player A and player B face each other with their fingers pointed at each other. A passes her hands through B's index finger loops. B draws his hands back, leaving the index loops on A's wrists. Now B passes his hands through A's index loops, and A draws her hands back, leaving the index loops on B's wrists.

A takes her hands out of the figure, and B points his hands up (don't stretch the figure). A gathers the loose strings in B's hands, twisting them into a rope. She passes the rope several times under the figure toward B and then over and away from B, wrapping it around loosely and allowing the end to hang down.

A uses her right hand to remove the loop from B's left thumb, and with her left hand removes the loop from B's left little finger. B removes his left hand from the wrist loop and uses his left hand to remove the loops from his right thumb and right little finger, removes his right hand from the wrist loop, and then takes the "little finger" loop in his right hand.

Draw and wiggle the loops apart to create a square within a rectangle with the corners cut off. (You may need to "help" it unroll.) A and B now sit opposite each other with their legs crossed. Each places the right-hand loop on the left foot and the left-hand loop on the right foot. Keep the loops secure by pressing the feet down. Notice that one pair of parallel inner strings lies over the other. Using one hand at each end of the square, pull the bottom pair together and lift them up to form the "ridgepole" of the house. The foot loops represent the stilts or stakes supporting the house.

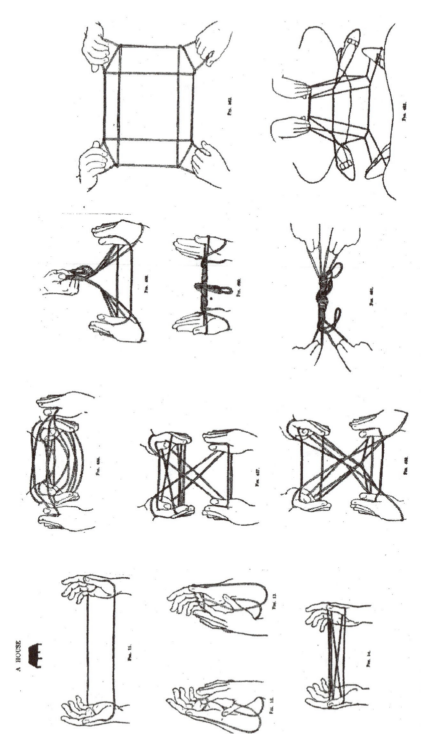

Figure 8.3. Naun was a two-person string game of the Yap and the Maori. *Source:* Adapted from Jayne (1906).

⊞ Puhenehene

This was the Hawaiian version of the universal hidden-object game. Adults and children of all classes played. Five large pieces of colored cloth and a stone, called a *no-a*, were the essential elements. Each player had a pointing stick, about three feet long, polished and decorated with a piece of fur or leaf attached at the end.

Two teams, usually of five players each, sat facing each other on the ground. The folded cloths were laid side by side between the teams so that the edges overlapped. Each color represented a *puu*, or watch of the night: sunset, early night, midnight, early morning, and sunrise. The team to go first selected a "hider," who held the stone in one hand and passed it back and forth under the cloths under the watchful eyes of the seeking team. Eventually the hider left the no-a in one puu, though continuing to move the hand for a while longer to help with the deception. Finally the hider separated the five cloths, rumpling them a bit to help hide the no-a.

Now the seeking team discussed the question, pointing with their sticks at the various piles and trying to guess from the hider's face which was correct. (The hider was allowed to cover her face with her hands during this process.) The seekers took turns tapping the piles of cloth, and a member of the hiding team whipped off each cloth as it was tapped, revealing the stone or the empty space.

The object could be either to find the stone on the fewest number of strikes, or to strike as many empty puu as possible before uncovering the stone. The first team to reach an agreed-upon total number of successes could be declared the winner, or play could continue all day, with the stakes distributed at the end on the basis of the number of rounds won. Young people often played the same game on the beach, with piles of sand and a piece of coral.

Collect five lengths of colorful cloth, and decorate pointing sticks with cloth and feathers to play puhenehene. You also need a stone and some shells for keeping score.

⊞ Ruke

This series of tricks was played with five smooth pebbles in the Maori version of the universal jackstones game. Throughout the game each move had to be done twice before moving on to the next level. A miss required starting over from the beginning, and if more than one player was playing a miss ended the turn.

For the first move four pebbles were lined up on the ground a few inches apart. The fifth stone was tossed into the air and one picked up before catching the tossed stone. The player next tried to pick up two stones while the tossed stone was in the air, then three, and finally all four. When all four stones had been successfully scooped up one at a time, the player set the stones on the ground with two off to one side and two on the other, making the game more difficult.

After successfully picking up all the stones in this alignment, the player began the third part of the game, which involved holding all the stones in the hand and tossing up first one, then two, then three, distributing the others on the ground and catching the tossed stones as they fell.

Finally the stones were spread out in four corners, and the player picked up and moved them to the center while the tossed stone was in the air, first one at a time and then increasing, and finally all four were picked up at once for the final move.

⊞ U (Palm Tree)

This kaikai (string game) was from the Torres Straits. This figure can be done alone if one is barefoot as the South Pacific Islanders were. Otherwise a helper is needed. A four- to six-foot string works best for this game.

To begin, stretch a loop around the little fingers. Turn your hands palm away from you, and slide thumbs up under the near (top) string. Turn your hands to face each other. Slide the right index finger under the left palm string and draw back. Slide the left index finger under the right palm string and draw back.

Have another person take the middle of the near thumb string and draw it away from you over all the other strings and hold it. Drop the loop from the right little finger over the left little finger, and draw the loop off the left little finger on to the right little finger (this is called "exchanging the loops"). Now exchange the loops on the index fingers.

Draw your hands up while the other person pulls down, and spread your fingers. To do this figure alone, instead of having a helper draw the string away from you, turn your hands toward your face and grab all the strings except the near thumb string with your fingers. Hold them tightly while you turn your hands away from you so the thumb string is out front. Bring your foot up and grab the thumb string from the inside with your toe. Pull down, then continue with exchanging the loops.

PLAY

⊞ Boorna Jokee

This Maori spear-dodging game resembled the familiar dodgeball, but the skills developed in this game could save a warrior's life in battle!

One player was "it." The others formed a circle and "it" stood in the center. On the signal, everyone tossed blunted spears at the player who was "it." He dodged and weaved to avoid being hit (ideally without moving his feet). In some versions, "it" held a shield to block spears. When the player was hit or everyone's spears had been tossed, another player became "it."

Younger boys played spear games using stiff reeds or light bamboo sticks for spears, and padded the ends with grass or chewed on them to make them soft. As their skills developed, they began to practice with heavier sticks before graduating to actual spears.

If cattails or rushes grow in your area, you may be able to play with these authentic practice spears. Even last year's ragweed or sunflower stalks will serve as practice spears. Or make soft-tipped spears: glue soft foam balls securely to the ends of lightweight bamboo or sumac sticks, five to six feet long. Shields made of corrugated cardboard should be long and narrow: about six to eight inches wide would be authentic. Put two holes in the center of the shield and thread both ends of a flexible twig through from the front: the two ends form the handle on the back of the shield. (Eye-protection such as lacrosse goggles would be a good modern addition to this game.)

▦ Bowgitee

Bowgitee was a ball game for a large group, not divided into teams. The ball was small, about three inches in diameter, and made of bark tied with string made of hair or plant fiber. The object of the game was simply to keep the ball moving as quickly as possible, tossing or hitting it from one player to another without letting it hit the ground.

You can make a bowgitee ball from bark if you have access to birch or beech logs (do not peel bark off living trees). Otherwise, use construction paper torn into strips about two inches wide for the covering. First, make a net of rough twine: cut twine into pieces about ten inches long. Take one piece as the center string. Tie other pieces around it about every inch along its length. Now tie other pieces into those, parallel to the center string. You will wind up with a "net" with holes about an inch square. (You can use a bag such as onions come in as a substitute.) Collect a couple of handfuls of grass or leaves for the center of the ball. Roll these into a fairly round core. Wrap the strips of bark or paper around the core. Wrap the net around the covering and tie the ends of the strings together.

▦ Kai-panukunuku

Although the South Seas do not have appreciable snowfall, sliding was as popular there as in other parts of the world. Large cabbage-type leaves, called *ti*, made slippery sleds. Children and adults alike would take the leaves to the top of a steep hill, sit on the wide part and twist the ends between the hands to steer. The ride could be quite speedy and sometimes riders landed amid thorns, adding to the excitement. On Hawaii, sleds were also made of wood, like very long skis on runners, and sledding tracks were built up to provide extra momentum. These tracks can still be seen today.

With a steep enough slope, today's plastic snow saucers will allow you to try some summer sliding, especially after a heavy rainfall.

▦ Kaiwhiuwhiu

Rope skipping was a game enjoyed by both adults and children among the Maori. The rope was a long piece of twisted flax. On Hawaii the skipping rope was a long piece of kowali vine. The rope was most often turned by two people while one or more players jumped, but it could be tied to a post or tree so that one person could swing it. The Maori also skipped with two ropes, one turning in each direction. In any case the game was to jump as many times as possible without missing. Singing or chanting helped the skippers to keep the rhythm, especially as the rope turned faster and faster.

▦ Kar Katu

Spindle tops were made throughout the Pacific Islands by piercing fruits and nuts and inserting long wooden spindles. These were set spinning by rolling the spindle between the palms. Adults frequently competed to see whose tops would spin the longest.

Experiment by making tops with a variety of fruits: different shapes will spin differently. Use an awl to make a hole through the fruit and insert a pointed stick (a pencil, a chopstick or even a knitting needle). (Only the tip of the spindle needs to come through the bottom of the fruit: the weight of the top needs to be near the ground.) Nuts are hard to pierce without cracking. Use a very small nail to make a hole, and a toothpick for a spindle.

▦ Ke-a-pua

Ke-a-pua was an arrow-throwing game from the Hawaiian Islands. It was generally played by teams of two, boys against girls. The arrows, called *pu-a*, were made of sugar cane. Pu-a were thrown by the use of a stick with a cord attached (*la-au-ke-a pu-a*). Wrapping the string made of twisted hair or vine around the middle of the arrow, the player would stand with the arrow lying on the ground and the stick held vertically, then whip the stick to pick the arrow up and fling it forward. The team whose arrows went the furthest won the game.

Thin bamboo canes, cut about a foot long, can serve in place of the sugar cane arrows. Cattail stalks or birch or maple twigs also work. The arrow thrower should be about four feet long (shoulder height from the ground). The string must be well-attached to the end of the thrower: slice the end of the stick and thread the string through the notch, then wrap it tightly before tying it. On the arrow, of course, the string is just wrapped around a few times, so that it can pick up the arrow and spin it as it flies. Be sure to try ke-a-pua in a wide open area, and try the motion a few times before competing: it takes practice to be able to launch the arrow in the intended direction.

▦ Kiolaolalena

People of all ages enjoyed this ring-toss game on the Hawaiian Islands. Each player had ten rings of coconut shell, an inch in diameter, and took turns tossing the rings at a pin set in the ground. The one who managed to put the most rings over the pin won a prize or stakes previously put up by all players.

▦ Kirra (Toy Boomerang)

What we think of as a boomerang, a curved stick that returns when thrown properly, is more accurately called a "toy" boomerang. Hunting boomerangs were larger and not designed to return to the thrower. The hunter tossed the boomerang so it "ran" along the ground to bring down an animal, a skill that was also practiced in the boomerang-polo game (see Sports).

Adults and children enjoyed games played with toy boomerangs (Figure 8.4). The simplest game was to throw the boomerang and have it return to the thrower. The player whose boomerang went the farthest and returned closest to his or her feet was the winner. In one variation, the player would catch the returning boomerang on a spear so it would spiral down to the ground.

More complex boomerang games included targets with varying point values. For one game a giant bull's-eye was traced on the ground, with the center circle about ten feet across and the outside circle almost one hundred feet in diameter. Players tossed their boomerangs and tried to land them inside the circle. The player whose boomerang came closest to the center point was the winner. Another target game had pegs set in different locations that players would try to hit in a particular order.

Plastic and foam boomerang toys are readily available at toy stores, and hand-crafted wooden boomerangs are available for those with a serious interest in the sport. You can also make boomerangs from cardboard or light wood. The simplest to build and fly are cross-boomerangs.

Figure 8.4. Men demonstrate throwing the boomerang and the spear. *Source*: Basedow (1925).

Cut two pieces of cardboard (cereal box weight or heavier) ten to twelve inches long and an inch or two wide, with rounded ends. Cross the two arms at the center and attach with glue. Fold the tip of each arm up, about one inch from the end. Or, cut similar shaped arms from light wood (paint stirring sticks work well). Use sandpaper to curve one side of each arm slightly (like an airplane wing). This thinner edge is the front of the boomerang, so attach the arms together so the leading edge is on the left if you are right-handed or on the right if you are left-handed.

Throw boomerangs on a day when there is little wind, and throw into the wind if there is any. Hold the boomerang with the curved side up, then turn your hand so the boomerang is tilted slightly off vertical (toward two o'clock if you are right-handed or ten o'clock if you are left-handed). The windier the day the more vertically you hold the boomerang, but you never throw it completely flat or completely vertically. The boomerang should rise as it moves away from you, turn at the height of the throw and then swoop down and return to you horizontally. You catch a boomerang by clapping your hands over and under it. Be sure to throw boomerangs in an open area and keep your spectators behind you!

Children also folded boomerangs from rushes or leaves and competed to see how far they would fly and how well they would return.

You can make them from rushes or stiff paper. To make a two-armed boomerang, take a single strip about three-fourths of an inch wide and eight to ten inches long. Tie it into a knot and flatten the knot, using glue to hold the folds tight in the center. The two arms should be at about a 60-degree angle. To make a four-armed boomerang, fold four strips six to ten inches long in half. Label each one: A, B, C and D. Place two strips (A and B) side by side, with their open ends pointed in opposite directions. Pass the branches of the third strip (C) around both branches of B and through the folded end of the A (A holds C closed, and C holds B closed). Finally pass the fourth strip (D) around the branches of A and insert it into the folded end of B. Try curving the ends of the arms to adjust the flight patterns. These small boomerangs can be used indoors.

▦ Kolap

For this game of battling tops Lake Eyre women in Australia made tops by flattening one side of a spinning ball (see Appendix) and inserting a wooden peg into the ball before baking it. Each player set her top spinning in a large wooden bowl, or *pirrha*. The woman whose top remained spinning the longest was the winner. In a variation of this game, the women would spin their tops together in the same pirrha. The tops bumped into each other and the one that remained spinning the longest was the winner. (A commercial version of this game became popular in the United States back in the 1970s.)

Use salt dough to make the body of the top and round toothpicks for pegs. A large wooden salad bowl with a fairly flat bottom makes a good pirrha. A mixing bowl is generally too rounded. A large wok will do.

▦ Koolchee

Koolchee was a man's game from the Lake Eyre region of Australia. It was very similar to the European boules. Koolchee balls were made from gypsum or other mud, rolled to a size of about three and one-half inches in diameter and baked or dried. Balls could be colored with ash, so that those of one team were distinct from those of the other. Players lined up one both sides of a smooth, flat piece of ground—the clay surface where a puddle had dried up was good. Each side attempted to roll their balls across the other team's line while at the same time trying to strike and break the opposing team's balls. Each ball that got across the opponent's line scored a point. Balls knocked out or which scored could be retrieved and put back into play. The game was over when there weren't enough balls left in one piece to keep going, and the winner was either the team with the most points or the one with the most balls left at the end!

Use salt dough to make koolchee balls (see Appendix).

⊞ Lelekoali

South Pacific peoples were very fond of swinging, and their versions were not for the fainthearted! The swinging rope was generally quite long, so that the arc of the swing was very large. The rope might be suspended high in a tree, or on a pole near a cliff, so that the arc carried the swinger out over the precipice. Other variations included hanging the rope from a pole held aloft by a couple of friends. In New Zealand the Maori suspended multiple ropes, as many as twelve, from the same pole, so that several people might swing around and around at the same time. If the cliff was along the seaside the game might include dropping from the rope into the water below.

On Fiji swings had a loop tied in the end for the swinger's foot. Tahitians tied a stout stick into the end of the rope, which the swinger sat upon with one leg on either side of the rope. Sometimes another person sat facing the first, with legs wrapped around her waist, while others pulled ropes tied around their waists to swing them back and forth.

⊞ Makamaka

This common game with many names in many places, involved simply tossing a stick back and forth from hand to hand as quickly as possible. Fancy moves (under the leg, around the back) such as a modern child might do with a basketball were encouraged, but by dropping the stick you were out!

Use a piece of branch about a foot long for makamaka. One with a crook in the end is even better.

⊞ Ngor-go

The ngor-go is a small gourd. To make this into a spinning toy the Mallanpara drilled two holes in one side of the dried gourd, threaded a string made from hair through the holes, and tied it to form a loop. Holding the looped string between the fingers and thumbs, the player spun the gourd around and around to twist the string. Pulling the hands apart made the string unwind and the gourd spin, and by his varying the tension on the string the gourd could be made to spin faster or slower and for a longer time. In some communities pairs of players held their ngor-go so they could "fight" until one or another broke, rather like the European game of conkers or Japanese fighting kites. This amusement could also be made into a game simply by having more than one player compete for the longest spin.

Toys like this are available for purchase but it would not be difficult to make one from a wooden disk. The small decorative gourds sold in the fall would make even more authentic ngor-go.

⊞ Panapanahua

This seed-shooting game was played with the seeds of the kakalaioa plant, often called *seabeans* or *nickernuts*. These are nearly round, and the game was almost identical to some marbles games from other cultures.

Players drew a ring ten to twelve feet across in the dirt, and each player put an equal number of seeds in the ring. Players took turns shooting from outside the ring, trying to knock the seeds out. Any that they succeeded in knocking out of the ring they kept. When the first player missed, he placed his shooter (a larger seed, called a *kini*) in the ring. If another player hit the kini before hitting any other marbles, that player would be out of the game. If another player hit the kini after hitting other marbles, the owner of the kini had to place another "starting" number of marbles in the ring.

You can play panapanahua with nickernuts collected at the beach or with marbles. You can also make marbles from paper maché.

⊞ Panapanalua

To play this seed-shooting game each player contributed an equal number of beans, called *papapa*. Players dug a small hole and piled the beans next to the hole. Then they took turns "flipping" the beans into the hole from a line some distance away, using the forefinger and thumb. A player continued flipping until he or she missed, passing the turn to the next player. The winner was not usually the player who put in the most beans but the player who put in the last bean.

⊞ Peepeeakua

Peepeeakua was a hide-and-seek game played on Hawaii. The player who was "it," called the ghost, was determined by counting out.

One Hawaiian counting-out rhyme goes like this:

A-ka-hi ou o-i ha
Pa-e-le pa-ki-ni
I-kau-a le-hei pa
Mai no a-la-ea
Mo-mo-na ka-pe-le-na
Ka-I-o-le wi-lu.

Then, while the others hid, the ghost would hide his eyes and another player chanted:

ku-i-ku-i
ka-mu-mu-mu
ho-lo i-u-ka
ho-lo-kai

and tapped out the rhythm on the ghost's back. Once all the others were hidden, the chanter stopped and the ghost began to search.

In Rotuma a home-based version of hide-and-seek was played on the beach. The base was marked with a circle or pole, and while the seekers searched for the hidden players, the hidden ones tried to sneak back to touch the base without being spied.

⊞ Poi

In New Zealand the Maori played several games of catch with balls made of rushes. Players sat or stood opposite each other and tossed the ball back and forth while singing a rhyming song. This game was also played in canoes (*waka-poi*), with players tossing the balls back and forth across the water. The balls sometimes had strings attached, and these could be used for a solo game of tossing the ball and then catching it as it rebounded on the string.

These balls were made from rushes or palm leaves braided into flat strips and folded into box shapes (they were more cubic than spherical). A piece of twine could be easily tied through two openings in the ball.

To make a palm-leaf ball, take a handful of flat leaves and braid three or four strips. (You may need to soak the palms if they are stiff, and you will almost certainly need to stitch or staple the ends together to start the braid, unless you're very accomplished at palm braiding.) The strips will tend to curve as you braid them. Draw the end of one palm through the braid to form a circle, and start the next one by threading a palm through the braid and perpendicular to that circle. Three or four braids will make a tennis-ball-sized ball, hollow and very light.

⊞ Po-po-jo

Spinning balls and tops were popular throughout Oceania, and even had ritual significance for some people. (A ball that spun for a long time was a good omen; one that stopped quickly could be considered a warning.) Spinning balls were usually small, up to one and one-half inches in diameter, and could be made from mixtures of clay, lime, ashes, or sand, sometimes with hair mixed in for strength. These would be rolled smooth and baked until hard.

The simplest spinning game was played by two or more players, each setting his or her balls spinning at the same time. The balls could be set to spin on a flat clay pan, hard-packed sand, or even a reed mat. The ball that spins the longest was the winner.

Use a smooth salt dough to make spinning balls (see Appendix).

▦ Potaka

Whipping tops were carved from various kinds of wood in the Pacific Islands, ranging from small tops that would fit in a child's hand to tops ten or more inches tall. Top whips were made of flax fibers attached to a stick. The preferred method of spinning the top was to hold it above the ground and drop it with one hand, catching it with the whip and setting it spinning as it fell.

▦ Pouturu

Stilts were a useful method of transportation that could be used for fun as well. Maori stilts were as much as six feet long, with flax loops for the feet. They were used for fording streams and making rapid progress over rough ground.

SPORTS

▦ Boogalah

This Juwalarai keep-away game was played by teams representing different totemic groups or clans. The ball was made of kangaroo skin and inflated. Any player tossed the ball into the air to begin the game. The first to catch the ball ran to the center of the field, and her team gathered around her. The opposing team formed a circle around the group. Now the team possessing the ball had to throw the ball back and forth, keeping it in the air, while the opposing team attempted to capture it. When the opposing team captured the ball, they converged on the center and the other team formed a circle around them, and so the game continued.

You can play boogalah with a small beach ball. For a more authentic ball, stitch strips of fake leather together: Form one strip into a circle. Put another around it, set off at an angle. Place a third strip beside the second, and so forth. Put a balloon or plastic bag inside the leather ball and inflate it. Stitch the ball closed (don't put a hole in the balloon!).

▦   Buroin:jin

Teams from different villages or tribes competed in this Jagara ball game, with as many as eight players on each side. The ball was made of kangaroo skin, stitched with sinew and stuffed with grass, not quite as big as a modern soccer ball.

A pole stuck in the ground was the goal and also the scoreboard. To begin, the ball would be tossed into the air and all players would try to catch it. Once a player caught the ball, he or she ran toward the pole, while the other team tried to catch the ball carrier. If an opponent tagged the carrier, he immediately had to get rid of the ball, passing it to a nearby teammate if possible, while the opposing players tried to intercept it. When a player reached the goal with the ball he pulled up the post. A notch was made in the post to mark the goal, and the post was replaced in the ground for the next play.

A modern football or rugby ball would work for this game, but don't inflate it, as it shouldn't bounce. The actual ball would be a bit lighter and easier to grab. You can make a buroin:jin ball in the same way as the boogalah ball (discussed earlier), but stuff it with cut grass instead of inflating it.

▦   Currum-currum

This disk-spearing game was also known as *gorri* and *wungoolay*. It had many different names as it was played throughout Australia. The game developed spear-throwing skills essential for hunting.

A *currum*, or disk, could be a slice of gum-tree bark or a thick piece of kelp. It could be as large as three feet in diameter, but one to two feet was more common and the size could be decreased to increase the challenge as the players became more skillful.

Players formed two teams and lined up facing each other with a clear path between them. The bowler stood at one end of the field, about fifteen feet from the lines of players, and called "are you ready?" When everyone responded "ready," the bowler sent the disk toward the path. Players flung their spears (sharpened sticks) to hit the disk and knock it over (Figure 8.5). The player who succeeded in spearing the disk was the next to bowl.

This game can be easily recreated with light sticks (bamboo or sumac would work well) and a toy flying disk or even a paint-can lid. The action of the currum will differ depending on how it is thrown: it can either bounce along the path or roll. Practice at both developed skills for hunting different kinds of animals. Uneven grass or dirt adds to the unpredictable behavior of the disk.

Figure 8.5. Men and boys chase down the currum. *Source*: Base-dow (1935).

⊞ Heiheiwaa

Canoe races in the Pacific Islands generally ran from the shore out to a marker set a mile or more out in the water, particularly in the smooth waters between a coral reef and the shore. The turning point could be marked with a bouy (a gourd floating on the surface tied to a stone anchor), or a swimmer on a surfboard. Several kinds of racing canoes were common in the Pacific. Long boats propelled by many oarsmen who coordinated their pulling could cover great distances with speed. Other smaller racing canoes (*tavane*) had long, low sails of woven mats that gave the single racers remarkable control. Both men and women competed in canoe races.

⊞ Hukihukikaula

For this Hawaiian rope-pulling competition, teams of seven arranged themselves at either end of a rope made of vine. In order to win one team had to pull the other across the center line.

⊞ Kokan

Games of striking a ball with a stick were very common among the local people in Australia and the Torres Straits before the arrival of the Europeans. In this Mabuiag version, the ball was made of wood, but in other locations a large nut was used. Some people used a wooden ball that was covered with clay and baked. Sticks made from branches or roots were curved and hardened in a fire. The playing field or pitch was a long stretch of sand. Goals could be marked at each end or not, as the teams agreed. Either way the object of the game was to keep the ball away from the other team while hitting and passing it into the other team's end of the field, through the marked goal or just across the end line. Any number of people could play but the teams were kept even, with players substituting in and out as they tired.

▦ Kylie (Hunting Boomerang)

In Australia the kylie, or hunting boomerang, was used not only for hunting but also for digging, hoeing, and even as a percussion instrument. They were not made to return to the thrower but were thrown to bring down game animals or to frighten birds into a net. The kylie could be tossed through the air or so that it "ran" or rolled along the ground. The hunter held the boomerang by its longer arm and threw it so that it spun, end over end, toward its target.

The community divided into two teams for a running game often described as *boomerang polo*. Teams were usually older men versus boys. A boomerang was rolled along the ground and both teams chased it. The first to catch the boomerang rolled it again, either in the same direction or back toward the crowd. It is not clear from the record how points were scored but the observers noted than the older men often won because of their better strategy, despite the boys' greater speed. It seems likely that a "point" was scored each time a team captured and threw the boomerang.

Instructions for constructing toy boomerangs may be found under kirra in this section. For polo the boomerang doesn't need a curved edge (because you're not trying to make it return through the air). A more authentic hunting-style boomerang can be made from a branch with a natural crook in it. The wood should be cut so that one arm is longer than the other, and the longer arm should be about the length of the thrower's forearm. (The shape of a traditional boomerang is frequently compared to a banana.) Remove the bark from the wood and sand the ends smooth.

▦ Litia

This distance competition was a common feature of intervillage tournaments in Samoa. Men and women both competed, and the losing team provided a feast at the end of the match.

The "spears" for the game were hibiscus sticks, eight to ten feet long and about as big around as a finger. With the bark peeled off to make them smooth and light they could be flung a surprising distance—one hundred feet or more. Contestants lined up and threw their spears on a signal, then the next set of competitors stepped up to take their turns. When all had thrown the results were tallied, and the team with the greatest number of winners after a set number of throws won the match.

■ Maika

This bowling game was played in the Warrina region of Australia using granite balls that did not break when struck (unlike koolchee, see Play). In Hawaii it was played with balls, called *ulu*, made of coral, lava, or other stone. Ulu ranged from golf-ball to bowling-ball size. The game required a smooth "alley," thirty to forty feet long, such as a stretch of sand. The first player would roll the ball as far as possible from the starting point. The second would attempt to strike the ball belonging to the first. If he was successful, he would roll again from that point. If not, the first player would win that turn and start again. On each turn the player who bowled the furthest won. In Hawaii the game was sometimes played with a goal, two upright sticks a few inches apart at the far end of the alley which the players tried to bowl through to win the game. The same alley could be used for maika and for pahee.

Croquet balls or softballs can be used to play maika.

■ Maona

Wrestling in the Pacific Islands was a popular sport for both casual participants and spectators at intervillage and interisland tournaments. It was called *maona* in Tahiti, *kulakulai* in Hawaii, and *te takaro* among the Maori.

A ring about thirty feet across was prepared on the beach or in a level field. Teams of wrestlers entered the ring, six to ten on a side. Each wore a *maro*, or girdle, and their bodies were oiled. They walked around the ring, scoping out their opponents, and finally an individual issued a challenge by thumping on his own chest to create a hollow sound in front of the chosen opponent, who accepted the challenge with the same motion. The other wrestlers stepped back to allow the two to begin their battle.

The wrestling stance in the Pacific Islands was to put one arm around the opponent's neck and the other around his waist. In some places the wrestlers assumed this position and then waited for the signal to begin grappling. In others they paced and dodged in the ring, each attempting to gain an advantage by catching the other offguard when grasping him. In either case the object of the match was to throw the opponent to the ground, and any fall counted (no particular part of the body had to touch the ground). When one went down the victor's fans began singing and shouting, while the loser's partisans hooted and yelled to try and drown them out. The loser was eliminated. The victor could remain in the ring to accept another challenge or withdraw.

⊞ Mokomoko

This Hawaiian festival game pitted village or island champions against each other in a weapons-throwing contest. (A similar contest, called *te paro mako*, was played by the Maori in New Zealand.) The contestants stood at opposite ends of a space marked on the sand. First one threw, and the other tried to dodge and jump clear to avoid being hit. Then they reversed roles. There were four rounds of seven throws each: seven spears, seven stones, seven axes, and seven knives. A single hit eliminated the contestant (and sometimes killed him).

You can play mokomoko with foam rubber weapons.

⊞ Nalu

Surfboards originated in the South Pacific, and surfing races (nalu) were a favorite sport from ancient times. Carved from the wood of the breadfruit tree, surfboards were five or six feet long on average and a bit more than a foot wide, although smaller ones were made for children and some large ones have been found which must have been for carrying multiple riders, since they were too heavy for one person to carry. Surfboards were stained and polished, rubbed with coconut oil, and dried carefully between uses.

Surf racing itself is virtually unchanged from its origins: the racers (both men and women) paddled away from shore on their boards, and when they reached the agreed-upon spot, lay or kneeled on the boards to await a good wave, then ride in propelled by the force of the wave. The more skilled the surfer the more upright he or she could remain on the board, and the truly expert could stand up as the wave lifted the board and ride in triumphantly on foot.

⊞ Oma-whakataetae

Various footraces were run for prizes in the Pacific Islands. Races of one-half to three-quarters of a mile were common, often run on the level sand of the beach. Sometimes the race course was out-and-back but more often it was a straight length.

In a Hawaiian race called *heiheihaawe* the runner carried a teammate on his shoulders as he ran.

⊞ Pahee

This was a Hawaiian game very similar to teka. The pahee was carved of heavy wood, carved and polished with a pointed head about six inches long and a tapered shaft, two to five feet long. These were balanced so when tossed they raced along the hard-packed ground. Villages would gather to compete, each represented by their best players, while spectators cheered and ran up and down the sidelines to mark the places where the darts stopped.

Pahee could be played just for distance but was more often the game was one of dexterity as well. Two pahee would be laid side by side partway along the track, and the throwers would have to aim their pahee so that it traveled between the two without touching them on its way.

The starting line was marked on the ground, and players would begin several yards back so that by running up to the line they added velocity to their throws. Each player would throw in turn, then the results would be tallied and another round played, until each player had thrown ten tries.

⊞ Pando

Pando was a football game from Australia for two large teams, often totaling anywhere from fifty to two hundred players. This game was played with a small ball (orange-sized) made of skin and stuffed with ground charcoal. The ball was kicked high into the air (reportedly as much as fifty feet). Once the ball was in play it could only be hit with the feet. The object of the game was to keep possession of the ball without letting it touch the ground. Players would leap high into the air to kick the ball to a teammate, and the game could range over a great expanse of ground.

⊞ Pekukinipopo

This was a form of football in Hawaii played with a single goal (a hole in the ground), and a large stuffed ball made of cloth or skin. Two teams of players would kick the ball, each trying to force it into the goal while the other tried to defend the goal and steal the ball.

⊞ Pelepele

On festival days in Hawaii and Tahiti boxing matches attracted huge crowds of spectators. Three judges oversaw each match. Players boxed bare-fisted or with their fists wrapped in strips of cloth and their arms stretched out in front of them. All blows were aimed at the face and head. Opponents avoided being hit by dodging blows rather than by parrying blows. Any fall, whether by being hit or by slipping, ended the fight, and the boxer left standing was the victor. In some of the Pacific Islands both men and women boxed, but in most places it was a man's sport.

⊞ Purru Purru

This keep-away ball game of the Jagara people of Australia was played by both men and women using a small ball of skin stuffed with grass. The group divided into two even teams. Once the ball was tossed into the air, the object was to keep the ball away from the other team without it touching the ground. Players would leap and catch the ball, tossing it back and forth to teammates. Allowing the ball to touch the ground awarded a point to the opposing team.

⊞ Teka

Teka, also known as weetweet and kukuru, was a game best played on the beach, though any open flat area would do. Many Pacific Island settlements had a carefully maintained grass track for playing teka.

A Maori dart was constructed out of a piece of kelp into which two sticks or stiff grasses were inserted to form about a forty-five degree angle. Each thrower inserted a stick into the point and tossed the dart, preferably underhand (*kokiri*) as far as it would go. The throwers chased the darts, scooping them up, and throwing them again and again until they crossed the finish line.

On Fiji the dart for teka was heavier—a stiff reed which when tossed properly would bounce off the ground and fly through the air toward the target.

A related game known as timata involved tossing a stick about one foot long with a cavity hollowed out at one end, into which the thrower inserted the end of the tossing stick: a sort of atlatl, but one that was only used as a toy, not a weapon.

▦ APPENDIX

MAKING AND FINDING PIECES FOR GAMES

▦ Things to Collect

Game pieces can be made from any number of found objects in a typical home or school. Sending out a request for bottle caps, erasers, straws, ice-cream sticks, broken crayons, and leftover pieces from old games generally results in a sizeable collection of suitable materials.

Colorful glass "stones" sold for fish tanks make wonderful game pieces. Choose the ones that are flat on one side.

Craft supply stores and unfinished wood stores often sell small wooden shapes that can be used for game pieces. You may find wood suitable for game boards there as well.

Wax collected from candle ends, crayons, and cheeses can be molded into a variety of game pieces.

Many games from Africa, Asia, and the Middle East use cowrie shells as counters or dice. These can be purchased inexpensively from craft stores.

Many ancient and medieval games used "knucklebones" as dice or playing pieces. A butcher or slaughterhouse will probably be willing to save these for you if you want to create authentic bone pieces. Otherwise, use modeling dough to recreate the bones.

⊞ Modeling Doughs

Many different game pieces can be molded from dough or paper maché. These are also available at craft supply shops, or you can use these recipes to make your own.

Coarse Salt and Flour Dough. A dough of one part salt to two parts flour will yield a fairly smooth dough. The more salt you add (up to equal parts salt and flour) the grainier the dough will be and the harder and more brittle the resulting object (some of the games require balls that will break when struck). Mix the dry ingredients and add water gradually. Use just enough water to make the mixture moldable (the more water you add, the longer the dough takes to dry). Depending on the thickness of the object, salt dough will dry in two or three days. You can dry salt dough in a low oven (about 200° F) but it may crack.

Smooth Salt and Flour Dough. Use two parts flour to one part salt, and as much water as salt. Add one tablespoon of cooking oil for each cup of flour used. Cook the dough over low heat while stirring until it becomes clay-like. As soon as it cools, knead the dough to a smooth consistency. (A teaspoon of alum for each cup of flour improves the consistency of the dough but isn't necessary.)

Wood "Dough." A mixture of fine sawdust and white glue will produce a dough that when dry looks like wood. This is a good way to reproduce "carved" playing pieces.

Stone "Dough." A mixture of one part cornstarch to two parts sand will produce a grainy dough that dries to resemble stone. Add one and one-half parts hot water to make a slurry, then cook the mixture over medium heat until the cornstarch thickens and the mixture becomes doughy. (A teaspoon of alum for each cup of cornstarch improves the consistency of the dough but isn't necessary.)

Paper Maché. A light paper maché dough made from paper napkins or tissue paper can be molded into imitation nickernuts. Medium-weight paper maché made from newsprint can be used for other playing pieces.

Tear the paper into small pieces and soak in warm water. Light paper will immediately dissolve and only requires a small amount of water. Newsprint takes longer to break down, so you will need to use extra water, and either let it soak overnight or boil it. You may want to use a blender or mixer to reduce the soggy newsprint to a pulp. Then drain out the excess water by pressing it through a sieve or squeezing it with your hands.

Once you have the paper pulp, add white glue for light dough or wallpaper paste for a heavier dough. Knead the pulp into a dough-like consistency and model into the pieces you need. Paper maché objects can be painted when they dry, or you can add coloring to the mash before the glue to color the whole batch. Some teachers recommend adding a few drops of oil of clove to the pulp to prevent mold from growing in the dough.

▦ Plant Materials and Wood

Garden supply stores stock lightweight wood and bamboo stakes that can be used for many of the spear/dart/arrow games included in this book. Inexpensive bamboo mats and window shades can be taken apart, and each will provide many lightweight splints. Chinese restaurants often have calendars printed on bamboo that are disposed of at the end of the year. They'll generally be happy to donate them instead. Rushes, reeds, raffia, and other plant materials are also available from basketmaking and chair-caning suppliers. A number of excellent paper substitutes for rushes are sold which are less expensive and easier to work with than the real thing.

You can buy wood in the form of dowels, boards, two-by-fours, and other lumber at building supply stores. You may also be able to find wood remnants inexpensively through sawmills and builders.

Most of the projects in this book that require wood can be completed using pieces of the size that are commonly pruned from trees under power lines and in landscaped areas. Small saplings that grow rapidly along the edges of fields and roadsides are generally of little value to landowners, who may in fact be glad to have someone cut them back. Ask!

Be sure to use tools, including chainsaws, saws, planers, and sanders according to manufacturers' instructions, and get help if you're not experienced with them.

MAKING BALLS

Many of the games described in this book used balls made of leather or cloth stitched and stuffed with such materials as hair, grass, sand, ash, or dried beans. These balls were not perfectly round! You can easily make an authentic ball from imitation or real leather or any heavy cloth.

There are several designs which result in a relatively round ball. The simplest is to cut a round piece of material, gather the edges and tie or stitch them (like a bag), fill the bag/ball with the stuffing, and then finish closing the hole. The edges can be tucked inside the opening before closing it for a rounder ball.

A slightly more complex design is made with two rectangular strips of material. The first is shaped into a loop and stitched. The next is wrapped around it and stitched in place at a perpendicular angle to the first, leaving one side open for stuffing. Using more strips and making each strip narrower will result in a rounder ball.

Finally, the ball's shape can be made more precisely round by tapering the ends of the strips before stitching them together. The panels of a plastic inflatable beach ball demonstrate this design.

MAKING BOWS, ATLATLS AND OTHER WEAPONS

Keep in mind that weapons are inherently dangerous! They were developed for hunting and for battle, and using weapons training exercises as sports doesn't change the basic nature of these tools. So use caution in both building and trying traditional weapons.

The most ancient weapons are sticks and stones. They could be thrown at a victim or held and used to hit the opponent. Over time these were refined, taking on distinctive forms in various parts of the world. Sticks in the hand became swords, axes, lances, and quarterstaffs. Thrown sticks became spears. Spears in turn were further refined and made more effective. Light spears developed into a specialized dart thrown with an atlatl, giving it much more force and distance. Heavier spears became javelins and harpoons, often thrown using a string to spin the spear, improving velocity and aim. Bows developed from the string, as a fixed string was found to give the hunter more control, and smaller arrows provided the hunter with more possible shots than a single spear. Darts, which probably developed later than arrows, and were either thrown or projected by air ("blow darts").

▦ Atlatls

For Central American Indians, especially the Aztec, and the peoples of the South Pacific, the atlatl was the preferred method of launching an arrow. An atlatl is often incorrectly called a spear thrower. A spear is heavier than a dart and rigid, and would be very difficult to launch with an atlatl. An atlatl is a short "handle" made of wood, with a notch or hollow in one end. The "dart" is essentially a very long arrow, complete with fletching ("feathers") and sometimes weights to correct its flight trajectory. The archer holds the atlatl with the dart lying along it, the fletched end of the dart resting in the notch. Raising the arm over his or her head, the archer launches the dart with a motion often compared to that of a fly-fisher casting. The final flick of the wrist frees the end of the dart from the atlatl notch and propels it forward.

To make an atlatl, you will need a piece of a branch about as long as your forearm, and half as big around. Cut the branch in half lengthwise, leaving just the back four or five inches around. If the heartwood comes away easily, the "trench" in the center of the atlatl will hold and guide the dart. Hollow out a shallow hole in the thicker portion of the atlatl to hold the end of the dart.

⊞ Bows

By the medieval period there were several distinctive types of bows in use around the world. Europeans used longbows, short bows, and mechanical crossbows. The Mongols used a very powerful short bow. Arab archers used small bows easily carried and fired on horseback. In Asia, Chinese archers used medium-length bows reinforced with horn, with a heavy bronze grip for the archer to grasp when drawing or re-stringing the bow. Japanese archery, kyudo, was notable for the use of very long bows made from layers of bamboo and wood, held so that two thirds of the bow was above the archer's bow hand when firing. In Africa, the Bambuti used small quick bows and relied on accuracy for their kills, while the Watutsi had longer, heavier bows. Some African people, such as the Maasi, preferred their traditional spears. In the Americas, most of the North American peoples relied on a longbow, but in Central America the atlatl ruled and in the far north, the harpoon. In the dense South American forests shorter bows and blowguns were more useful. Hunters in the South Pacific used atlatls and boomerangs.

Europeans and the people of the Americas used self-bows, the body of the bow made from a single piece of wood or many layers of wood glued together along the length of the bow. Asian and Middle Eastern bows were composite bows, made in sections: a handle and two "arms," notched and glued together, with pieces or horn attached at the ends. Turkish and Persian archers generally wore a "thumb ring" with which to draw back the string.

You can make a simple self-bow just for fun from a straight green sapling and ordinary string, although a real bow would be made from carefully seasoned wood, cut and carved to take advantage of the grain, the strength of the heartwood, and the flexibility of the sapwood. Notch the ends of the bow to hold the string tight, wrapping the string several times around the notch after bringing the string through it.

Thanks to the popularity of renaissance recreations and primitive skills courses, complete instructions for making bows are readily available if you want to make a more authentic reproduction. Be aware that it is a task that will take many months to complete, including time spent sea-soning the wood.

▦ Arrows and Darts

An arrow at its simplest is just a long, lightweight stick with a point. The addition of stone or metal points at one end makes it a more effective weapon, and fletching, or feathers, at the other end makes its flight truer. Softwoods such as pine or hemlock are lightest and will fly the furthest. Birch and alder grow straighter and are a bit sturdier. Choose the straightest pieces you can find, about one-quarter inch in diameter. Remove any bark and sand away rough spots. Whittle a slight point at one end and a nock (notch) in the other. Feathers for fletching may be purchased from craft stores or collected at the beach or fields. Trim feathers so they will lie flat against the shaft and bind them tightly to it. Note: the fletching should not reach beyond the end of the arrow or it will interfere with the archer's ability to place the nock against the string.

Darts for throwing with atlatls should be four or five feet long for the South American style, even longer to recreate those of Oceania. They can be thicker than arrows for bow shooting, but should still be flexible.

Recreational darts were probably originally broken arrows with the broken shafts whittled down to take a point. In the corn-growing regions of North America and Central America, darts were often made from pieces of corncob, with a pointed stick or thorn inserted in one end and the quills of feathers stuck into the other.

▦ Spears, Lances, Javelins, Quarterstaffs, and Fighting Sticks

These weapons were generally an inch or more in diameter and rigid. Broomsticks and dowels can often be used to represent these weapons, or they can be cut from saplings. Staffs and sticks were generally straight. Spears, lances, and javelins were tapered to a point for aerodynamics as much as for stabbing.

A NOTE ABOUT GAMBLING

In several chapters of this book mention was made of the condemnation and prohibition of games because of religious and moral objections to gambling. These issues are not simply historical curiosities. Some people today have religious objections to gambling. Strictly religious Muslims will not participate in any game that has an element of chance and risk. Some Protestants will not participate in games that have components associated with gambling or fortune-telling, such as dice and cards. Other people avoid gambling games because of their own bad experiences or those of family members.

Most people are not opposed to games that are not played for money, and most games are fun to play with no stakes involved. If a stake is necessary for the game or desirable in order to be authentic, the stakes can be made part of the game equipment rather than something provided by the players, eliminating the element of risk. Stick counters, poker chips, play money, sunflower seeds, and corn kernels are all possibilities. If the game is being played as part of a party or festival, consider providing small candies or chocolate coins for stakes.

⊞ BIBLIOGRAPHY

Ahsan, Muhammed Manazir. *Social Life under the Abbasids*. London: Longman Group, 1979.

Ares, Philippe. *Centuries of Childhood: A Social History of Family Life*. New York: Random House, 1962.

Avedon, Elliott, webmaster. "Museum and Archive of Games." Waterloo, Ontario: University of Waterloo, 2001. <http://www.ahs.uwaterloo.ca/~museum/index.html>.

Avedon, Elliott Morton, and Brian Sutton-Smith. *The Study of Games*. New York: John Wiley & Sons, 1971.

Baker, William J. *Sports in the Western World*. Totowa, NJ: Rowman and Littlefield, 1982.

Baker, William, and James A. Mangan. *Sport in Africa*. New York: Africana Publishing Co., 1987.

Basedow, Herbert. *The Aboriginal Australian*. Adelaide: F.W. Preece and Sons, 1925.

Basedow, Herbert. *Knights of the Boomerang*. Sydney: Endeavor Press, 1935.

Basso, Ellen B. *The Kalapalo Indians of Central Brazil*. New York: Holt, Rinehart and Winston, 1973.

Bean, Lowell John, and Lisa J. Bourgeault. *Indians of North America: The Cahuilla*. New York: Chelsea House Publishers, 1989.

Beattie, James Herries. *Traditional Lifeways of the Southern Maori*. Dunedin, New Zealand: University of Otago Press, 1994.

Beavers, Anthony F., and Hiten Sonpal, designers. "Argos: Area Search of the Ancient and Medieval Internet." Evansville, IN: Evansville University, 2001. <http://argos.evansville.edu/>.

Beckwith, Carol, and Angela Fisher. *African Ceremonies*. New York: Harry N. Abrams, 1999.

Bell, Richard C. *Board and Table Games from Many Civilizations*. Facsimile. New

York: Dover Publications, 1979 (original, Oxford, UK: Oxford University Press, 1960, 1969).

Bell, Richard C. *The Boardgame Book*. London: Marshall Cavendish, 1979.

Berdan, Frances F. *Indians of North America: The Aztecs*. New York: Chelsea House Publishers, 1989.

Bett, Henry. *The Games of Children, Their Origin and History*. London: Methuen & Co., 1929.

Blanchard, Kendall, and Alyce Taylor Cheska. *The Anthropology of Sport*. South Hadley, MA: Bergin and Garvey, 1985.

Blanchard, Laura V., and Carolyn Schriber. "ORB: The Online Reference Book for Medieval Studies." Memphis, TN: Rhodes College, 2001. <http://orb.rhodes.edu/>.

Bloom, Jonathan, and Sheila Blair. *Islam: A Thousand Years of Faith and Power*. New York: Gardner Films, 2000.

Brown, John Macmillan. *The Riddle of the Pacific*. Kepton, IL: Adventures Unlimited Press, 1996.

Bureau of Indian Affairs. *Indians, Eskimos and Aleuts of Alaska*. Washington, DC: Government Printing Office, 1968.

Calloway, Colin G. *Indians of North America: The Abenaki*. New York: Chelsea House Publishers, 1989.

Cantor, Norman F., general editor. *The Encyclopedia of the Middle Ages*. New York: Viking, 1999.

Carter, J.M. *Medieval Games: Sports and Recreations in Feudal Society*. Westport, CT: Greenwood Press, 1992.

Carter, J.M. *Sports and Pastimes of the Middle Ages*. New York: University Press of America, 1988.

Carter, J.M., and A. Krüger. *Ritual and Record: Sports Records and Quantification in Pre-modern Societies*. Westport, CT: Greenwood Press, 1990.

Chagnon, Napoleon. *Yanomamö: The Fierce People*. New York: Holt, Rinehart and Winston, 1968.

Chelminski, Rudolph. "Jeu de Paume, Anyone?" Washington, DC: Smithsonian Institute, 2000. <http://www.smithsonianmag.si.edu/smithsonian/issues00/jan00/tennis.html>.

Cheska, Alyce Taylor. *Traditional Games and Dances in West African Nations*. Schorndorf, Germany: K. Hofmann, 1987.

Clendinnen, Inga. *Aztecs*. Cambridge, UK: Cambridge University Press, 1991.

Coe, Michael D. *The Maya*. New York: Thames and Hudson, 1999.

Coe, Michael D. *Mexico, from the Olmecs to the Aztecs*. 4th ed. London: Thames and Hudson, 1962.

Cole, Joanna, and Stephanie Calmenson. *Marbles: 101 Ways to Play*. New York: Morrow Junior Books, 1998.

Cotlow, Lewis. *In Search of the Primitive*. Boston: Little, Brown, 1942, 1966.

Cotton, Charles. *The Compleat Gamester*. Facsimile. Barre, MA: The Imprint Society, 1970 (original, London, 1709).

Cox, Richard William, director. "British Society of Sports History." Manchester, England: The University of Science and Technology in Manchester, 2001. <http://www.umist.ac.uk/sport/index2.html>.

Crompton, Paul. *The Complete Martial Arts*. New York: McGraw-Hill Publishing, 1989.

Culin, Stewart. "Ceremonial Diversions in Japan," *Journal of American Folklore* (October 1919): 1026–1031.

Culin, Stewart. "Chess and Playing Cards." Report of the National Museum, Washington DC: Government Printing Office, 1896.

Culin, Stewart. *Games of the North American Indians*. Facsimile. New York: Dover Publications, 1975 (original 1907).

Culin, Stewart. "Hawaiian Games." *American Anthropology*, new series, 1:2, (1899): 201–247.

Culin, Stewart. *Korean Games*. Facsimile. New York: Dover Publications, 1991 (original 1895).

Culin, Stewart. "Philippine Games." *American Anthropology*, new series 2:2 (1900): 643–656.

Cuyler, Patricia L. *Sumo: From Rite to Sport*. New York, Tokyo: John Weatherhill, 1979.

Dale, T. F. *Polo Past and Present*. London: Country Life, and New York: Chas. Scribners, 1905.

Day, Jane S. "The Mesoamerican Ballgame." Denver: Museum of Natural History, 1992. <http://linux1.tlc.north.denver.k12.co.us/~gmoreno/gmoreno/Mesoamerican_Ballgame.html>.

Diagram Group. *Family Fun and Games*. New York: Sterling Publishing, 1992.

Diagram Group. *The Official World Encyclopedia of Sports and Games*. New York: Paddington Press, 1979.

Diagram Group. *Rules of the Game*. New York: Paddington Press, 1974.

Draeger, Donn F., and Robert W. Smith. *Comprehensive Asian Fighting Arts*. Tokyo: Kodansha International, 1980.

Dumitru, Petru, coordinator. "I*EARN International Project: Children's Folk Games Project." Foscani, Romania: School No. 10, 2001. <http://www.estcomp.ro/~cfg/home.html>.

Dummett, Michael. *The Game of Tarot*. London: Duckworth, 1980.

Endrei, Walter, and László Zolnay. *Fun and Games in Old Europe*. Budapest: Corvina Kiado, 1986.

Everhart, Deborah, and Martin Irvine, codirectors. "The Labyrinth: Resources for Medieval Studies." Washington, DC: Georgetown University, 2001. <http://www.georgetown.edu/labyrinth/>.

Fage, J.D. *A History of Africa*. New York: Alfred A. Knopf, 1978.

Falkener, Edward. *Games Ancient and Oriental and How to Play Them*. Facsimile. New York: Dover Publications, 1961 (original 1892).

Feest, Christian. *Indians of North America: The Powhatan Tribes*. New York: Chelsea House Publishers, 1989.

Flower, Raymond. *The History of Skiing and Other Winter Sports*. New York: Methuen, 1976.

Fortin, Francois. *Sports: The Complete Visual Reference*. Willowdale, Ontario: Firefly Books, 2000.

Frantzen, Allen J., general editor of online version. "Essays in Medieval Studies." Chicago: Loyola University, 2001. <http://www.luc.edu/publications/medieval/index.html>.

Friedman, David, and Elizabeth Cook. *Cariadoc's Miscellany*. San Jose, CA: Friedman and Cook, 1992.

Gabriel, Kathryn. *Gambler Way*. Boulder, CO: Johnson Books, 1996.

Geis, Joseph, and Francis Geis. *Life in a Medieval City*. New York: Harper and Row, 1969.

Geis, Joseph, and Francis Geis. *Life in a Medieval Family*. New York: Harper and Row, 1998.

Geis, Joseph, and Francis Geis. *Life in a Medieval Village*. New York: Harper and Row, 1990.

George, Michael W., webmaster. "The WWW Virtual Library History Index, Medieval Europe." East Lansing: The Michigan State University Graduate Student Medieval and Renaissance Consortium, 2001. <http://www.msu.edu/~georgem1/history/medieval.htm>.

Gibson, Robert O. *Indians of North America: The Cumash*. New York: Chelsea House Publishers, 1990.

Gomme, Alice. *Traditional Games of England, Scotland and Ireland*. London: Thames and Hudson, 1984.

Gorini, Pietro. *Encyclopedia of Traditional Games*. Rome: Gremese International, 1994.

Gould, D. W. *The Top: Universal Toy, Enduring Pastime*. New York: Clarkson N. Potter, 1973.

Graham, Steven. "Boomerang Lesson Plans." Bartlesville, OK: Jane Phillips Elementary School, 2001. <http://www.bartlesville.k12.ok.us/jp/graham/>.

Grunfeld, Frederic V., ed. *Games of the World: How to Make Them, How to Play Them, How They Came to Be*. New York: Ballantine Books, 1977.

Haagen, Claudia. *Bush Toys: Aboriginal Children at Play*. Canberra: Aboriginal Studies Press, 1994.

Hale, Duane K., and Arrell M. Gibson. *Indians of North America: The Chickasaw*. New York: Chelsea House Publishers, 1990.

Haley, James L. *Apaches: A History and Culture Portrait*. Garden City, NY: Doubleday, 1981.

Halsall, Paul, ed. "Byzantine Studies." New York: Fordham University, 2001. <http://www.fordham.edu/halsall/byzantium/index.html>.

Halsall, Paul, ed. "Internet Medieval Sourcebook." New York: Fordham University, 2001. <http://www.fordham.edu/halsall/sbook.html>.

Hanawalt, Barbara A. *Growing Up in Medieval London*. London: Oxford University Press, 1993.

Harbin, Beau A.C., webmaster. "Netserf: The Internet Connection for Medieval Resources." 2001. <http://www.netserf.org/>.

Harbin, E.O. *Games of Many Nations*. New York: Abingdon Press, 1954.

Harris, Harold Arthur. *Greek Athletes and Athletics*. Bloomington, IN: Indiana University Press, 1966.

Harris, Harold Arthur. *Sport in Greece and Rome*. London: Thames and Hudson, 1972.

Harris, Mark, webmaster. "Stefan's Florilegium." 2001. <http://www.florilegium.org/>.

Harris, Nathaniel. *The Earliest Explorers*. Danbury, CT: Grolier Educational, 1998.

Hassrick, Royal B. *The Sioux: Life and Customs of a Warrior Society*. Norman, OK: University of Oklahoma Press, 1964.

Hendricks, T.S. "Sport and Social Hierarchy in Medieval England." *Journal of Sport History* (1982): 20–37.

Hickcock Sports History. "Hickcock Sports." 2001. <http://www.hickcocksports.com/history>.

Hodgson, Pat. *Growing Up with the North American Indians*. London: Batsford Academic and Educational, 1980.

Huxley, Francis. *Affable Savages*. London: Travel Book Club, 1958.

imThurn, Everard F. "Primitive Games." *Argosy: Journal of the Royal Agricultural and Commercial Society* (1890).

Ingpen, Robert, and Philip Wilkinson. *A Celebration of Customs and Rituals of the World*. New York: Facts on File, 1996.

Jayne, Caroline Furness. *String Figures*. New York: Chas. Scribners Sons, 1906.

Jewell, Brian. *Sports and Games: History and Origins*. Tunbridge Wells, England: Midas Books, 1977.

Jonas, Gerald. *Dancing: The Pleasure, Power and Art of Movement*. New York: Harry N. Abrams, 1992.

Jue, David F. *Chinese Kites: How to Make and Fly Them*. Rutland, VT, and Tokyo: Charles E. Tuttle Company, 1967.

Kenyon, Sherilyn. *The Writers Guide to Everyday Life in the Middle Ages*. Cincinnati: Writers Digest Books, 1995.

Kidd, Dudley. *Savage Children*. New York: Negro Universities Press, 1969 (original, London: Adam and Charles Black, 1909).

Knuttgen, Howard G., M.A. Qiwei, and W.U. Zhongyuan. *Sport in China*. Champaign, IL: Human Kinetics Books, 1990.

Leonard, Jonathan Norton. *Great Ages of Man: Ancient America*. New York: Time, 1967.

Lewis, Peter. *Martial Arts of the Orient*. New York: W.H. Smith, 1985.

Lychack, William. *Games People Play: England*. New York: Children's Press, 1995.

MacGregor, Charles, webmaster. "Alphonso X Book of Games." Minneapolis, MN: MacGregor Historic Games, 2001. <http://games.rengeek.central.com>, <http://www.historicgames.com/index.html>.

Mandell, Richard D. *Sport, A Cultural History*. New York: Columbia University Press, 1984.

Manesse Liederhandscrift Manuscript. University of Heidelberg, circa 1350. <http://www.aemma.org>.

Maranda, Lynn. *Coast Salish Gambling Games*. Canadian Ethnology Service, no. 93. National Museums of Canada, 1984.

Marcus, Rebecca B. *Survivors of the Stone Age: Nine Tribes Today*. New York: Hastings House, 1975.

Masters, James. "Traditional Games." London: Masters Games, 2001. <http://web.ukonline.co.uk/james.masters/TraditionalGames/index.htm>.

Maxwell, James A., ed. *America's Fascinating Indian Heritage*. Pleasantville, NY: The Reader's Digest Association, 1978.

Mayer, L.A. *Mamluk Playing Cards*. Leiden: Brill, 1971.

McComb, David G. *Sports: An Illustrated History*. London: Oxford University Press, 1998.

McLean, Teresa. *The English at Play in the Middle Ages*. Windsor Forest, Berkshire: Kensal Press, 1988.

Mead, Margaret, ed. *Cooperation and Competition among Primitive People*. New York: McGraw-Hill, 1937.

Morencos, Garcia. *Pilar: Libro de Ajedrez, Dados y Tablas de Alfonso X el Sabio: Estudio*. Madrid: Patrimonio Nacional, 1977. (original circa 1275)

Muchembled, Robert, supervising editor. *Roots of Western Civilization: Games and Sports*. Danbury, CT: Grolier Educational Corporation, 1993.

Mueller, Bruno. "Boomerang Throwing for Boomerang Beginners." Speyer, Germany: Bruno Mueller, 1998. <http://www.bumerang-sport.de/throwing/throw.html>.

Murray, Grace A. *Ancient Rites and Ceremonies*. London: Senate, 1996 (original, London: Alston Rivers, 1929).

Murray, H.J.R. *A History of Board Games Other than Chess*. Oxford: Clarendon Press, 1952.

"Native American Technology and Art." <http://www.nativetech.org>.

Natkiel, Richard, and Anthony Preston. *Atlas of Maritime History*. New York: Facts on File, 1986.

Nieboer, Geof, webmaster. "Games Kids Play." 2001. <www.gameskidsplay.net>.

Nile, Richard. *Cultural Atlas of Australia, New Zealand and the South Pacific*. Abingdon, England: Andromeda Oxford, 1996.

North American Society for Sport History. *Journal of Sports History*. Los Angeles: Amateur Athletic Association, 2001. <http://www.aafla.org>.

Olivová Věra. *Sports and Games in the Ancient World*. New York: St. Martin's Press, 1984.

Opie, I.A., and P. Opie. *Children's Games in Street and Playground*. Oxford: Clarendon Press, 1969.

Opie, I.A. and P. Opie. *Children's Games with Things*. London: Oxford University Press, 1997.

Oxendine, Joseph. *American Indian Sports Heritage*. Lincoln: University of Nebraska Press, 1988.

Parlett, David. *A History of Card Games*. London: Oxford University Press, 1991.

Poliakoff, Michael. "Jacob, Job, and Other Wrestlers: Reception of Greek Athletics by Jews and Christians in Antiquity." *Journal of Sports History*, 11, no. 2 (1984): 48–65.

Pugh, Marion D. *Games of the NEFA*. Shillong: North East Frontier Agency, 1958.

Raum, O. F. *Chaga Childhood*. London: Oxford University Press, 1940, 1967.

Reeves, Compton. *Pleasures and Pastimes in Medieval England*. Stroud: Alan Sutton, 1995.

Riche, Pierre. *Daily Life in the World of Charlemagne*. Translated by JoAnn McNamara. Philadelphia: University of Pennsylvania Press, 1988.

Roberts, David. "In the Land of the Long Distance Runners" Washington, DC: Smithsonian Institution, 1998. <www.smithsonianmag.si.edu>.

Rosenthal, Franz. *Gambling in Islam*. Leiden: E. J. Brill, 1975.

Rules of the Konane. Lapakahi State Historical Park Brochure. 2000.

Scalley, David P., webmaster. "Dagonell's Web Page." Buffalo, NY: Canisius College, 2001. <http://www.cs.canisius.edu/~salley/articles.html>.

Schrodt, Barbara. "Sports of the Byzantine Empire." *Journal of Sports History* 8 (1981): 40–59.

Selby, Stephen. *Chinese Archery*. Hong Kong: Hong Kong University Press, 2000.

Shadbolt, Maurice, and Olaf Ruhen. *Isles of the South Pacific*. Washington, DC: The National Geographic Society, 1968.

Siegel, Morris. *A Study of West African Carved Gambling Chips*. Menasha, WI: American Anthropological Association. No. 55, 1940.

Singman, Jeffrey L., and Will McLean. *Daily Life in Chaucer's England*. Westport, CT: Greenwood Press, 1995.

Skidmore, Joel, webmaster, with Merle Greene Robertson, Jorge Pérez de Lara, and Mark Van Stone. Mesoweb. San Francisco, CA: Pre-Colombian Art Research Institute, 2001. <http://www.mesoweb.com/>.

Smith, Anthony. *Mato Grosso: Last Virgin Land*. London: The Royal Society, 1971.

Somogyi, Jozef. "Muslim Table Games." *Islamic Quarterly* 3/4, (1958): 236–299.

Staples, Michael P., and Anthony K. Chan. *Wu Shu of China*. Van Nuys, CA: Michael P. Staples and Anthony K. Chan, 1976.

Stern, Theodore. *The Rubber-Ball Games of the Americas*. Monographs of the American Ethnological Society, Number 17. Seattle, WA: University of Washington Press, 1949.

Thomas, Carissa, webmaster. Medieval World. 2001 <http://www.geocities.com/MedievalWorld/>.

Thomas, E. M. *The Harmless People: The Bushmen of South-West Africa*. New York: Alfred Knopf, 1959.

Traditional Games and Martial Arts. "Discover India." 2001. <http://www.indiagov.org/sports>.

Trench, Charles Chenevix. *A History of Marksmanship*. Chicago: Follet Publishing Company, 1972.

Von Leyden, Rudolf. *Ganjifa: The Playing Cards of India*. London: Victoria and Albert Museum, 1982.

Wagner, Eric A. *Sport in Asia and Africa: A Comparative Handbook*. Westport, CT: Greenwood Press, 1989.

Waks, Mark, webmaster. "Medieval & Renaissance Games Home Page." 2001. <http://waks.ne.mediaone.net//game-hist/>.

Whitehead, Ruth Holmes, and Harold McGee. *The Micmac*. Halifax, NS: Nimbus Publishing, 1983.

Zaslavsky, Claudia. *Africa Counts: Number and Pattern in African Culture*. Boston: Prindle, Weber and Schmidt, 1973.

Zevin, Jack, and Charlotte Evans, eds. *Kingfisher Illustrated History of the World*. New York: Kingfisher Books, 1993.

▦ GEOGRAPHICAL INDEX

Most of the national boundaries we know today did not exist in the Middle Ages. In addition, games crossed lines of tribe, region, and even language. It is not uncommon to read of people who could not understand one another's languages playing games together.

This index organizes discussions of games in the text by region as well as by individual nations or peoples. Some games are listed only under the main region because they were played in all parts of the region. Page numbers in *italics* indicate figures.

▦ GENERAL INDEX

Page numbers in *italics* indicate figures.

About the Author

SALLY WILKINS is a freelance writer and has contributed to Greenwood's *The Louisa May Alcott Encyclopedia* (2001).